Praise for *Myanmar's Enemy Within*

"A book of impressive historical depth and intellectual acuity. Francis Wade shatters many clichés about religious violence as he explores its tangled roots in Buddhist Myanmar."

Pankaj Mishra, author of *Age of Anger:*
A History of the Present

"Francis Wade has invested immense energy in pursuit of the truth about the tragedy of Myanmar and its Muslim population. There is no other writer on this topic with the same moral courage and intellectual insight. His work demands serious attention."

Fergal Keane, BBC Correspondent and author of
Road of Bones: The Epic Siege of Kohima

"This gripping investigation into the plight of Myanmar's Muslim community reads like a forensic case history, uncovering the full extent of a nation's festering wound. Lucid, compassionate, admirably researched and reasoned, here is scholarly reportage at its best."

Wendy Law-Yone, author of *Golden Parasol:*
A Daughter's Memoir Of Burma

"Elegantly written, empirically rich, and analytically nuanced, the book combines in-depth, on-the-ground reportage with a solid command of the scholarship. An excellent book."

John T. Sidel, LSE, and author of *Riots,*
Pogroms, Jihad: Religious Violence in Indonesia

"A fine, engrossing work, at the centre of which is that all too common enmity and conflict between people of different religious and ethnic adherences."

Paul Brass, author of *The Production of*
Hindu-Muslim Violence in Contemporary India

Asian Arguments

Asian Arguments is a series of short books about Asia today. Aimed at the growing number of students and general readers who want to know more about the region, these books will highlight community involvement from the ground up in issues of the day usually discussed by authors in terms of top–down government policy. The aim is to better understand how ordinary Asian citizens are confronting problems such as the environment, democracy and their societies' development, either with or without government support. The books are scholarly but engaged, substantive as well as topical and written by authors with direct experience of their subject matter.

Series Editor: Paul French

Previous Titles:

Forthcoming:

Thailand: Shifting Ground between the US and a Rising China by Benjamin Zawacki

On the New Silk Road: Journeying through China's Artery of Power by Wade Shepard

Last Days of the Mekong by Brian Eyler

Hong Kong: Markets, Street Hawkers and the Fight against Gentrification by Maurizio Marinelli

Myanmar's Enemy Within

Buddhist Violence and the Making of a Muslim 'Other'

FRANCIS WADE

ZED

Myanmar's Enemy Within: Buddhist Violence and the Making of a Muslim 'Other' was first published in 2017 by Zed Books Ltd, The Foundry, 17 Oval Way, London SE11 5RR, UK.

www.zedbooks.net

Typeset in Bembo Std by Swales & Willis Ltd, Exeter, Devon
Cover design by Emma J. Hardy
Cover photo © Nic Dunlop/Panos

A catalogue record for this book is available from the British Library.

ISBN 978-1-78360-528-6 hb
ISBN 978-1-78360-527-9 pb
ISBN 978-1-78360-529-3 pdf
ISBN 978-1-78360-530-9 epub
ISBN 978-1-78360-531-6 mobi

Printed and bound by CPI Group (UK) Ltd, Croydon, CR0 4YY

For my mother and father,
whose love and support underpins all this.

Contents

Acknowledgements

Numerous people have helped, from near and afar, with the research and writing of this book. The characters featured in these pages, who form the backbone of the story I've tried to tell, were often approached in roadside teashops or at the doorways of their homes, unaware they would be drawn into a conversation of a deeply personal, and sometimes painful, nature. But all were generous with their time and thoughts, and I owe a great debt to them.

Friends and colleagues offered valuable feedback on structure and content, and plugged important gaps in my reading of the events documented in these pages. In particular I am grateful to Carlos Sardiña Galache, Matthew Schissler, Aung Tun, Elliott Prasse-Freeman, Sai Latt, David Mathieson, Matthew Walton, Maung Zarni, Taylor O'Connor and Charlie Campbell for their input on key, and complex, topics. At Zed Books, Kim Walker and Paul French provided useful advice on drafts, and patiently postponed the deadline more than once. Chris Lewa has, since I first began exploring this issue, kindly provided invaluable material and information, and I am lucky to have been able to bounce ideas around with the team at the International State Crime Initiative – Penny Green, Thomas McManus and Alicia de la Cour-Venning – whose own research has been vital to informing my own.

Some of the content of this book, particularly in Chapters 5, 7 and 8, drew on reporting I had undertaken for *TIME*, *Los Angeles Review of Books*, *The Irrawaddy* and ucanews.com. I am grateful for their permission to rework the material in here. Elsewhere, firsthand accounts I collected of the violence and its aftermath were furnished with information from reports published by Human Rights Watch, Fortify Rights, Amnesty International and Physicians for Human Rights, all of which have carried out important research into the events of recent years.

Many thanks to those in Yangon and elsewhere in the country who gave crucial contributions to this book that cannot be acknowledged in its pages – Sophia Naing, Harry Myo Lin, U Soe Oo and Saw Nang in particular. In Yangon, Sam Aung Moon provided important translations, often sitting patiently through inordinately long interviews. Ali Fowle has been endlessly helpful over the years, somehow weathering my incessant pestering, while Joseph Allchin has provided a wealth of thoughts and ideas. I am also grateful to the staff at the Democratic Voice of Burma, where I joined as a journalist in 2009 and, in time, came to learn a great deal from colleagues there, many of whom had fled from the very same system of oppression and the horrors it brought that I would report on in the years afterwards. My experience there provided a foundation for all that followed.

Yetike and KH have been vital to my understanding of Myanmar, and have sacrificed a great deal of their time to translate, to guide, to support, to provide an intellectual crutch … it goes on. Their grasp of the murky politics of their country has greatly strengthened my own, and without their generosity and friendship this book would have been that much harder to complete.

I owe a great debt to friends and family across the world who have provided much-needed support and a welcome distraction throughout. I've been groaning about this project for too long, and now I'll finally stop. Above all else, my mother and father, Kristin Wade and Malcolm Andrews, have, since long before I learned to pick up a pen, taught me to look, to listen and to question. And, eventually, to write. They were present throughout this book, steering me through a testing year and more, and offering the finest advice on drafts. Words cannot express how grateful I am for this and everything else they have done.

Author's note

This book is the product of research undertaken over numerous trips to Myanmar between 2012 and 2016 to report on the violence and its aftermath. Some lasted weeks, others months. Care has been taken to change the names of characters who requested it, or who I felt could not be safely identified. Close surveillance of the population has continued well into the era of civilian rule, and brings with it often horrific consequences for those considered to have slandered the military, the government and now, even, the monkhood.

Regarding the use of local names, I have opted for Myanmar over Burma. Although it was the military that arbitrarily made the switch in 1989, Myanmar is the name most commonly used now by those inside the country. To maintain consistency, I have also used the current names for states and divisions, rather than those introduced by the British but also dropped in 1989. As such, Yangon refers to Rangoon, Rakhine State refers to the old Arakan State, and Kayin State to Karen State. The majority Bamar ethnic group had once been known as the Burman. I have opted to use Bamar, but its old incarnation appears in quotes throughout this book.

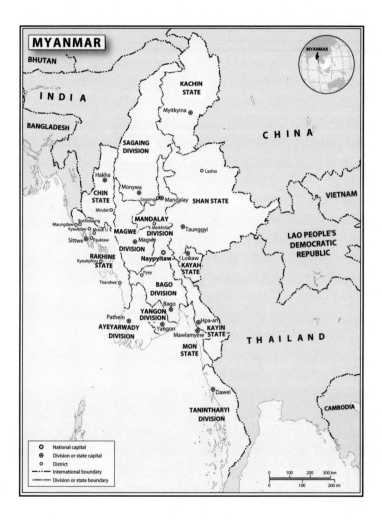

Prologue

"We aren't saying that violence is necessarily required. What we are saying is that we need to defend ourselves by building a fence with our bones, if it's necessary to do so."

Lunchtime in the teashops of Yangon always provided an orchestra of sounds – the call and response of the cooks and the busboys, the clattering of plates and the traffic grinding noisily past outside – that made conversation difficult, and I had to lean in close. The young man I sat with was articulate, educated to university level, and warm, if somewhat direct. Rarely did he pause between question and answer; instead, he spoke in rapid fire: rat-a-tat, rat-a-rat, never missing a beat. It seemed that he had been party to this line of conversation many times before.

"It's a misunderstanding that we are extremists. It's like that. The main thing is that we would defend our race and religion by building a fence with our bones. It's for the safety of our homes; we are not burning down those of others."

I had been introduced to him through an old colleague who had grown up in Yangon but who, a decade or so back, moved with his family to Thailand. In his day, the traffic in the old capital hadn't been nearly so loud, and my taxi ride to this teashop in the sprawling northern suburbs would have taken half the time it did that morning. But that was a long time ago. Much had since changed, and was still changing. Myanmar was opening to the world and all it offered and, so it seemed from afar, the military that ruled it for so long was haltingly, cautiously, making way for a new civilian order. I wanted to know what that change felt like – the full spectrum of fears, anxieties and anticipations that were being stirred as the country moved into the light. Transitions like this one don't manifest only at the political level, among the people at the top who engineer them. The whole building shakes, right down to its foundations, and in Myanmar, in the years after the transfer of power began in 2011, the entire structure was shifting.

The colleague had introduced me to this man for a particular reason. Amid the flowering of this new era, violence, often ferocious in nature, had broken out between Buddhists and Muslims, and it had taken many by surprise. It felt new. Civilians were attacking civilians en masse, in fits of bloody rage that often seemed unbridled by forces either internal or external to the participants. And the military, for once, appeared to have suspended its monopoly on violence.

The dynamics of the violence didn't fit the usual narrative ascribed to Myanmar by the international press, in which there was a seeming unity, whether spoken or not, forged in opposition to the junta by the vast mass of peoples who had all, with varying degrees, experienced the pains of life under it. Seemingly new fissures were opening and tensions rising between communities that had lived alongside one another for generations. A new anger was being directed away from the men in their greens and their jackboots, and towards one another. Neighbour turned on neighbour, until the blood began to run.

These communal fissures weren't entirely new, but to many outside observers, they were unknowns. And before a deeper analysis of their causes began to arrive, they had caught many off guard. Certain aspects of what unfolded after the first wave of violence in the middle of 2012 didn't seem to add up: the bulk of attacks were coming from Buddhists, but it was surely impossible that they, and particularly the venerated monks with their gospel of peace, could support or even perpetrate such acts of violence; or that the passage from authoritarian rule to democracy could emerge as the site of efforts to exclude an entire religious community from the country. And what about democracy itself, a term so synonymous with the movements for change that had come and gone throughout the decades of military rule in Myanmar? Perhaps it wasn't a step in the direction of equality, but instead the pursuit of an ideal nation, arbitrarily defined but so delicate a conception that any obstacles in the way of it needed removing.

The young man I met that day was a member of a movement known as the Organisation for the Protection of Race and Religion, led by Buddhist monks and known better by its local acronym, Ma Ba Tha. Not far from the teashop where we hunkered down amid the crowds lay its headquarters, in a monastery set back from a busy road in the north of Yangon. It was founded in 2013, and it had quickly become a well-oiled machine, present in townships across the country and boasting a support base that stretched into the millions. I took the man's fluency with the subject matter to be reflective of the conviction that underpinned the movement's ambitions. It cast itself as chief protector of Buddhism in one of the few countries in the region in which the faith had, in the eyes of many, remained largely

intact against the corrosive influence of foreign ideas –
modernism, Islam, or whatever other forces had brought
about its demise elsewhere in the world. But as the transition
advanced many of the country's devoted Buddhists feared
that this was beginning to change, and unravel. Society had
been thrown into a state of flux, and the Buddhist values
that for so many centuries had provided a strong moral and
intellectual foundation were under threat.

I'd kept him at the table for two hours already, in the
heat of high summer. There was a bit of tea left in the
pot and I poured another round, hoping it might sate him
for long enough to ask one last round of questions. But
he had begun to tire. I often found during exchanges like
this that I was interrogating feelings that were difficult for
others to express in words, particularly to a foreigner. The
story of what unfolded in Myanmar upon its transition is,
perhaps more than anything else, one about identity and
belonging, yet I was a visitor to Myanmar, an outsider
with no pretensions otherwise. Whatever sense of group
belonging I myself felt adhered much more to my family
and friends than the land within the borders of the country
where I grew up. Those nationalist loyalties were largely
abstract to me, especially when they fused with religion
– another point of reference I didn't share with the young
man. How could he explain something so subjective and
intimate to someone like me?

Still, important questions remained, and I pressed
him one last time. As much as the violence had shocked,
it also compelled a deeper look, for in many ways this
wasn't unique to Myanmar. There were echoes from
ethno-religious conflicts elsewhere in the world, where
fears about the resilience of identities and belief systems

had been whipped up into bloody fury, with profound consequences. And there were lessons to be learned for other diverse societies undergoing rapid change. But what was unfolding in Myanmar felt particularly perplexing because the violence seemed to go so heavily against the grain of the country and its majority faith. Why was Buddhism in such need of protection? Why, in the changing landscape of Myanmar, had there emerged actors so fierce in their fervour that they would build a fence with their bones, or that they would, contrary to his words, seek to kill off whatever threat to their religion lurked amidst them? The violence that had erupted in towns across Myanmar after 2012 had been vicious and terrifying – heads were severed by machete in broad daylight, on corners of streets in busy towns; young Muslim students were massacred. I'd wanted to understand how that turn to violence could occur. But to get into the mind of radical nationalists like him, who functioned with such singularity of vision, perhaps it would be better to explore what he feared might be lost if Buddhism hadn't been defended, with the fence of bones or with the machete.

"Buddhism stands for the truth and peace," he replied. "Therefore, if the Buddhist cultures vanish, truth and the peace would vanish steadily as well. If there's no Buddhism in Yangon …."

For once he drifted off, pausing for a moment. But then he quickly came back in. I hadn't asked him specifically about Islam, yet still …

"Even now, you can see kufi caps everywhere. It can't be good at all. This country was founded with the Buddhist ideology. And if the Buddhist cultures vanish, Yangon will become like Saudi and Mecca. Then, there wouldn't be the influence of peace and truth. There will be more discrimination and violence."

What would happen then, to him, his home – everything?

"It can be the fall of Yangon. It can also be the fall of Buddhism. And our race will be eliminated."

1

The first wave: the murder, the smoke and the ruins

In Sittwe, on the western coast of Myanmar, there is a road that runs out of the town centre, bound towards the vast blue of the Bay of Bengal. On either side the road is lined with buildings, one or two storeys high, some made of brick, others wood – teashops, houses, barbers. But the road then hits a straight, and the buildings abruptly stop. In their place come fields – scrubby, and dotted with small wooden huts. They are oddly spaced apart, as if built in haste and not to last. From the road, you can look south between the dwellings to a distant line of trees that mark the neighbourhood limit. The area is called Nasi, but it bears little resemblance to the Nasi of old. The wooden huts, occupied by squatters and interspersed among unkempt bush, have replaced what used to be clusters of houses and shops connected by narrow lanes and alleyways. There had been 11 sub-quarters here – some housed Buddhists, some Muslims; others were mixed. In the centre, beside the road, sat a high school where students from all over Nasi would study together.

On the morning of 12 June 2012, Ko Myat had been in his village 10 kilometres north of Sittwe. The 43-year-old was, like the majority of men in Par Da Lek, a longtime fisherman in the nearby tributaries that feed into the Bay of Bengal. He had divorced from his wife several years before, and now lived alone in a stilted wooden house towards the back of the village, past the market and the dusty pitch where children would always play football. As far back as he knew the village had been only Buddhist, but Muslims would come here to trade. They too fished in the nearby creeks, and would move from one village market to another each day until the morning's catch was sold.

That month of June hadn't thus far been what Ko Myat would describe as normal. In the days before 12 June, talk had swept through the village of fits of violence underway not so far away. These weren't newspaper reports, but rumours that passed from mouth to mouth. They said that Rakhine, the Buddhist ethnic group to whom he belonged, were being attacked. It was the Muslims.

Par Da Lek hadn't seen any of this violence, but none-theless there were strange rumblings in the village. Over the two days prior to 12 June 2012, men had been shuttled on buses to downtown Sittwe. Ko Myat would watch them go in wave after wave. They were goaded onto the buses and away, he said, by the village administrator, the chief author-ity there. For those two days he had stood at the entrance to the village, where the road rises up on a bank above the busy marketplace. Buses would come and go; the men who stood there waiting empty handed would be given weapons – sticks and machetes – before climbing aboard.

The village was six miles from the nearest Muslim community and he hadn't worried about similar running battles erupting closer to home. But where these men were heading, the fighting had been particularly fierce. Having finished lunch on 12 June he went to the village entrance and volunteered to go. A monastery in Sittwe would offer food to participants later that day, he was told. Ko Myat had been unable to count the numbers of villagers that had departed in the days before, but he soon understood the scale of the wider operation. Upon arriving at Nasi quarter that afternoon, other buses that had ferried Buddhist Rakhine into Sittwe from villages elsewhere in the area were parked near that straight section of road, like tourist coaches waiting outside a site of natural beauty. On either side, the smoke from burning homes climbed in narrow towers into the sky. He remembers a light drizzle falling that day as all around him the embers of razed houses glowed. The smoke had blanketed the landscape in a surreal haze. "It was like a movie," he recalls.

Only three days before, Nasi had been home to several hundred families; by the time Ko Myat arrived, the majority had fled, and many structures had been levelled, leaving him with little else to do. Even so, the men aboard the buses who had encouraged him and other villagers on had divided his bus into two teams, one to steal into the quarter and torch the remaining houses and another to amass at exit points, armed and under orders to attack anyone who escaped. He joined the second group, and remained on the roadside for several hours while others carried flaming torches inside the quarter and held them to any buildings still standing. He felt tense, anxious. Five hours passed. He saw little physical violence, he said, save for the fires started by the mob. "Our group was standing on the road but most of the Muslims who were still inside Nasi stayed there. They were too scared to come out." Upon hearing a signal later that afternoon, the two teams withdrew from the area and boarded one of the waiting buses. It wound its way back through the Sittwe outskirts before heading north. Twenty minutes later, they were back at the entrance to the village. Behind them, Nasi quarter lay in smoke and ruins.

★ ★ ★

More than three years had passed by the time I met with Ko Myat. We sat together on the deck of his house in Par Da Lek and spoke for several hours about the events of June 2012. Like many communities embroiled in intergroup violence, Buddhists and Muslims in and around Sittwe immediately broke off interaction. In Sittwe town, the residents of Nasi and other Muslim quarters were either herded into displacement camps that sprang up along the coast or confined within the two remaining neighbourhoods, Aung Mingalar and Bumay, that hadn't been razed. Police checkpoints erected at the entrances to these neighbourhoods ensured that, thereafter, they would not be able to leave. In villages to the north of Sittwe, contact between Buddhists and Muslims was largely put to a stop. Those fellow fishermen whom Ko Myat would see arriving at the village each day to trade at the market ceased coming, and across this township and beyond, the two communities retreated within themselves. The shift in the social dynamic of Sittwe and its surrounds had been radical. Where interaction had once been commonplace, it was now utterly severed.

The violence of early June 2012 was the first major wave of conflict between Buddhists and Muslims to strike Myanmar as it transitioned away from military rule. In October that year, a second wave occurred, beginning on the morning of 22 October with orchestrated mob attacks on Muslim communities in nine townships across Rakhine State. Like June, these attacks focused predominantly on the Rohingya, a Muslim minority that many Buddhist Rakhine like Ko Myat thought to be illegal immigrants. In the decades past, so the narrative went, they had slipped over the border from Bangladesh at the point where it meets Rakhine State and settled on their land. They were growing in number, diluting the concentration of the Buddhist population, and providing the vanguard of a crusade to turn Myanmar into a Muslim country.

Around the same time Ko Myat boarded the bus and made for Sittwe, I was over on the other side of the country, holed up in a hotel in Laiza on Myanmar's northeastern border with China. It was the headquarters of the Kachin Independence Army, one of a number of ethnic armed groups that had been fighting the military on and off for nearly half a century. I had already been working on Myanmar for several years, and those were the conflicts I was used to reporting, and thought I understood. Within them was a seemingly clear delineation between actors and their loyalties: the ethnic armed group and its constituency on one side, the Myanmar army on the other, and in between a scattering of allies of each. These conflicts, long running and often brutal, had been romanticised by the foreign press as a battle of good versus evil, a "just war" being fought by rebels against a derided junta. And with the overwhelming majority of the population of Myanmar holding a deep disdain for the military that had ruled them for so long, there was little doubt where the broad support of the public lay: no one wished the military success in the borderlands.

But the violence in Rakhine State didn't fit that neat, if overly simplified, plotline of bad military versus good citizenry. Instead this was the first of a number of local contestations over who did and did not belong in a country that was undergoing great upheaval. There was no one big battle, no condensed mass of fury from which a single solution emerged. Instead, from 2012 onwards, the violence jumped from village to town to city, from the western coast of Myanmar to the mountains of the northeast. The dynamics and nature of it differed as time went on. Unlike the first outbreak in Rakhine State, where ethnicity was a major cleavage, the Buddhist-on-Muslim unrest that began in central Myanmar the following year often saw communities from the same ethnicity that had experienced no prior conflict pitted against one another. In the tumult of the transition, broader demarcations of "us" and "them," outsiders and sons of the soil, were forming. For a large cross-section of the Buddhist population, the Muslims of Myanmar had come to be seen as the outsiders bent on bringing the nation, and its majority Buddhist belief system, to ruin.

As I sat with Ko Myat on the deck of his house, he considered the motive for his participation. He was a timid, hesitant man. He spoke little, and rarely made eye contact. When I pictured him outside Nasi quarter scoping the lanes and alleyways for any fleeing Muslims, his face didn't wear the expression of a determined killer. Rather, it was timor-ous, frightened even. But when he outlined the rationale for boarding the bus that afternoon several years earlier he did so with a quiet conviction. As a Rakhine Buddhist, he felt threatened by the Muslims who lived in the state. "If I don't protect my race then it will disappear," he believed. The Muslims had come here to take over the land that ethnic Rakhine had inhabited for centuries. The stirrings of democratic change in Myanmar might level the playing field, allowing communities who felt long disenfranchised by the military to assert greater claims to the nation. These particular Muslims might take advantage of this, and if they did, Buddhists would suffer, as they had elsewhere in the world – in Malaysia, in Indonesia – where Islam had taken root.

We spoke for a while about the details of the Nasi attack and the broader anxieties he felt. But the violence had come on so suddenly, and I asked him if he could locate a particular trigger. There had been an incident in late May 2012, he explained, that not just for Ko Myat but for many Rakhine I spoke with in the years afterwards fed latent anxieties about the intentions of the Muslims living among them. "It started because Muslims attacked a Buddhist," he said.

The catalyst was the rape and murder of 26-year-old Ma Thida Htwe. The young Rakhine seamstress had been walking home from work in Kyaungnimaw village on Ramree Island, 100 miles south of Sittwe, when, according to police reports, she was gang-raped and her throat slit. It was the evening of 28 May 2012, and her contorted body was left in long grass under a rain tree by the side of the road leading into her village. Three men, identified variously in state media as "Bengali Muslim" or "Islam followers," were arrested two days later, found guilty of the attack and sentenced to jail. But then, on 3 June, a bus carrying Muslims through the town of Taungup, west of Ramree Island, was set upon by some 300 Rakhine Buddhists, many wielding wooden poles. Ten passengers were dragged off the bus and beaten to death. Why the perpetrators had targeted that bus was never made clear. The men deemed guilty of Ma Thida Htwe's murder were already in police custody. Moreover, those on the bus were not Rohingya. They were Muslim missionaries, from Magwe Division, from Ayeyarwady Division – none of them from Rakhine State. It appeared to be a random revenge attack on Muslims, one that, in conjunction with the rape and murder of the seamstress, would have a catastrophic effect on relations between Buddhists and Muslims across the state. Five days later, Rohingya mobs in Maungdaw in northern Rakhine State finished their Friday morning prayers and attacked Buddhist properties across the town and in outlying villages. Shortly afterwards, Nasi quarter burned.

So it had begun with a rape and murder. But in the days after Ma Thida Htwe's body was found on the roadside, information began to circulate on leaflets and DVDs and in local and state media that framed it not as an act isolated from the broader pre-violence dynamic between the Rakhine and Rohingya, but as a direct expression of all that was dangerous in it. That particular attack would carry huge symbolic weight among Rakhine – rape is the act that, perhaps above all else, signals a bid for conquest of one group by another, and this interpretation would become a driving force in the mayhem that followed.

For Ko Myat, his decision to board the bus that afternoon in June 2012 and head to Nasi quarter had in large part resulted from the linking of an event that occurred 100 miles away to the broader fate of his entire race. He wouldn't be alone in doing this. Time and again in the years after, when the violence had spread beyond Rakhine State into areas where historic relations between the two religious communities had been more harmonious, small incidents came to be indicative of a much larger campaign being waged by Muslims against Buddhists. Suddenly, with the smallest disturbance, communities were injected with a palpable enmity towards their neighbours that hadn't been so present before.

I found this intriguing. Some people spoke of their fears as if they were dormant, and always susceptible to activation. At particular moments in Myanmar's not so distant past, that dread of the consequences of its most cherished belief system coming under attack was, to many, very present and very real. Perhaps the attacks being carried out against Muslims in response to these incidents were echoes of a deeply uncertain past, one that I'd learn about only as time went on. But to others, that apprehension seemed to have arisen rather more recently. The military that took power in 1962, ending the brief spell of parliamentary democracy that the country enjoyed following independence in 1948, had used these fears of the demise of Buddhism and the break up of the nation as a principal tool in its efforts to cultivate loyalty among a resentful population. It knew how to manufacture communal violence that appeared, from a distance, spontaneous, and that warranted the presence of the military as protector of the nation. Perhaps this needed to be factored into understandings of what unfolded after 2012.

But there was a bitter irony to the violence of the transition, and it was this that drew me in the most. Ko Myat and the fellow villagers that descended on Nasi quarter during those early days of June 2012, turning an entire neighbourhood to rubble and sending thousands fleeing to camps, were exercising a newfound agency that arrived with the commencement of the passage to civilian rule. For some, old scores, given greater urgency in the clear light of day, were being settled. For others, heightened anxieties brought about by the political changes and everything they carried needed addressing.

But the military, in its retreat from power, seemed to have passed a torch onto the masses of people who had spent so many years opposing its mercurial rule. Its deft manipulation of lines of difference among and between the myriad communities in Myanmar had seemed to bleed into the new landscape, empowering civilians to take up where it had left off. As the transition advanced and the violence crossed the mountain range separating Rakhine State from central Myanmar, monks and their legions of followers began to preach the same message of national unity – or ethno-religious uniformity – that their jailers of old had done. Under their watch, the new Myanmar would be a nation of one religion, one blood. The razed neighbourhoods and the segregation of Buddhists and Muslims, physical and psychological, were the immediate results of this vision. But the how and why – the mental processes undertaken to turn neighbours into enemies, the political machinations that gave rise to the killings and everything that followed – would in the years after 2012 only gradually come into view.

2

Sons of whose soil? Britain and the birth of a fractured nation

More than a millennium before the camps sprang up along the Rakhine State coastline, its beaches had providing a landing point for some of the first Muslims to arrive in the territory known today as Myanmar. They came in boats, as traders from India and Persia who set up a string of small colonies along the western and southern coastlines. These settlers may not have intended to stay, but the laws of nature and the technologies of seafaring in the ninth century were against them. The monsoons that whip in across the Bay of Bengal around May each year effectively trapped many of these early arrivals, and so they remained, married and provided among the first evidence of Islam in Myanmar.[1]

At the time the coastal kingdom of Rakhine, then independent from Myanmar and predominantly Buddhist, by and large looked to the Muslim kingdoms to the west for trade. The lengthy Rakhine Yoma mountain range running north to south along its eastern flank had prevented the development of close ties with the Bamar kingdoms, but that began to change with the mass migration of the peoples of the Ayeyarwady Valley into the coastal region around the eleventh century. This new community intermingled with the Buddhist population already settled there, and came to form the bulk of the Rakhine ethnicity. For much of the past millennium, they lived among the Muslim descendants of the Persian and Indian traders in relative harmony, and governors encouraged courtship between the men and women of each religious community. But the arrival of the early Muslim settlers coincided with a period of rapid Islamic expansionism eastwards, into kingdoms of Asia that had hitherto been predominantly Hindu or Buddhist. The chronicles of travellers who in the late ninth century ventured through southern China towards Myanmar's northern frontiers also note the presence of Muslims along the China–Myanmar border, at around the same time trading posts were being set up on Myanmar's western coast.[2] Gradually these people spread inwards. The early kings of Myanmar launched routine slave-raiding campaigns on Muslim villages in the periphery, resettling captives in the interior and, over the centuries, widening the network of inland Muslim communities.

That was all before Buddhism became the *de facto* state religion of the country, and long before religion became the point of violent division it has come to be in recent years. Myanmar's past is coloured by stories of conquest, but there are few tales of large-scale violence being fought predominantly along lines of faith. The conflicts of yesteryear were projects of territorial defence and expansion that drew on the manpower of whatever communities lived under the purview of the kings executing them, largely regardless of their ethnic or religious identity.

But in the late nineteenth century, a major demographic shift began, slowly, to impinge on the religious dynamic in the country. Myanmar fell in its entirety to the British in 1885, and the western border separating it from India

– then controlled by Britain – was done away with. Yangon came under the authority of the Bengal Presidency, whose rule at one point extended as far as Peshawar to the west and Singapore to the east. The colonial power encouraged a free flow of Indians into Myanmar from Bengal and beyond, as it had done in Sri Lanka, Malaysia and elsewhere, planting the seeds for communal tensions well into the future. In Myanmar this immigrant workforce took up jobs at every rung of the economic ladder: day labourers, office clerks, civil servants and soldiers, but also money lenders, who began to play an authoritative role in the provision of finance to locals. A number settled in that first port of call in Myanmar's west, Rakhine State, moving freely back and forth across the erased border as the changing seasons dictated work patterns. Others moved further towards Yangon and the paddy fields of the Ayeyarwady delta, and by the early 1930s, as anti-colonial movements were mobilising with vigour against the British, more than half the population of Yangon was Indian, both Muslim and Hindu. Bamar, the majority ethnic group in Myanmar, grew increasingly aggrieved at their minority status – by 1931, there were 212,000 Indians in Yangon alone, versus 128,000 Bamar,[3] and the capital had developed the feel of an Indian city. At a time when the global recession of the 1930s was hitting the already indebted rice farmers of the Ayeyarwady delta, more than half of the arable land in the delta was controlled by "non-resident landlords," the majority Indian. This compounded the feeling that not only were livelihoods being drained by foreigners, but that the actual land of Myanmar was being lost, and with it not just the economic worth it carried, but the emotional attachments Bamar had to it.

The targets of the resentment that fuelled those nationalist movements began, over the course of the 1920s and 1930s, to widen to include the country's Muslims, particularly the new arrivals from the subcontinent. Hindus were spared much of the ire, for they were better able to assimilate, but local Buddhist women who married Muslim men often converted, and raised their children as Muslims. They were seen to be diluting the bloodline. But there was a second catalyst for the anger that began to be directed at them: these new communities were seen as stooges of the British – an additional foreign presence that might, if left unchecked, eat away at the Buddhist values that for so long had provided a bedrock for Myanmar society.

★ ★ ★

From the beginning, religion meant a great deal to Myanmar's rulers. The attempts to consolidate something approaching a national identity arguably began a millennium ago with the ascension to the throne of King Anawratha, a late convert to Buddhism who used the scriptures to help achieve what had eluded all rulers before him: the uniting of the disparate peoples of the Ayeyarwady Valley, that long, snaking north–south backbone of the country, into one functioning, governable kingdom. They would form the basis of the Bagan Empire, Myanmar's first, and one that provided an arena in which the majority Bamar ethnicity could begin to organise into a dominant force. These were the originals, so it went – the Bamar and the Buddhist; the first of the real Myanmar.

Such a close fusion of religion and national identity has two broad effects: it provides a sense of unity and security in times of war and conquest and lends a moral justness to the defence of borders, but it also narrows the spectrum of identities that people can express and still rightly claim membership of the nation. The frequency with which scholars of Myanmar attribute the consolidation of the Ayeyarwady Valley communities in the twelfth century to the beginnings of the country's modern history speaks to the widespread belief, heavily reinforced by the junta after it took power in 1962, that Myanmar is and always was a Bamar Buddhist country – that to be Bamar, and therefore a true son of the soil, means to be Buddhist, and that a threat to one was a threat to the other.

Despite all the anxieties that seemed to rise to the surface upon the start of Myanmar's transition from military rule after 2011, a visitor to the country wouldn't be mistaken for thinking that Buddhism's run over the nearly one thousand years since Anawratha took the throne remains unbroken. Official tallies put close to 90 per cent of the country as Buddhist – not only the majority Bamar, but a number of other ethnic groupings too. The tens of thousands of golden pagodas that dot the cities, the plains and the mountains illuminate the degree to which it is, in all but law, the national religion. Yet while it may be of central importance to a large chunk of the population today, its position has at key points in the country's recent history appeared threatened by foreign influences. To its most devoted followers, these influences had a profound effect on the breakdown and reconfiguration of a national identity, a process that the violence of recent years showed was still in motion.

When the forces of the East India Company moved to take Upper Burma in 1885, having already conquered the rest of country in successive stages since 1824, a battalion of troops was sent to the Royal Palace in Mandalay where King Thibaw Min sat. Thibaw Min had been the last in a line of kings that had ruled the country since the reign of Anawratha, but the British knew that any hope of achieving preeminence in Myanmar would be realised only by dispatching him and removing would-be challengers to their rule. After his dethroning on 28 November 1885 and his hurried exit from the Royal Palace, he was shipped along with his family to the port city of Ratnagiri on India's western coast, where he lived out his days a recluse in a residence built for him by the British.

His fall, and the final end of monarchical rule in Myanmar, were to have dramatic consequences for the long-term viability of the colonial project, but it also impacted on a local dynamic little understood by the British at the time. Unlike the kings and queens of western nations whose powers, although more or less total, were largely administrative, Myanmar's rulers enjoyed an added quasi-spiritual dimension. Up until Anawratha's reign in the eleventh century, Myanmar played host to a number of religions, including Hindu and Theravada Buddhist sects, as well as the worship of *nat* spirits – an indigenous form of animism. None were dominant, nor did their followers seek to make them so. This changed with Anawratha's arrival on the throne. Like the Indian kings who took up the word of the Buddha in the first millennium BC, he considered himself a *bodhisattva* on the path to Awakening, and sought to institutionalise Buddhism as the *de facto* state religion of his empire. Pali, the language of the Buddhist scriptures, had a strong influence on the Old Burmese that developed in that area from the twelfth century onwards. Anawratha ordained himself, and all kings thereafter, as the chief preserver of Buddhist law, and made special provisions for Myanmar's order of monks – the Sangha – so that it came to rely on the monarchy for protection. Kings would support the Sangha and settle any problems within it by royal decree,[4] and in return the monks endowed the monarchy with the legitimacy that only a body as revered as the clergy could muster. As the monks encouraged loyalty to the state, one historian noted, so "the Order became the conscience of the government, ensuring that it ruled, at least to some extent, in accordance with Buddhist ethical principles."[5]

What the British hadn't banked on when it rode its cavalry towards the Royal Palace in 1885 was the profound effect that the severing of that symbiosis between Myanmar's monarchy and its Buddhist clergy would have. Not only was a bullish foreign power now calling the shots, but the sacrosanct belief system that unified those in Myanmar living under the king had been threatened.

★ ★ ★

Today a visitor to Mandalay can cross one of the four bridges spanning the moat in the city's downtown and wander through the grounds of the Royal Palace where Thibaw Min sat. Much of it was rebuilt from the ruins of a bombing campaign during World War Two, and artefacts from the Konbaung Dynasty, of which Thibaw Min was the final incarnation, are on display. It remains a site of immense cosmological import to Buddhists in Myanmar. But following the removal of the king, parts of it were transformed by the British into an Anglican chapel and the Upper Burma Club, where colonial officers would play snooker and waltz into the night. Thereafter, the British showed little interest in investing time and energy in keeping the Buddhist order onside. Despite warnings from British administrators that "the extinction of the monarchy left the nation ... without a religion,"[6] colonial administrators had largely failed to comprehend the fact that Myanmar's points of power were not independent of one another, but instead comprised a mutually enforcing network of authorities, both religious and political, that would all be weakened considerably without the support of one another.

Decades later, the effects of this rupture were to be Britain's undoing. The decision by the British to terminate 800 years of kingship and, in the eyes of the Buddhist nationalist groups that gradually began to mobilise, trigger the gradual retreat of Buddhism from its central place in Myanmar society, did little to endear many in Myanmar to its rule. Over time, monastic schools lessened in number and influence, while funds were channelled instead to Christian missionary schools, those same institutions that were seen as an additional threat to Buddhism in a period of rapid modernisation for the country. Nationalist groups, like the Young Men's Buddhist Association, that were at the forefront of the first major wave of independence agitation in the 1920s sought as much to drive Britain out as to bring Buddhism back in, thereby galvanising what came to be a parallel campaign to independence – that of a Buddhist revival that provided a second axis of solidarity within the movement. In the eyes of these movements, the British had colonised not just the administrative apparatus of the country but also the mental and spiritual space of its citizens by displacing their devotion to Buddhism with the more mundane concerns of a modernising society.

It was the monks who had perhaps first seen the potential for this development: dressed in their robes, they had led bands of armed rebels in attacks on British troops in Upper Myanmar shortly after King Thibaw Min's fall. For centuries, as Donald Eugene Smith notes in *Religion and Politics in Burma*, the monk was held aloft as a leading moral force in society, but that had changed with the arrival of the British.

> There was no place for him in the new western-oriented social hierarchy, his educational functions were assumed by other agencies, an unknown foreign language prevented him from understanding what was going on, and westernized Burmese laymen increasingly regarded him as irrelevant to modern life.[7]

★ ★ ★

A day before Ko Myat armed himself and took the bus to Sittwe from his home in Par Da Lek village, a video was uploaded to YouTube entitled "Disappearance of the Race is a Thing to Fear." On the screen a flaming skull sat against a jet-black background. A distant voice read the words of a lengthy sermon given by a monk in the late 1990s that detailed the threat posed by Muslims to Myanmar.

"My lay followers, do not be complacent about protecting our race from extinction," it began. The Muslims are "relentlessly working to swallow up Burma's ethnic populations," and swallow up Buddhism too. "Our people of Burma are not very aware of this. Our ethnic people are kind hearted and hospitable. They treat everyone as their close friends, very trusting. The Muslims know this very well. They take advantage by marrying ethnic women and persuading them to practise their religion."

Yet Muslims hadn't always been the pariah community they seemed by 2012 to have become. Although Buddhism had long ago become the *de facto* state religion, followers of Islam were present in successive royal courts from the time of King Anawratha onwards. These rulers knew the value in keeping the country's various religious communities onside, and in doing so they cultivated a degree of communal harmony that would be unfamiliar to those watching the country today. It was in the coastal region of Rakhine, an independent kingdom until it was annexed to Myanmar in the late eighteenth century, that the presence of Islam would come to be despised the most. Yet the Rakhine kings of old patronised the religion as much as their counterparts had done in the centre. Mosques were built in the ancient Rakhine capital of Mrauk U, and the Kaman, the Muslim minority group that was eventually swept up in the violence of 2012 alongside the Rohingya, descended from a unit of archers that provided a key pillar of defence in the predominantly Buddhist court of Mrauk U from the seventeenth century onwards. Under the rein of King Pagan Min in the mid-nineteenth century, a Muslim served as governor of Amarapura, the old capital. Although they were never significant political movers and shakers, Muslims had been close to the centres of power, and the country had on the whole enjoyed a pluralistic society.

Yet the sentiment contained in "Disappearance of the Race is a Thing to Fear" wasn't altogether new. As nationalist fury built in the 1920s and 1930s, it began to fix on those communities that were considered stooges of the colonial power, which had aided the departure of Buddhism from its central place in society. Chinese immigration into Myanmar during the colonial period had also been a major point of contention for locals, who felt they were being dispossessed of their businesses, but the arrival of this immigrant community hadn't been encouraged by the British so excitedly as the Indians had. Colonial authorities believed Indians to be hard workers, loyal to their masters, and as the border with India was done away with towards the end of the nineteenth century, they came over in droves – 250,000 each year, on average.[8] By the early 1920s, the Indian community had become a major economic powerhouse, able to pay higher rents than their Myanmar counterparts and to buy up swathes of land in Yangon and the delta, which had been transformed by the colonial power into a hugely lucrative rice bowl. Not only had Indians been the source of a major demographic shift, but their economic muscle and their favouring by the British meant they were seen by the local population to have displaced Buddhists from their work in their tens of thousands.

Grievances among the Buddhist population of Yangon only intensified as colonial rule dragged on and a feeling hardened that they were being subordinated to foreigners. And in time, a strange phenomenon began to occur: Muslim communities in Myanmar that could trace their roots back centuries suddenly came to be lumped together with the more recent arrivals, and all they stood for as threats to the "traditional" order that the early kings had crafted.

Perhaps the clearest instance of this shift came on 26 July 1938, as anti-colonial sentiment was reaching its crescendo. As the sun burned through the afternoon sky, crowds began to collect inside the perimeter of Shwedagon Pagoda in Yangon, the country's most revered totem to the Buddha. They arrived first in small groups, but as the afternoon wore on the numbers built. By early evening close to 10,000 people had amassed there. Various speakers, some of them monks, others political leaders, took to an elevated platform and, one by one, launched a tirade against a Muslim man writing under the pseudonym Maung Shwe Hpi. Until several weeks before the writer had been known only to a small number of Muslim intellectuals in Yangon. Seven years earlier, he had penned a response to a pamphlet issued by a Buddhist that criticised Islamic teachings. Maung Shwe Hpi's offering had, according to those who later rounded on him, deliberately disparaged the Buddha. Around 1,000 copies of his response were circulated, and garnered little attention. Then in 1936, another print run saw an additional 2,500 copies distributed, but still it gained little traction. It was only in July 1938 that people began to take notice. First it caught the attention of staff at *The Sun* newspaper. An article dated 19 July called for "drastic action" to be taken on him,[9] while on the same day the *New Light of Burma* decried it as "an insult to the Burmese nation as a whole."[10] Significant page space was given over to polemics focusing on the insult to Buddha inherent in the text, meaning that the crowds who had arrived already incensed at Shwedagon Pagoda that afternoon were primed for what they were about to hear. On the platform, speakers had only to explain over and again what Maung Shwe Hpi's writing symbolised for the situation to turn violent. As the sun dipped in the sky, the audience made for the Muslim marketplace of Surti Bazar in downtown Yangon, chanting anti-Muslim slogans along the way. Battalions of police, among them Muslims installed by the British, tried to disperse them. In the process, two monks were hurt. The next day, attacks on Muslim communities erupted across Yangon.

The carnage was fuelled in part by the way the injuries to the monks were framed in the morning newspapers. They were not a localised incident, but instead were symptomatic of a broad and violent hostility towards Buddhists among Muslims. Fast forward nearly a century, and that same framing would goad on the mobs that attacked Nasi and other Muslim neighbourhoods across the country.

But the rioters of the late 1930s were propelled by a second force. Towards the end of the preceding day, as the speeches at Shwedagon had come to an end, a resolution was passed. It warned that unless police tracked down and arrested Maung Shwe Hpi, "steps will be taken to treat the Muslims as enemy No. 1 who insult the Buddhist community and their religion, and to bring about the extermination of the Muslims and the extinction of their religion and language."[11]

★ ★ ★

The idea that Myanmar could only survive as a nation if foreign influences were purged and Buddhism returned to centre stage characterised much of nationalist thinking throughout the twentieth century. But even long after the end of colonial rule, it continues. The young man I met in the teashop in northern Yangon had been a member of Ma Ba Tha, the monk-led organisation that took its name from a popular anti-colonial rallying cry of the 1920s and 1930s: "Amyo, Batha, Thathana!" – race, language/religion, and Sāsana, the teachings of the Buddha. These were the three pivots on which Myanmar society revolved, each one as inviolable as the other. One of the leading secular anti-colonial organisations, the We Burman Association, founded in 1930 and later headed by General Aung San, father of Aung San Suu Kyi and leader of the independence movement, printed the cry on pamphlets circulated around Yangon and other major cities. But it implied by its name that the independence movement would be a Bamar-centric one.[12] Other ethnicities were involved in the broader quest for independence, and political figureheads of various creeds rose to seniority in the post-independence government, but theirs would be a marginal presence in the new political landscape, for they too were seen as lackeys of the colonial power, and not fully Myanmar.

Partly in response to the campaigns of agitation led by predominantly Bamar figures, the British had drafted soldiers from the Kayin, the Kachin and other smaller ethnicities into their army, as well as Muslims, and awarded them positions above that of Bamar. They were seen as more trustworthy than these other dissenters who had led the charge against British rule. But that ill-thought-out policy of the British backfired in more ways than one. Not only were the flames of resentment towards them further fanned, but the independence movement of the 1920s and 1930s developed an ethnic and religious chauvinism towards non-Bamar and non-Buddhist that would carry well into the post-independence era, splitting the country along multiple lines and paving the way for decades of conflict.

The rallying cry of "Amyo, Batha, Thathana!" spoke to a need for the homogenisation of Myanmar society after decades of corrosive foreign rule. But the linking of those three elements into a singular vision of society meant that conceptions of who truly belonged were greatly narrowed, thereby enlarging the pool of those who did not. Just as these nationalist movements knew those three pivots to have been threatened by the British and its immigrant workforce more than a century ago, the monks of Ma Ba Tha believed them now to be threatened by Islam. The imams and their followers were the new colonisers, doing in their own way what had nearly been achieved by the imperial power long before.

Watching the violence of 2012 and afterwards unfold, it felt as if history was repeating itself. The waves of attacks in Rakhine State and central Myanmar seemed to echo that of 1938 – an attempt to avenge and correct the weakening of Buddhism by people of different religions and nationalities. But not all was as straightforward as it first appeared. In the months after Muslim quarters were torched in Rakhine State I wrote of the historic streak of Islamophobia coursing through Myanmar society – that the violence of today was merely the latest eruption of long-dormant tensions. With hindsight that appeared too simplistic. Anxieties, if they are latent, can be awakened, giving the illusion that the conflicts of today are the natural progression of historic enmities. But they can also be manufactured or appear as the logical response to new circumstances. In the years after 2012 I met Buddhists, young and old, as well as Muslims, whose sense of foreboding about that Other seemed very new. Fed by stories from the past, fears were activated so that old friends suddenly took on sinister qualities that turned them into enemies – for some of such malicious intent that the use of violence against them seemed morally just. Looking back on the Myanmar of the twentieth century, however, good relations between Buddhists and Muslims have been the norm, and violence an aberration. What had caused those aberrations? And why, in the years after the transition began, did Myanmar feel like such a divided society? There had seemed to be unity in opposition to the junta, but suddenly, as the junta began to step back, that crumbled.

There did however appear to be one clear similarity between the Myanmar of the early twentieth century and the country of today. The notion of ethnic and religious superiority promoted by the Bamar Buddhist nationalists of the independence movement was seized upon by the military when it took power in 1962. The British, eager to administer as effectively as possible such a diverse population, had already created its own ill-fated taxonomy of ethnic groups, hardening boundaries between communities that before had been fluid, and preparing the ground for conflict well into the future. All it took was a paranoid clique of generals to further manipulate lines of difference so that it could sell to the population the idea that Myanmar was still, long after the British left, infested with internal enemies. The quest for national unity became one of national uniformity, with the military seeking to assimilate vast swathes of the population into the Bamar Buddhist core – all the better to create a nation of one voice, one blood. But those that could never conform to the vision of the ideal society suffered their own particular fate. They were too different to ever truly belong, and in time were pushed further and further towards the edges of Myanmar society.

3

The art of belonging: a peculiar transaction in Yangon

Not so long ago, a visitor to an immigration office in Myanmar will have encountered a signboard on the wall, its inscription rendered in bold lettering, that warned of a particular peril facing the country: "The Earth will not swallow a race to extinction but another race will." It had become the slogan of the Ministry of Immigration during the long years of military rule, when the country retreated inwards, walling itself off from the outside world. Like much of the rhetoric of that age, it was abrupt and deliberately stark, and the message it contained was simple: save for strong borders and the vigilant offices of the state, the country would be overrun by outsiders. In time, the national race might cease to exist.

I only learnt of the slogan some time after the signboards had begun, bit by bit, to be taken down. As the transition progressed, these remnants of military rule, though still present, appeared less frequently. Now, with hindsight, there seemed an eerie prescience to the slogan, a warning of what might, with the right forces awakened, happen when those vigilant offices came under new management and the society around them began to shift. The military may have stepped back, but the violence of 2012 and thereafter showed that the fears it encouraged did not depart with the men in green.

The junta that ruled Myanmar in various guises for nearly half a century did so with a particular vision in mind, taken from a motto used by the independence movement: "One voice, one blood, one nation." On giant red billboards planted at intersections of busy roads it spoke of the "People's Desire," imploring loyal subjects to "Crush all internal and external destructive elements as the common enemy." They implied that there was an undercurrent of existential anxiety running throughout the population, common to all the people. Or perhaps, where that anxiety wasn't present, it could be cultivated. Fear has always been a powerful unifier, and if the authors of these slogans could sell the idea that a threat to the nation lurked just beyond its borders, or perhaps even within them, then the project to bring disparate peoples under one flag might bear fruit.

In the decades after the coup of 1962 that brought Ne Win to power, a narrative developed which saw the military not so much as nation builders but nation restorers. They would return Myanmar to its supposed pre-colonial glory, when a Buddhist order thrived, uncontaminated by foreign influence, and all subjects of the king enjoyed an abiding sense of national unity. It saw that past as a blueprint for the future, one that fed much of the propaganda circulated in the decades after the coup that carried an underlying warning of the dangers of cultural diversity. The billboards and signboards had a particular bluntness to them, not to be easily forgotten, but others were more lyrical. They evoked a fanciful picture of what had been, and what, with some work, could be.

"Moving about in the manner of whirlpools," so began one passage in *Minye Kaungbon*, a text issued in the mid-1990s by the State Law and Order Restoration Council, the successor to Ne Win's regime, "racial groups have assimilated to a large extent and just as one major [one] was about to emerge, Myanmar fell under imperialist rule. Some currents of water that had not yet completely assimilated with others were prevented from reaching the journey's end and were left half way."

The British sabotaged that project, so the story went, and drove a deep wedge between the different racial and religious groups of the country.

> They spread false tales of differences in race and in culture as if they were merely defending minority rights … Let all national groups have complete faith, trust and love among themselves. They are blood-brothers and let them be united just like water is united and indivisible.[1]

The quest the military embarked upon was to restore that sense of purity and homogeneity to the country. But of course it never existed. King Anawratha may have achieved a degree of unity of the valley peoples that none before him had managed, but after the fall of his dynasty, the country's centre was embroiled in centuries of conflict between rival kingdoms, as the power of the Bamar kingdoms waxed and waned greatly.

There was, however, some truth to the accusations. Myanmar has always been a nation of innumerable porous and interchangeable identity groups, each with divergent loyalties. Yet Britain imported its obsession with racial classification, one that had been used to such deleterious effect in its colonies elsewhere in the world. Boundaries were drawn between peoples where they hadn't previously existed, and over time, the human landscape in Myanmar began to change. Once fluid notions of ethnicity calcified into hard distinctions between groups. Myanmar emerged from colonial rule with an emboldened sense of diversity, but it was of a sort that was imposed, rather than having developed organically. The colonial administration's carving up of the population meant that allegiances, and all that came with them – competition and conflict – were directed along ethnic lines, and for a military elite consisting almost solely of the Bamar Buddhist majority that sought to control every inch of the land, this posed a particular problem. It would be the job of the post-independence rulers to re-build the nation. They would construct from this mosaic of groups a single identity and bring together those currents of water as they headed towards the journey's end. What began after the coup in 1962 was a process of forced assimilation of different identity groups into the ethnic majority sphere, and the banishing of those that would never conform to the ideal nation. In doing so, the dangers posed by other races, internal or external, to the "national race" would lessen, and the sense of unity and harmony that had been so disrupted by foreign rule would be finally returned to the country. Or so the logic went.

It is from this starting point, of illuminating the broader processes of statecraft in Myanmar over the past half century that have affected all communities, not just Muslims, that the violence of the transition is perhaps best understood. The mobs that began visiting Muslim neighbourhoods in 2012 may have done so long after these processes had started, but they signalled that the project of national unification was by no means finished.

★ ★ ★

One evening in Yangon I had dinner with a friend on the northern edge of Inya Lake. A stone's throw from the restaurant sat the compound where Ne Win had lived out his final days. From the roadside you can peer across a spit of water and, through a clump of trees that rise up from the lip of the lake, see snatches of what had once been the former general's house-cum-prison. He was confined there in March 2002, 14 years after he resigned from office. Several months before, the new regime, formed of members of his inner circle that took power after his fall, had gotten wind of his involvement in an alleged plot crafted by his son-in-law and grandsons to overthrow the then junta leader Than Shwe and return the family to power. The former general would die there nine months later, a recluse in a home that, walled off from the life going on outside the compound, mirrored the isolation he had forced on Myanmar.

The friend I met that evening had been 18 when Ne Win died. Save for a small obituary in the state-run *New Light of Myanmar* newspaper, the death had gone largely unannounced in media. Perhaps the new clique of generals saw the indignity of an unmarked death as an appropriate posthumous punishment for his treason; perhaps they feared it might stimulate some sort of response from the populace. Either way, he had been an immensely unpopular leader, and this had only grown with his time in office. His paranoiac superstition and fear of usurpation made him a highly erratic ruler, prone to irrational decisions that verged on the maniacal. Twice in the 1980s he demonetised the Myanmar currency in a bid to exorcise from it number combinations he felt would bring bad luck, in a stroke wiping out the already meagre savings of millions.

★ ★ ★

Hla Hla moved to Yangon from a small village in Mon State to the southeast at the age of four. It was 1988, the year of the nationwide uprising that, although eventually put down by the military, would ultimately force Ne Win from power. His fall in July that year, after a resignation speech that included the infamous warning to student protestors, "If the army shoots ... it shoots to hit," was followed briefly by the rule of his Chief Justice, U Maung Maung, before a coup in September marked the beginning of the era of the State Law and Order Restoration Council and the eventual rise to power of Senior General Than Shwe, Myanmar's last outright dictator.

Hla Hla had come to Yangon with her mother and father, leaving her extended family – cousins, aunts, uncles – behind in their village just south of the Mon capital, Mawlamyine. "In the summer holidays I would return to the village and I loved it there," she recalls. It was a remote location, made all the more so by the woefully under-maintained roads that wound their way through the border regions. "Thirty-five cousins were there; the whole village was full of my kind. But in Yangon I felt lonely. I couldn't make any friends."

In the four decades between independence and Hla Hla's arrival in Yangon, the dynamic between the dominant Bamar ethnic bloc and the minority groups scattered around the country's periphery had changed. Shortly before Myanmar became an independent nation in 1948, several of the ethnic groups residing in the border regions were guaranteed the freedom to secede from Myanmar, and others, although not all, to be granted self-determination and rights equal to those of the Bamar. But those promises were gradually withdrawn, first by the post-independence civilian government of U Nu, and then by the dictatorship that arrived with Ne Win in 1962. As it became increasingly evident that self-determination would not be granted, ethnic rebellions intensified in the country's periphery, and the military responded in kind. Despite Myanmar having no external enemies, the army grew to become the country's best resourced institution, channelling all its energy into putting down the revolts and launching a decades-long effort to subvert the status of ethnic minorities and suppress the markers of their cultural identity – their language, their freedom to practise their religions or celebrate their National Day.

Hla Hla hailed from one of these minorities, but one with a particularly proud heritage whose decline had embittered its leaders all the more. At various points over the past millennium the Mon kingdom had covered vast territory in southern Myanmar and into Thailand. Its contact with Theravada Buddhist schools in Sri Lanka had provided a transmission line for Buddhism to enter Myanmar, and it was through the influence of a Mon monk, Shin Arahan, that King Anawratha had converted in the eleventh century, paving the way for Buddhism's eventual preeminence. There were lengthy periods in which the Mon had enjoyed great prestige, but as the Bamar sphere expanded, the Mon were gradually reduced to a minority, in both size and clout. The Mon Freedom League had formed the year prior to independence, and launched its own revolt shortly after the British departed. And when the military came to power, all Mon – like ethnic minority groups the country over – were considered potential saboteurs of the nation-building project.

After the family had settled in a suburb in northern Yangon, Hla Hla was enrolled at school. It wasn't an easy induction into life in the then capital. The school was populated mainly with Bamar children from northern Yangon, and she found it difficult to integrate. "They all made fun of me because I'm not Bamar. My Mon accent was quite strong and people laughed at it," she remembers.

At the age of ten, she was taken by her parents to the local immigration office to apply for a National Registration Card. The small laminated card is obligatory for all citizens – proof that you belong in Myanmar. "When the time came to get my identity card my mum wasn't sure what to do," Hla Hla recalled. Her mother knew that ethnicity had long ago become a chief determinant of one's fortunes, and either granted or denied freedoms at a time in Myanmar when freedom was a prized asset, to be snatched at any opportunity. Like religion, it was stamped on the ID card. For the military, it provided an indicator of the carrier's supposed allegiances, and thus put any non-Bamar at an immediate disadvantage. They were deemed worthy of a level of surveillance far beyond that of the majority group.

"If you go travelling somewhere the police will ask where you register and what race you are and that's the problem," she said. "I didn't change my ID because of social pressure, but because of the way the government tried to control and discriminate and separate people. So although we are Mon, when we moved to Yangon my mother said, 'No, we must be Bamar Buddhist because this is the highest identity we can get'."

★ ★ ★

When the British arrived in the early nineteenth century they knew virtually nothing of the rich and complex tapestry of cultural norms and belief systems that made up the territory they sought control of. At the time of its early incursions into lower Myanmar in the first quarter of the century, the Konbaung Dynasty ruled over much of the lowland territory, and as far to the west as Bengal and Assam. To the north and east, in the mountainous borderlands that ring Myanmar, lay a patchwork of microstates that remained largely independent of the central kingdoms. While the kings would dispatch their armies into the mountains to round up slaves and to levy taxes on upland populations, they were never subject to direct rule. Their communities were too remote to be of much economic or strategic value and their land too rugged for the farming techniques that had developed on the flat terrain below them. Unlike the townspeople of the central plains who had intermingled for centuries, these "hill people" had developed their own economic and political systems in comparative isolation, both from the lowlanders and from one another, making their incorporation into mainland societies all the more difficult.

In the Myanmar of that age there were ethnic groups, so to speak, and each looked to longstanding distinctions that extended back well before colonial rule. Texts from the pre-modern era speak of Mon or Shan, and they note their different customs, dress and language – those features that comprise the identifying cultural "material" of ethnicity. But rulers of the time also understood that these distinctions were not hard and fast, and nor did they necessarily determine allegiances. Instead, boundaries between groups in the pre-colonial era were porous, and subject to shifting political loyalties. The distinguishing features of the two major lowland ethnicities, the Mon and

Bamar, could be swapped back and forth at will: ponytails would be adjusted, dress would be changed, and a Mon could become a Bamar if it meant that the marauding armies of one kingdom would spare them.[2] There is a rich archive of stories that illuminate this. A time traveller sent back to the court of Ava in 1740 may have been surprised to see battalions of the Mon king, Smin Dhaw, who had launched a final bid to expand his power, being led by ethnic Bamar, only to be repelled by Mon soldiers fighting on the behest of the ruler of the kingdom of Ava, himself a Bamar[3] – a scene that would be entirely alien to watchers of Myanmar today.

While ethnicity still carried great significance as a marker of identity, if one could "become" another, perhaps by changing clothes or switching loyalties, then it brought into question a claim so often repeated by the nationalists of today: that members of each group were defined by innate characteristics that had remained unchanged across millennia and that established members of one as the natural ruler of the country, the master race, and all others as secondary citizens, or worse. Somewhere in between the battles of Ava and the conflicts in modern-day Myanmar, this had come to be, and it meant a politicisation of ethnicity that locked groups in a state of perpetual competition, and often violent conflict, with one another.

Much of this was owed to the British. At the time of their arrival in Myanmar, the science of racial classification was popular in Europe. It was a science that sought order and coherence where there appeared none, and tried to replicate the hierarchical social relations that were common to Western societies. While at its core was the belief that groups of people could be defined along biological lines, and that these then determined behaviour and thus social status, it was also used to categorise people for more functional purposes. Unlike the Mon or Bamar defectors of the pre-colonial period who could alter their identity when circumstances demanded it, this science emphasised that different ethnicities, or "races," as the British then referred to them, were fixed in time, the boundaries between them yielding not to external events. It ignored the preexisting nuances in relations between groups, yet it would make the job of administrating foreign lands that much easier. Although woefully uneducated as to the complex dynamics between the different communities of Myanmar, enumerators were dispatched by the British into the hills to conduct censuses of the population, encountering what political scientist James C. Scott describes as "a baroque complexity that all but defeated their mania for classificatory order."[4] Yet still they were classified: groups became groups because of the languages they spoke, and sometimes because of their geographical location. The more salient preexisting allegiances based on kinship, or even political and economic opportunism, were largely ignored.

This artificial construction and ordering of communities was necessary because of the way the colonial power had divided Myanmar into two territories: Burma Proper, the central region that was governed by Bamar under the auspices of the British, and the mountainous Frontier Areas of Kayah (Karenni), Kachin and Chin. The latter contained many different sub-groups, all of which developed in comparative isolation as a result of the rugged topography of their lands. Over time, broad umbrella groups evolved as communities that had before considered themselves rather more discrete but now came to see themselves as part of a greater whole.[5] The British had, in effect, "ethnicised" the landscape in Myanmar by greatly politicising ethnicity, and what had been more nuanced relations that traversed these moving lines began to stiffen.

It echoed the work undertaken by European powers in Africa long before. "To control a people's culture is to control their tools of self-definition in relationship to others," the Kenyan writer, Ngugi wa Thiong'o, once observed of the effects of colonial divide and rule policies there.[6] In Myanmar, as in European-administered countries the world over in the eighteenth and nineteenth centuries, ethnicity became the major cleavage between, and an instrument of exclusion of, different groups.

This reengineering of the landscape was to have a toxic effect on relations between the centre of Myanmar and its periphery after colonial rule ended. By codifying these newly drawn boundaries, what distinctions did exist soon hardened into divisions. The national identity that had started to coalesce around Bamar Buddhism during the independence movement of the 1920s and 1930s took a more rigid form after the British departed, when the legacy of its classification began to play out in violent forms. It fed the idea, so amplified by the junta, that ethnicity was an unassailable point of difference, and that Others – whether ethnic, racial or religious – were necessarily threatening to the Bamar Buddhist majority.

★ ★ ★

"We were so scared that they would find out we were Mon," Hla Hla said of the first visit to immigration. "When we went there they looked at me and asked, 'Where are you from?' I said Yangon. 'Where were you born?' I said Mawlamyine. 'Are you Mon?' No."

The grilling was to last several hours. She remembers the careful instructions detailed to her beforehand, to ensure no clues were given as to her origins. "My mum had told me not to say anything. I was so scared. It was like sitting in an interview – am I going to fail or pass?"

By that age, Hla Hla had mastered how to speak with a Yangon accent. It was partly a conscious effort, to stem the bullying at school, and partly strategic. "I got comments and corrections back from friends and picked up the accent that way. I had to adapt to the flow of how they speak Burmese." But she still felt sidelined at school. Her teachers would call her "Mon Ma," or "Mon girl." "They would say to others, 'Let's ask Mon Ma to do it', and I'd have to go and buy food for them."

But her parents also knew that in order to present a compelling case to immigration officials that she was indeed Bamar and not Mon they would need to take additional measures. Were she to continue as a Mon, then the discrimination would persist; not just in school, but afterwards – her career might suffer, and she would come under undue attention from authorities. What followed was a complete rewriting of her family tree, going back generations. "When you go to the immigration they look at you and if you don't look Burmese they say 'No. You can't be Burmese – you look Karen, or Mon. Are you Karen? Show me your family tree.'"

The document she would eventually produce was a lie. It had erased her complex ancestry – a father who was "half Muslim," a grandfather who was Chinese Mon, and written as such on his ID card. "We paid and completely made it up

– we Burmanised names completely." The local authorities in her village were friends, and a bribe to them meant they could alter the ID cards of everyone in her family. The process effectively homogenised her identity, bracketing her into a category, that of Bamar Buddhist, that spoke little to her true lineage. But more changes to her character lay ahead. I asked Hla Hla how exactly people made fun of her at school. Was the underlying belief in the science of racial classification introduced by the British – that ethnicity determined behaviour, and therefore that it should have a bearing on social status – alive in Myanmar during Hla Hla's early years? It seemed so.

"Me being dark. Also the way I sit and walk. The way you dress, the way you hold yourself and behave. You have to be a city girl, not like in the village," she replied.

Hla Hla eventually got the ID card and became, in the eyes of officialdom in Myanmar, a Bamar. She was able to convince the immigration officials that she belonged to this group, even though she didn't. It took some work – the changing of her accent, her posture, the rewriting of her family tree. But it wasn't a wholly lived experience. "We still think we belong to where we come from," she said. "We feel we migrated into Yangon and away from our town. But the food we still eat, and the traditions we still keep. We do not forget about it. This is us."

Yet the changes she did have to make – those that showed to immigration officials in Yangon her apparently true orientation – were essentially cosmetic. She hadn't needed to transform anything innate within her, regardless of the fact that the country's rulers have built the whole discourse of identity and belonging in Myanmar on the idea that ethnicity runs in the veins, and is therefore a key determinant of the character of the people – their goodness, or their wicked ways – that it seeks to rule over.

★ ★ ★

Another development occurred shortly before Hla Hla's birth. The regime began to vigorously peddle the idea that within the borders of Myanmar lived precisely 135 distinct "national races," or *taingyintha*, who were indigenous to the country. This provided the foundation for the discourse of belonging, but it had been a volatile discourse. The British had counted, or indeed created, 139 ethnic groups in its 1931 census; when General Ne Win ordered a fresh census in 1973, it found there to be 144. The numbers were in continual flux, and by 1983, even before a new round of enumerators were sent out into the valleys and hills, it was set at 135. But at no point was clear evidence provided for the source for that number.

By utilising a trick of the light that illuminates histories of ethnicity, the regime was able to lock in a taxonomy of ethnic groups that had little basis in reality. Implicit in the indexing of 135 groups was the belief that they, unlike others who were excluded, were composed of fixed bodies of people that had existed unbroken for centuries, or longer, and could be defined consistently across time. But all identity groups are the product of human mobilisation, and their boundaries, as Hla Hla and countless others showed, are not permanently set. Rather than degrees of construction – that some groups are natural and others artificial – there are instead degrees of chronology. Some came together earlier than others, but none rose up as one from the earth. Yet the intent of the national races discourse was to sell this idea of primordialism and to clean up the country after the mess and divisions left by the British. Any false claimants to the nation were weeded out, thereby denying them a place in that vaunted index.

Despite the mythology that underpins it, the concept of 135 "national races" set the framework for deciding who was and was not a citizen of the country. To be a citizen, one effectively had to be a member of a recognised group. The merits of individual claims, perhaps that one had an ancestry stretching back generations in Myanmar, mattered little unless the entire ethnicity the claimant subscribed to was certified indigenous. So derided were the "non-ethnics" inhabiting the land that immigration officials would by and large dismiss their claims to a legal status, for anyone who wore the badge of an unrecognised group simply could not be native to Myanmar.

Moreover, it echoed one of the great fictions of nationalism – the idea that there could ever be "one nation," in the sense of a contiguous grouping of people, in Myanmar or any other country; that all within a country's borders share a set of commonalities outside of their mere membership of the national community that unites them together. Some communities in Myanmar's periphery have as much, if not more, in common with populations in neighbouring countries than they do with their fellow "nationals," for the borderline pays little respect to the lineages of people who long before settled in the regions through which it was drawn. There, family lines still cut across that divider, and the cultural markers of those populations – the customs, the dialect – were largely unbroken by it.

For all its shakiness, the discourse of "national races" became perhaps the most powerful political tool in the

regime's armoury. After Ne Win had come to power in 1962
and launched his ideological crusade under the banner of
the "Burmese Way to Socialism," industry was nationalised
across the country. The resulting capital, he claimed, would
be redistributed to all indigenous communities. Despite the
fact that Ne Win himself was a *kabyer*, of mixed Chinese-
Bamar ancestry, his paeans to the pure Myanmar of old
belied a deeply ingrained xenophobia that drew a sharp
line between those he considered native to Myanmar, and
those who were deemed foreign. Hundreds of thousands of
Indians and Chinese were forced out of the country in the
mid-1960s and their businesses returned to their supposedly
rightful owners. Those who remained were issued with
Foreign Registration Certificates (FRCs), and when the
general unveiled a new constitution in 1974, all holders
of FRCs were required to hand them in and await a new
one.

When the first set of National Registration Cards were
issued in 1952, they hadn't included details of the holder's
ethnicity or religion. This meant that all who could prove a
family presence in the country going back two generations,
or who had lived in the country for eight years prior to
independence, were granted citizenship, regardless of their
group identity. Thirty years later, when Ne Win announced
the new Citizenship Act of 1982, that changed, and before
long ethnicity was flagged on the cards. Yet the military
government, it later became clear, would ignore the law
it crafted. After 1982, people were refused citizenship on
account of their not being among the 135 national races,
even though the index was created after the Citizenship Act
was promulgated. That Act had made no mention of it, but
as the 1980s wore on, the index became such a prominent

decider of who was and was not native to the country that it, and not the legal criteria for citizenship, came to determine the make-up of the national community.[7]

The most visible victims of this were the Rohingya. Under British rule, many who now identify as Rohingya were likely bracketed under different designators: as native "Rakhine Muslims," or as "Chittagonian Muslims" who arrived during the time of the British. Both categories were included in British censuses but later dropped by Ne Win. Why they disappeared is unclear, but for "Rakhine Muslim," it was likely a product of Ne Win's increasingly aggressive xenophobia. It might have been that the general was unable to countenance having a "foreign" religion alongside an indigenous ethnic label, or perhaps it gave Muslims a claim to Rakhine that he believed to be false. But because the group was absent from the list of 135 groups, so its members would be absented from the nation. In 1989, as their security grew increasingly imperilled, immigration officers went among Rohingya communities in Rakhine State demanding they turn in the Foreign Registration Cards they too had been given in the mid-1970s and await a new Citizenship Scrutiny Card. But those who still argued for a Rohingya identity, or who the government considered to be in the country illegally, were not given ID cards, and were refused re-registration. From that point on, the legal status of anyone who subscribed to the Rohingya identity began to crumble.

It appeared that they too were considered foreigners, first introduced by the British Empire, whose loyalty to the nation was in doubt. Their ethnicity was considered to be an artificial creation, in contrast to the supposedly "natural" groups listed on the index. It was created in order to give these supposed Bengali interlopers a claim to citizenship and, so it went, a platform on which to begin the Islamisation of Myanmar. Over time, the Rohingya would become that type of race warned of in the immigration slogan, one that, through the spread of their sinister ideas and their irreconcilable differences, would swallow the Myanmar people in their entirety. As a result, anyone who self-identified as Rohingya was pushed off the national map, even those who lay claim to deep roots in the country.

But it wasn't only they who were affected by the turn of events in 1982. Their denial of a place in society would manifest in the most insidious form, leaving them stateless, beyond the scope of law and justice, and the object of widespread resentment. But tiers of belonging were created that impacted on large sections of the population all over the country: "full citizens" looked down on "associate citizens," who in turn held a place of privilege, limited as it was, over "naturalised citizens." Bamar formed the bulk of the first category. Their ancestry in Myanmar prior to 1823, the year before Britain's arrival, when the country's demographic make-up began to shudder and shake, was never questioned. They were granted full political rights, albeit greatly curtailed in that era, but other minority groups fared worse. To gain full citizenship required the presentation of ID cards and a knowledge of procedures, but for populations embroiled in conflict or who didn't speak the mother tongue, these were often not issued, and so many in the ethnic states became associate citizens.[8]

"This is not because we hate them," Ne Win stated in 1982, shortly after the law was announced. "If we were to allow them to get into positions where they can decide the destiny of the State and if they were to betray us we would be in trouble."[9] They weren't Bamar, and were therefore untrustworthy – that was clear to the general. And with it, the distinction between the civilised Bamar centre and the unruly border peoples, amplified first by the British and then reified by the military, again came to determine the fortunes of millions.

* * *

The antagonism between the centre and periphery had been a slow-burning development. Armed conflict along ethnic lines began in 1949. The Kayin, which had provided vital military manpower for the colonial government, had been promised an independent state by the British as it was readying for departure. But as it became clear upon independence that this would not be granted, small-scale uprisings began in Kayin State, soon coalescing into a broad armed resistance movement. By the beginning of 1949 Kayin insurgents had taken several towns in central Myanmar and the delta region, and in response, soldiers from that ethnic group were purged from the military's ranks. The Karen National Union, formed in the hills of Kayin State close to the border with Thailand, then declared war on the Myanmar government.

Others soon followed. As negotiations for independence had gotten underway and a new constitution was drawn up, General Aung San had resisted pressure from within his party to make Buddhism the state religion. The father of the independence movement feared that it would stir anger among the significant portion of the non-Buddhist populace at a time when national harmony was a key priority.

At the hour of Myanmar's independence in January 1948, with the by then deceased Aung San having stood firm during discussions the year before, it remained a secular state. But by the mid 1950s, the issue had become hot. In May 1956 three Sangha organisations threatened mass protests unless Buddhism was elevated to the state religion. Prime Minister U Nu, then in his eighth year of the premiership, responded in an address to elder monks that he was anxious to meet their demands. Yet he worried that it might only worsen the already bitter grievances held by ethnic minorities, among whom were sizeable non-Buddhist communities, towards a government that was showing clear signs of reneging on its pledges of self-determination for minority groups.

But U Nu pushed ahead. He was known to be a committed Buddhist; one writer claimed his administration "could not be distinguished from one long Buddhist ceremony,"[10] and he entered the monkhood for a brief spell in the mid-1950s. As he toured the country in the build-up to elections in 1960, monks campaigned in his favour, taking to villages and towns to rally support for his party. Two months later, U Nu formed a special commission to gauge public opinion on making Buddhism the state religion. It canvassed communities of the four major religious groups – Buddhism, Hinduism, Islam and Christianity, as well as animism – but gave disproportionate voice to Buddhists. But when it travelled to the northernmost state of Kachin, the train carrying the commission into the state capital Myitkyina was attacked by rock-throwing protestors and forced to turn back. These were the first salvos in a popular revolt that the following year would crystallise into the Kachin armed rebellion. Also denied self-determination and the accompanying guarantees for respect of their cultural practices, the Kachin, a sizeable proportion of whom were Christian, understood that if Buddhism were to become the state religion in a country populated by multiple faith groups then it would codify the predominance of those who subscribed to Buddhism. The result would be to further push ethnic and religious minorities to the periphery.

Buddhism never did make it that far. U Nu managed to pass a watered-down bill in 1961, but he was ousted the following year by Ne Win. While the general, who would rule for the next 26 years, understood the power that the faith held over the majority population, he believed that church and state should remain separate, and so it was revoked.

Instead Ne Win embarked on a different strategy of unification. U Nu's manoeuvrings, undertaken in the wake of the mess left by the British, whose rule laid waste to social structures and redrew lines of authority and allegiance, had pushed non-Bamar Buddhists further away. This weakened what potential there was for the government to rule over the entirety of Myanmar. Instead, under the general's watch, minority groups would be drawn closer towards the centre, coercively assimilated into the majority. Doing so, he believed, would cultivate a loyalty within them that would serve to hold the country together in these volatile times. Over and again he affirmed the ethnic and religious hierarchy that had come to be in Myanmar, with Bamar Buddhists as the true heirs to the land, and all others, whether indigenous or not, as threats to the master ethnicity.

"Today you can see that even people of pure blood are being disloyal to the race and country but are being loyal to others," he said in a speech in 1979.

If people of pure blood act this way, we must carefully watch people of mixed blood. Some people are of pure blood, pure Burmese heritage and descendants of genuine citizens. Karen, Kachin and so forth, are of genuine pure blood. But we must consider whether these people are completely for our race, our Burmese people: and our country, our Burma.[11]

Under the general's logic, there was an obstacle in the way of unity – that of diversity. And as the many different ethnic rebellions showed, that diversity was the source of a violence that would gradually eat away at the nation, threatening the realisation of a pure Myanmar.

Hla Hla had been one of these obstacles. And when she came to Yangon, a transaction of sorts occurred: she would give them her identity and in return be granted a degree of agency she would otherwise not have as a non-Bamar. That was the transformation she must undergo to develop loyalty to the nation. Elsewhere the process of assimilation – of pulling people into the Bamar Buddhist sphere, and doing away with those who resisted – took on different, more explicit forms: the teaching of ethnic minority languages in schools was replaced by Bamar language classes; non-Buddhists were coerced into converting to the majority faith, while Buddhist communities were planted in regions populated by Christians and Muslims, becoming pawns in large-scale social engineering projects. And ethnic minority women were forced to marry Bamar soldiers deployed to the border regions, thereby diluting the concentration of their own communities. Accompanying those projects were campaigns of violence, led by the military, that had as their ultimate goal the eradication of these differences, whether by exclusion from society through mass flight to other countries, or by the killing of those considered different.

But Hla Hla's was a peculiar transaction, for at its core lay a seeming contradiction: with those adjustments she was able to become part of the master ethnicity, even though the conversation surrounding identity in Myanmar since the dawn of military rule emphasised the timelessness of ethnic categories – that Bamar was an entity unto itself, purer than all others and the pivot around which the nation revolved, and always had.

There were other people, whom we'll meet later, who underwent such wholesale shifts in their outward identity that they were pitched from the far fringes of society right into the core: Rohingya who "became" Rakhine, Muslims who "became" Buddhists. Or for one man, both. It seemed to be the only way they could become members of a society to which the criteria for belonging had narrowed so greatly.

There was, however, an important message to take from the stories of those who experienced this transformation. If particular traits can be activated that allow us to join other groups, then it shows that none of us is one singular identity. Instead we each stand as composites of different characteristics, loyalties and attachments that are modified greatly over time, and that link us to others in many different and interchangeable ways. When particular identity labels bring power and prestige, individuals often cleave tighter to them. But for others, like Hla Hla or anyone that comes from a subordinated group, there is often a compulsion to morph from one to another. Rather than this providing evidence of an innate superiority in the master ethnicity, this phenomenon shows that the identity, or identities, we subscribe to have less of a bearing on our inner nature than some might like to think. Our ability to move between groups is surely a reflection of that old dictum, that our similarities are more powerful than our differences.

Yet for the nationalist project to succeed in distinguishing those who belong from those who do not, it requires differences to be emphasised in ways that make them appear threatening, and those cross-cutting ties to be obfuscated entirely. The most barbaric crimes of the past century have been, above all else, expressions of common hatred for people considered to be different to us, and whose difference runs so deep that the only way to exorcise it is to banish it from this world. That can happen only when the common ground is obliterated and the dynamics between groups rewritten entirely.

The rape and murder of Ma Thida Htwe on 28 May 2012 provided a catalyst to drive this process forward – not just between the Buddhists and Muslim communities of Rakhine State but, gradually, all over the country. When newspapers and social media began to identify the culprits by their religion, it made victims of Muslims who neither had any link to the assailants nor to the Rohingya ethnicity generally. Islam, rather than particular individuals who subscribed to it, became the new threat in Myanmar. No longer were Muslims members of the same local and national community; instead they were cast as utterly opposed, and this reality was asserted again and again by Buddhist nationalists over the years that followed 2012, thereby encouraging the violence to move into areas of the country with little prior history of communal tension. The Muslims, it soon became apparent, were not just another obstacle in the way of unity. They were the race that would swallow the people of Myanmar – the true people, the Buddhists – to extinction.

4

Us and them: making identities, manipulating divides

The construction of an identity is often done by antithesis – I am what you are not. When, in the wake of the first wave of violence in western Myanmar, the Buddhist Rakhine and Muslim Rohingya retreated sharply to within their own communities, the process of differentiation took on a new force. It seemed natural that any fear of a collective identity being weakened would be met with vigorous efforts to refine and assert that identity. But as relations quickly worsened, the psychological polarisation that followed gathered an altogether new momentum, setting in motion a break-up of the local society whose consequences would be both profound and lasting.

That process hadn't begun with the violence of June 2012, however. Rather, a hardened notion of what it meant to "be Rakhine" had been in the making long before, as the inhabitants of the state faced off against three successive colonising powers: the pre-colonial kings of mainland Myanmar, the British and the Bamar-dominated military. For the Buddhist population, who claimed with the greatest vigour to be the rightful owners of the state, this unrelenting colonisation drive fuelled a siege mentality that eventually came to be directed at Muslims. Today, Rakhine Buddhists

of all stripes often speak of being "caught between Islamisation and Burmanisation" – the drive to stamp a Bamar,
or Burman, identity on ethnic minority groups. Yet while
the conflict with Muslims may have dominated the news
coming out of Myanmar in recent years, the manoeuvrings
of different political powers long before that were instru-
mental in planting the seeds for the violence and fuelling
the separation of an "us" from a "them" – a clearly defined
in-group ranged against multiple out-groups, with Rakhine
primed to see any perceived outsiders as threatening. So
forceful did the separation become that whatever shared
sense of victimhood might have developed between the
Buddhists and Muslims of the state under the dictatorship
was quickly forgotten. As the transition away from military
rule progressed, nationalist Rakhine leaders amplified the
looming threat of further subordination, this time to Islam,
and in the process created a narrative that centred on the
need purify the Rakhine identity and finally rid their land
of any foreign contaminants.

It was a powerful narrative, for it drew on a centuries-
old campaign to suppress the identity and autonomy of
Rakhine, thereby giving their present-day condition a
painful historical backdrop. And it had substantial merit.
Long before Islam became the dominant threat in the
Rakhine imagination, the independence of the Rakhine
people, and their freedom to follow their own customs
and traditions, was snatched from them. Their once mighty
kingdom, encompassing much of present-day eastern
Bangladesh as well as the western flank of Myanmar, was
annexed by a king who sat on a throne hundreds of miles
away and ruled with little regard for the traditional norms of
his new subjects. They came to be managed by his people,

under his strictures. Yet the power of this new and remote authority, projected from afar, had a curious effect, for it began to erode the tradition of inclusivity that had once been a marker of Rakhine culture.

For much of the past millennium the busy trade along the shores of western Myanmar meant that the Rakhine kingdom was populated by a large and transient immigrant community. In the centuries that followed the migration there of communities from the Ayeyarwady Valley, and before its annexation by King Bodawpaya in 1784, the kings of Rakhine had been compelled to cultivate an inclusive attitude towards their subjects on account of the myriad different religious and ethnic communities that lived there. The early Persian and Indian seafarers who arrived from the ninth century onwards were small in number and had made only a minor impact on local society, but this began to change around the fifteenth century. Bengali kings that ruled territories to the west of Rakhine had helped several of their Rakhine counterparts retain the throne against the manoeuvring of rivals. The Rakhine king, Min Saw Mon Narameikhla, fled to Bengal in the early fifteenth century following attacks by Bamar armies from the east, and spent 24 years under the protection of the Sultan of Bengal. When he returned to establish the city of Mrauk U, he built mosques alongside the pagodas that dotted in their hundreds the hills surrounding the city. For two centuries after, Rakhine kings would use Muslim designations for their names and mint coins with Persian inscriptions to make the bountiful trade with westerly kingdoms easier. Despite the region soon bearing the marks of strong Islamic influence, religious differences hadn't provided the source of violent contestation they do now.

By the early eighteenth century, however, the coastal region had fallen into a state of anarchy, as the many peoples – Christian Portuguese and Dutch traders, Buddhist Siamese mercenaries, Hindu and Muslim Bengali settlers and slaves – that had joined the existing population vied against one another to place in power a ruler that would safeguard their interests.[1] The kingdom's frontiers were greatly weakened, and this allowed King Bodawpaya to make his move. In late 1784 a band of Rakhine ventured to Amarapura in central Myanmar, where he then sat, to request his intervention. The Bamar king needed little prompting – he would execute a "just war" that would ensure the return of Buddhism to its central position in Rakhine culture, and remedy the foreign influence that was eroding the cohesion of society there. The invasion he launched brought the Rakhine kingdom under his rule, and used violence of a kind so grisly that it left an indelible mark in the Rakhine imagination.

"They united on the west coast, swept the Arakanese royal army out of Ramree Island, and camped along the Dalet River northwest of An, receiving the homage of the surrounding country," the historian G.E Harvey wrote of the 1784 invasion.

> Subsequent fighting took place through the creeks and islands, and the Arakanese came out to offer resistance both on land and sea; but they were outnumbered three to one and never succeeded in seriously checking the Burmese who occupied the capital Mrohaung [Mrauk U] without difficulty, inflicting wanton cruelties on the population, leaving them tied to stakes at low-water mark, or burying them up to their chin in fields which they then proceeded to harrow.[2]

The routing of the kingdom upended the social order, already weakened by the lengthy internal unrest that preceded Bodawpaya's invasion, and his soldiers looted its most sacred relics. Among them was the Mahamuni statue. Legend has it that the figure of the Great Sage had been sculpted during the time of the Buddha, who "breathed life upon it" when he visited Rakhine and gave it special powers to protect the kingdom.[3] Bodawpaya evidently wanted its guardianship for himself. When his soldiers returned to Amarapura, they brought with them a band of Kaman Muslims – those specially trained archers who had guarded the court of Mrauk U – who trailed behind them sections of the Mahamuni statue, to be reassembled at a temple on the sparse northern fringes of the old city. Nowadays the area is swallowed up by the suburbs of Mandalay, but visitors can still meander their way through the streets south of the moat and, once at the Mahamuni Buddha Temple, behold the onetime protector of the Rakhine kingdom, now fattened by the volumes of gold leaf that devotees – Bamar, Rakhine, Mon – have encased it in over the centuries since.[4]

When the British eventually departed Myanmar in the mid-twentieth century and the border with India was redrawn, the process of annexing Rakhine and bringing its people under Bamar authority was complete. When Ne Win later began his expansion into the periphery, he appointed only Bamar officials to regional military and administrative postings. If the recipe for a unified Myanmar state required domination by a single ethnicity and religion, then better that members of the superior group serve as the regime's tentacles in the hinterlands. Non-Bamar or non-Buddhist figures could not be trusted in positions of authority – their "kind" was deeply antagonistic towards the regime, and would not willingly act in its interests.

Ne Win seemed to have borrowed from the blueprints of his predecessor, for Bodawpaya had done something very similar two centuries before when he took control of the Rakhine kingdom and wholly purged it of Rakhine authority. After his invasion, political leaders and military commanders, monks and local officials, were all supplanted by Bodawpaya's own men, nearly all of them Bamar, and Maha Thammada, the last of the Rakhine kings, was exiled along with his entire court to Amarapura.

The effort undertaken by the military after 1962 to expand its control into the ethnic states that ring Myanmar earned the name "Burmanisation" on account of its bid to assert a Bamar identity and authority in these regions. Bodawpaya's conquest of the eighteenth century was an early incarnation of this: Bamar monks were sent to Rakhine with their Bamar language texts to set up Sangha networks that would bring the practice of Buddhism into their framework, and it centralised Rakhine political institutions under the Bamar royal court.[5] Ne Win later followed suit. Where the king had planted officials from his court in positions of power across Rakhine, so did the general appoint Bamar to the vast majority of senior administrative and ministerial posts, not just in Rakhine but all over the country. As Bodawpaya left a garrison of several thousand soldiers in Mrauk U to ensure his authority there remained paramount, so were troops loyal to Ne Win stationed in barracks across the state to monitor civilians and deliver the military's security objectives.

Similar processes have occurred across all ethnic states in Myanmar, in many ways mirroring the colonisation of sacked kingdoms in the centuries prior to British rule. This campaign to remove the collective agency of ethnic Rakhine – and ethnic minorities the country over – has occurred persistently across generations, providing the foundations for a deep-seated fear of subordination to "outsiders," whoever they may be.

★ ★ ★

Fuelling the gradual polarisation of religious and ethnic communities in western Myanmar was a transformation of the country's political landscape. As two of the major lowland kingdoms of the territory, Rakhine and Mon, were both annexed to the Bamar-dominated mainland in the latter eighteenth century, and as the British moved in and imposed their own designs on this foreign land, borders were drawn in place of porous frontiers. Those frontiers had once shifted regularly, causing communities to "belong" to different territories at different times, or sometimes to none at all.[6] Yet over time, what had been somewhat arbitrary boundaries came to be accepted as natural lines of division between nations and the people that inhabited them.

Western Myanmar came to know this well. Long before the border separating it from Bangladesh, and before that India, was finally demarcated in 1985, two-way traffic moved regularly across it. After Rakhine was annexed to Myanmar at the close of the eighteenth century, some 200,000 Rakhine, both Buddhist and Muslims, fled west, crossing the Naf River and the mountains that roll down from Chittagong, to areas of sanctuary where they wouldn't be reached by Bodawpaya's marauding forces. Later convulsions of violence on either side of the border would cause communities to move back and forth repeatedly. Sometimes they stayed and settled, sometimes not. But by the time it was redrawn after the departure of the British in the middle of the twentieth century, the communities of each country had developed a degree of attachment to their land, as did the peoples of post-colonial societies the world over, that only a modern-day nation state could generate. Long forgotten was the relative ease of movement between the territories of present-day Rakhine State and Bangladesh; anyone who arrived after the establishment of that border was considered alien to the land, and thus a threat to those who claimed it as their own.

At around the same time those ethnic Rakhine were fleeing into Bangladesh in the late eighteenth century, a Scottish physician by the name of Francis Buchanan was moving between the communities of Myanmar document-ing the various groups that lived there. Under the title *A Comparative Vocabulary of Some of the Languages Spoken in the Burma Empire*, he produced perhaps one of the most com-prehensive studies of the peoples of the region prior to the beginnings of colonial rule. In it he noted "three dialects, spoken in the Burma Empire, but evidently derived from the language of the Hindu nation. The first is that spoken by the Mohammedans, who have long settled in Arakan, and who call themselves Rooinga, or natives of Arakan."

Rohingya cite this, and subsequent references in Euro-pean texts to Buchanan's findings, as evidence of their pres-ence in the region prior to the British conquest of Rakhine in 1826 and the influx of workers from the subcontinent that followed it. They also point to the fact that Rohingya were recognised, at least vocally, by U Nu, and served as members of parliament, and even ministers, in the post-independence government.[7] Throughout the 1950s, 1960s and into the 1970s official documents referenced the Rohingya as inhabitants of northern Rakhine State. The denialism that is so pervasive now wasn't commonplace within the government after independence. The Rohingya could organise politically – the government sanctioned the Rohingya Students Association at Rangoon University – and the group had its own thrice-weekly Rohingya-language radio broadcast.

But as the regime sought to fix the ethnic landscape of Myanmar with a rigidity that bore little resemblance to the Myanmar of old, groups considered foreign to the country were gradually excluded. The hardening of an exclusive Rakhine Buddhist identity that resulted from the Burmanisation project, coupled with the removal of the "Rakhine Muslim" category from the 135-strong index of ethnic groups, compelled the Muslims of the state to cleave more tightly to another label, one that had a history in Myanmar going back to at least the late eighteenth century, and one that, at least initially, the government recognised. The Rohingya ethnicity should therefore have stood up to the test of the general's 1982 citizenship criteria: that of a presence in Myanmar prior to the advent of British rule in 1824. But its absence from British records provided Ne Win, who pushed the notion of an ethno-religiously "pure" Myanmar harder as time went on, with a pretext to exclude an entire group from the nation.

In an environment such as that shaped by the military in Myanmar, where ethnic groupings reified by the colonial power were cemented as primordial "facts," the longevity of a particular identity label was seen to determine, quite wrongly, the individual lineages of those who subscribed to it. So fixed have these supposed facts about Myanmar's ethnic make-up become – that the history of a group name corresponds directly to the history of its adherents – that public opinion is wholly pitched against the notion that anyone within the Rohingya group might have a longstanding presence there. It is a "new" label, and therefore its members must be new. Opponents of the label claim it gained traction in the 1950s as part of a bid by Bengalis who crossed over the border and settled on the land to support the separatist ambitions of the Mujahids. While illegal immigration from Bangladesh did occur throughout military rule, aggravating the siege mentality felt by Rakhine Buddhists, whose predominance in the state had already been threatened by British-engineered immigration, a powerful narrative developed that saw all who identified as Rohingya as interlopers there to support the campaign for a separate Muslim state.

Because the Rohingya label is a fabrication, so it goes, then every individual claim to citizenship under it is scrutinised like no other. The logic that, as Rohingya, they simply cannot belong, underpins their statelessness, but it doesn't stop at the legal sphere. Instead, it has provided a rationale for denying them even the inalienable human rights that should be conferred regardless of ones political status. "It seems," so wrote the German political theorist Hannah Arendt, who herself was rendered stateless by the Nazis, "that a man who is nothing but a man has lost the very qualities which make it possible for other people to treat him as a fellow-man."[8]

The architects of Rohingya statelessness would know this too. The alienation of this community from the once-plural society of Rakhine State, and the nation more broadly, and the loss of dignity that accompanied the stripping of their basic rights fuelled a process that, over the decades, has come to see the group dehumanised and ostracised altogether.

The clique of generals that took Ne Win's place in the late 1980s continued his push into the country's periphery, but when it came to the strategies used to manage ethnic minorities, they began to chart a somewhat different course. Ambitious new schemes were developed to encourage even more aggressively the systematic weakening of the Rohingya, and shortly after the turn of the decade, a project to re-engineer the social landscape of northern Rakhine State took shape. The animosities that began to simmer more intensively caused Buddhists and Muslims there to grow even further apart, and provided kindling for the fire that started years later, when the body of Ma Thida Htwe was discovered beneath the rain tree.

5

Ruling the unruly: social engineering and the village of prisoners

If you happened to be a common criminal in Myanmar's prison system in the mid-1990s you may have been approached with a compelling, if unlikely, offer. The wardens of jails in Yangon and elsewhere had begun visiting Buddhist inmates to gauge their interest in a peculiar bargain deal: would they accept early release in exchange for their relocation to a far corner of the country, 350 miles from the former capital? Those who agreed, and many did, would gather their belongings and, within days, be driven to the main port in Yangon, where a hulking freightliner was docked. They would sail west, hugging the coastline for four days until they reached Sittwe on Myanmar's western coast. And from there, they journeyed further north, slicing through the floodplains of the Mayu River until they reached Buthidaung, in northernmost Rakhine State.

In the hills and plains surrounding the town lay a network of newly built model villages developed solely for these new arrivals. The men and women who just days before had been crammed into filthy, overcrowded prison cells were gifted not just a new house, but a cow, a small stipend and promises of monthly food rations – cooking oil, fish paste, beans and rice. The paddy fields that surrounded the villages were theirs to till, and the land theirs to roam. Soon they would be joined by others – inmates from jails elsewhere in central Myanmar, and homeless families that had been recruited from squatter camps on the outskirts of Yangon. Rakhine from further south in the state would swell the numbers even more.

By the late 1980s the regime had grown increasingly concerned that this area of the country was being "lost" to Muslims. There were the descendants of the early Muslim settlers and the captives brought over in their hundreds of thousands from Bengal between the sixteenth and eighteenth centuries,[1] and there were the labourers who crossed over from India and bore families during the time of the British. But of greater concern was a perception among many Rakhine, and the regime, that the weak border separating Rakhine State from Bangladesh had allowed Bengalis to pour over since independence and settle. It was these more recent arrivals who were identifying as ethnic Rohingya, so it was claimed, and who became the chief drivers of a political and demographic crisis in Rakhine State.

The regime's rescue plan took shape in the elaborate model village scheme, which over the years would see Buddhists, invariably the poor or condemned, shifted out from their hometowns and organised into new communities. They would correct the demographic imbalance, one that was considered proof enough that Islam was gaining strength in Myanmar. Buddhists had by then become a minority in northern Rakhine State, and for the regime, that meant a weakening of its ability to project its power there. So the Buddhist prisoners were brought out of their cells to begin new lives far away.

It was an audacious idea, one whose roots are found in a document drawn up in 1988, several years before the first inmates were approached. Circulated around the Ministry for the Progress of Border Areas and National Races, known by its local acronym, Na Ta La, was an 11-point strategy to turn back the tide against an encroaching Islam. The 170-mile border between Bangladesh and Rakhine State had long before earned itself the appellation of the "western gate," where a fragile separation between the Muslim and Buddhist worlds had become increasingly imperilled. The plan would stem that danger. Stage three served as a basic blueprint for the resettlement scheme: "To strive for the increase in Buddhist population to be more than the number of Muslim people by way of establishing Natala villages in Arakan with Buddhist settlers from different townships and from out of the country."[2]

The directive was authored by one Colonel Tha Kyaw, chairman of the National Unity Party, which was formed that same year from the ashes of Ne Win's Burma Socialist Programme Party to contest elections scheduled for 1990. Little is known of the colonel, except that he had been Minister for Transport under Ne Win, and that he was an ethnic Rakhine Buddhist. His prescription for taking northern Rakhine State back into Buddhist hands fused more institutional modes of suppression of the Rohingya identity with outright persecutory ones. He, like many other Rakhine, and indeed the seeming majority of people in Myanmar by the late 1980s, believed the "Rohingya" label to be part of a conspiracy to bring the Muslim world further into Myanmar. Were these Bengalis to be officially recognised as an ethnic minority of the country, rather than the illegal interlopers many thought them to be, then Myanmar would suddenly have a sizeable Muslim constituency to deal with. They would serve as lackeys for the expansion of Islam further into Southeast Asia, and Buddhism would once again be threatened.

They needed containing, and the plan outlined how this might be done. Among other strategies listed was the denial of higher education to Rohingya and a ban on construction, even repair, of mosques and madrasas. But Rohingya would also be persistently referred to as insurgents in order to strengthen justification for their denial of citizenship after 1982, while marriages would be restricted "and all possible methods of repression and suppression [used] against them … to reduce the population growth."

★ ★ ★

The model villages that lie scattered throughout the hills and low-lying plains of northern Rakhine State by and large replicate the nature of the communities that make them up. The prisoners, like the homeless transferred there in the 1990s and 2000s, were sent as groups, and placed in villages designated only for them. If they left within three years of arriving, they would be returned to jail. The regime intended to make these villages permanent fixtures on the landscape; proof that Buddhism was there to stay.

Towards the end of the rainy season, one that had been marked by particularly fierce storms that had swept in from the Bay of Bengal, causing landslides and flooding, a colleague and I went in search of a village of former prisoners. Only one remained. Aung Thar Yar had been settled in 2004, at the foot of a small hill surrounded by paddy fields. The approach was along a heavily rutted road running past a barracks that once housed soldiers of the Na Sa Ka border force. It was formed in 1992 to man Myanmar's five borders, but its operations in northern Rakhine State, where it enforced control measures on the Rohingya and was regularly accused of brutality towards the community, gained it particular notoriety.

Long before you see the village, the eyes are drawn to a small golden pagoda that sits atop a 20-foot boulder. It is a feature that marks the entrance to many of the Na Ta La villages in the area. Other villages housing former inmates once existed nearby, but are no longer. Many inhabitants had stuck out the required three-year minimum stay, but once that passage of time had passed, they sold their properties and left.

The establishment of the Ministry for the Progress of Border Areas and National Races in 1988 took place after Ne Win's fall. Yet it indicated that the new clique of generals that regrouped under the State Law and Order Restoration Council had shared their predecessor's enthusiasm for the "national races" discourse. Soon after its inception, it began a programme it claimed was geared towards the advancement of the 135 recognised groups. They had, it said, "suffered throughout successive eras the atrocities of local terrorists."[3] The statement was intended to play ethnic minority civilians off against the armed movements that claimed to represent them, as well as the opposition Burma Communist Party whose forces were involved in campaigns against the military across the country. By that stage, rebellions in the border states – the work of these so-called "terrorists" – had been in motion for four decades, and continued to pose that same problem that had hounded the regime since it assumed power in March 1962: how to unify the country in the face of continued obvious resistance towards unification?

Behind the rhetoric of "national races" development, however, lurked a different agenda. The areas targeted for "progress" were those in which the regime's scope of authority was limited by the presence of communities that were deeply resentful of this national project. Northern Rakhine State may not have been in outright rebellion when the Na Ta La project was first mooted, but its demographic make-up was not one that favoured either Bamar or Buddhist, and was therefore a point of anxiety for the regime.

Just as Hla Hla would reorient herself towards the centre, so to speak – by "becoming" a Bamar and embedding herself firmly in the Bamar-centric Yangon culture – so too would the centre expand out to the periphery. In areas where Buddhism, that millennium-old social glue, had been uprooted and cast to the fringes of local society, it would be replanted. The Buddhist settlers that made the journey to the Muslim-dominated northern Rakhine State would be the necessary demographic corrective; the seeds that, in time, would flower into a meadow and beautify the hills and plains of northern Rakhine State.

It was an ambitious attempt at the social re-engineering of the landscape. Around 50 model villages were built between the three towns of Maungdaw, Buthidaung and Rathedaung. In a country known for its stark absence of state welfare, the benefits their inhabitants received – the cows, the food, the money – were unheard of.

★ ★ ★

We arrived at the prisoner village around midday, and the groups of men that began to trail us from house to house carried on their breath the sharp whiff of cheap liquor. Beneath the stilted houses, the rains of the morning had collected in fetid pools that teamed with mosquitoes. Fierce winds that had arrived with the monsoon that year had barrelled again and again across the land with a force too powerful for the structures of Aung Thar Yar to withstand. Through large holes that had been torn in their latticed wooden walls, bedrooms and kitchens were visible. Despite the damage, their inhabitants remained – no other options were available to them.

It was a bleak illustration of the lengths to which the regime went to expand its sphere of influence. The villagers came from prisons in Bago, in Mandalay, from Insein Prison in Yangon – from all across central Myanmar. Others were enticed from their cells in Sittwe and brought up here. The village head, across whose face were etched deep scars, one running just below his left eye, explained that the wardens had approached anyone with less than a five-year sentence. With two years left on his three-year term for army desertion, he signed on.

As the mandatory three-year period of stay ended and prisoners sold off their properties here and vacated, the village's population needed replenishing. This meant that every few years, the process would begin again, with wardens visiting prison cells and dangling in front of their occupants' eyes the prospect of free housing, and freedom – a home at the foot of that hill, beneath the golden pagoda. So keen was the Ministry to keep this Buddhist presence there that the rules governing who was and was not eligible for relocation to the prisoner village appeared far from hard and fast. One woman who had stood nearby as we spoke to the village head told us later that her husband had been released early from a murder conviction and sent to the village, but for whatever reason was no longer there.

Some inhabitants had moved repeatedly back and forth between village and jail. Among them was Kaung Latt. He had been here twice, first in August 2004, upon early release from Myaungmya Prison in the delta, and then again in 2013.

"I came here and stayed for some time, but then I was arrested again for robbery and they sent me back to jail, over in Buthidaung. I was given a seven-year sentence." Two and a half years in, he was offered early release once again on the proviso that he would return to Aung Thar Yar. "I was told that in Rakhine there are so many Muslims so we want to balance that out by sending Buddhists here," he recalled of the conversation with wardens the second time round.

His two children played on the wooden steps of his house as we spoke. During the conversation a young boy, no more than 12, came past on the dirt road and lingered outside the house. He had a deep gash in his scalp and a swollen eye. A woman nearby said his mother had beaten him with a rock several days before. The patterns of abuse that had taken many of these people to prison had been brought to this village: domestic violence was evidently routine, and the police were called there regularly to break up fights.

In the Na Ta La villages, people recalled vague mentions of a "border area ethnicity development" project that they were to be a part of. The prospect of a newly built house and guaranteed food for a year easily bettered the squalid conditions many had endured at home for too long. But the merits of that trade-off soon began to fade. A little over a decade after it was settled many inhabitants of Aye Thar Aung wanted to return to their original homes. The rations had stopped years before and work was difficult to find. These people hadn't been trained in the arts of paddy farming and had struggled to adapt to new demands, yet knew that they could neither afford the journey back to their town in central Myanmar nor risk not being able to find work once they arrived.

Other villages in the network soon went the way of Aye Thar Aung. Further south, Shwe Yin Aye had been built for the eleventh wave of settlers in 2005, who came largely from Yangon and who, this time around, were gifted two acres of land and a trailer. But as the years passed the original inhabitants left and the village came to be populated by down-and-outs – alcoholics and gamblers who brawled into the night, and who found relief from the harshness of life there in a brothel set up in one of the stilted wooden houses, where young women from surrounding villages would service them until dawn came round again.

And the malaria had taken person after person; not just in Shwe Yin Aye, but all across this condemned pocket of northern Rakhine State. In one tiny village just outside of Buthidaung we stumbled across the headman lying on his floor beneath thick blankets, shivering violently. We asked for permission to meet with other villagers. He waved us on and remained on the floor. As we spoke with one family of former homeless in the yard outside their storm-beaten house, an elderly woman emerged from a nearby doorway and struggled across a narrow street pockmarked with oily black puddles. She was likewise covered in blankets and racked with malarial fever, and disappeared inside a neighbouring house.

By swamping the area with a new demographic, the regime hoped to exercise greater control over a region where its authority was weak. The only quality required of participants was that they be Buddhist. It mattered little that some were violent criminals, or that they might hold no sympathy towards the regime's expansionist aims. Religion, like ethnicity, had long before become a principal barometer in determining, if not allegiance to, then affiliation with, the state, and the recruits would play the role of purifiers of a land being steadily swallowed up by Muslims. These villages, like the Israeli settler enclaves in the West Bank, would become the "facts on the ground" that served as proof that Buddhism was alive and well there.

* * *

Some months after visiting the prisoner village I travelled to a suburb of northern Yangon to meet with U Maung Maung Ohn. A retired army general and former head of the Na Sa Ka border force, he had once been Deputy Minister for Border Affairs in Rakhine State before being appointed Chief Minster in 2014, tasked by former President Thein Sein with stabilising the region once and for all as the unrest continued after 2012. I wanted to know whether the explanation given to prisoners decades before when they relocated to that corner of the country had chimed with official policy for the area. His answers were always careful and considered. Like many former high-ranking members of the military, he sought to construct an image of the

monolithic institution as one that acted only in the interests
of the people it ruled for half a century.

"It's about Buddhist, Myanmar citizens," U Maung
Maung Ohn had said of the Na Ta La villages, denying
the presence of any ulterior strategic motive for a regime
concerned about its grip on the area and its people. "It's for
both Rakhine and Burmese." Buddhists felt their land was
being taken from them, and the events of the late 1940s and
1950s, which would be recalled by Rakhine over and again
to justify the violence of 2012, provided historical evidence
that this had been in motion for too long.

> It goes like this. Maungdaw area has belonged to Rakhine
> State since long ago. And it still does. Even some of the
> Bengali villages still have Rakhine names and there are many
> pagodas in their villages. This means that these areas used to
> be places where Rakhine people once lived.

Yet the Muslim population had grown dramatically, he
said, and had begun to take over.

> The government established the Na Ta La villages to make
> sure all the Rakhine people are spread all over Rakhine
> and to make it look like Rakhine people are living densely
> in their state, otherwise there will be no Rakhine. Instead,
> Bengali will be everywhere and they will demand their own
> territory.

The fear that northern Rakhine State was being lost to
Muslims hadn't solely been a ruse to expand regime control
to the far edges of the country. It had an historical basis
that seemed to underpin many of the anxieties that burst to
the surface in 2012. Nearly half a century before Colonel
Tha Kyaw drew up his list of strategies to reclaim the land,

Rakhine State had been convulsed by fighting between the British Army and the Japanese. World War Two arrived in Myanmar in 1942, and as Japanese forces swept across to Rakhine State, the British organised battalions of Rohingya to counter them. The Japanese in turn sought the support of Rakhine Buddhists, with varying degrees of success. Marshalled by opposing foreign powers, armed mobs from either side inflicted bloody massacres on one another. Sittwe district, then known as Akyab, saw a particularly intense wave of fighting in April 1942 which marked the beginning of a geographical divide between Rakhine and Rohingya, with the Japanese holding *de facto* control of the mostly Buddhist south and the British holding the Muslim north.[4]

There the Na Ta La villages would later be built, preceded decades earlier by the movement of tens of thousands of Muslims north as they fled fighting around Sittwe. That migration radically altered the demography of towns like Maungdaw and Buthidaung, but it coincided with an upsurge in the movement of peoples across the border into Rakhine State from what was then India, most likely among them Muslims who had fled west at the onset of war in 1942.[5] They brought with them tales of massacres by Rakhine Buddhists in the chaotic aftermath of World War Two, just as Buddhists would do the same of Muslims.

"The stories of atrocities told by refugees reaching Maungdaw aroused the wrath of the local Muslims, who vented it on the Buddhist minority in their midst," wrote Moshe Yegar, an Israeli diplomat posted to Yangon in the 1970s, who conducted several in-depth studies of the history of the Muslim presence in Myanmar. "Soon the Buddhists were streaming in droves from the north as the Muslims were streaming from the south, and Arakan stood divided into two distinct territories, a Muslim and a Buddhist one."[6]

Amid the maelstrom that followed World War Two in Myanmar a Muslim insurgency developed in Rakhine State, focused predominantly in the north. Known as the Mujahids, many of its members had been trained by the British during the war to battle the Japanese and their erstwhile Rakhine collaborators. Fearful of the prospect that the British would soon leave Myanmar, and aware that nearby Muslim-majority regions like Chittagong in present-day Bangladesh would soon join East Pakistan, they too demanded the inclusion of northern Rakhine State in the newly formed Muslim nation. Some even called for an entirely independent Muslim country.[7]

At one point in 1948 the Mujahids held complete control of Buthidaung and Maungdaw, capitalising on the fact that the Myanmar army's resources were diverted towards tackling the much larger rebellions in the east of the country. Over the subsequent six years the Mujahids struck further south, launching raids on Buddhist villages and levying heavy taxes on both Buddhists and Muslims. The suffering of local populations on both sides was compounded by the actions of government troops deployed to the area towards the end of 1948, where they burnt mosques and villages and sent close to 30,000 fleeing across the border to East Pakistan.

Buddhist Rakhine had an additional reason to be fearful of Muslim supremacy in Rakhine State, and this fed a narrative of Rakhine subordination that, by 2012, had become highly combustible. Aggravating the crisis that followed World War Two was an ill-conceived decision by the British to reward the loyalty of its proxy Rohingya forces by offering all top administrative posts in the north of the state to Muslims, thereby entirely sidelining Rakhine from positions of power. This planted the seeds of a deep resentment among Rakhine, not only towards Muslims but towards any non-Rakhine authority imposing itself on the state.

The demands of the Mujahids for independence of the northern district never came close to materialising, for neither the outgoing colonial administration nor the post-independence government saw any reason to let go of it entirely. Additionally, the movement had lacked popular support and manpower, numbering at its peak only around 1,000 soldiers. Muslims had suffered too at the hands of the Mujahids,[8] but there were also residual loyalties among Muslims to the central state that meant that support for secession was slim. "Many of the Rwangyas, as distinct from the 'Indian Muslims', remained loyal to the Burmese Government,"[9] R.B. Pearn, a professor at Rangoon University before the Japanese occupation, who later joined the Foreign Office Research Department where he studied the Mujahid revolt, wrote in 1952.

Even so, the events of the late 1940s and early 1950s were to leave a deep and pervasive suspicion towards Rohingya aspirations. These were sharpened by several subsequent attempts, most notably by the Rohingya Patriotic Front in 1974 and its successor, the Rohingya Solidarity Organisation (RSO), to launch armed insurgencies that many Rakhine believed had separatism as their ultimate goal. The RSO, established in 1982 with the stated aim of securing citizenship and greater political rights for Rohingya, had bases in Bangladesh, and carried out various cross-border attacks on police and army posts in northern Rakhine State in the 1980s and early 1990s. But it never posed much of a security threat, and by the late 1990s it was considered largely defunct.

Yet the historical existence of several different militant movements became a reference point for assertions by Rakhine and the regime that Rohingya were seeking to gain a foothold in the north, both through armed mobilisation, and by claiming an indigenous ethnic status. The view that another armed Rohingya uprising was inevitable was reinforced in the years after the 2012 violence, when a number of international terrorist groups, including the Pakistan Taliban and the Islamic State, called upon Rohingya to take up arms against the government. If terrorist groups prey on aggrieved populations who feel they have little recourse to political expression other than violence, then perhaps they thought the conditions in Rakhine State were ripe for recruitment. But there had never been evidence of a broad sympathy among Rohingya for armed warfare, even when the RSO was at its peak. The population was too vulnerable, and any mobilisation would invite the full wrath of the military, as well as local Rakhine. Yet in the eyes of many in Myanmar, the threat always lurked. Strict controls, and a strategy to dilute the population using Buddhist settlers, were therefore needed to prevent them from completing the project begun by their alleged forebears, the Mujahids, half a century ago.

★ ★ ★

The Muslims of northern Rakhine State hadn't been the only population of concern for the regime. As time went on it pushed out into "unaligned" communities elsewhere in the country, using Buddhism as a transmission line to bridge ethnic divides and draw disparate communities closer towards the centre. Where the Na Ta La scheme was intended to weaken rather than assimilate the Rohingya, who long before were judged to be too alien to be incorporated into the nation, other projects sought to actively cultivate an ideological alignment.

Above Rakhine State lies Chin State, and if you were to travel northeast from the Na Ta La villages, across the Kaladan River floodplain and up into the Chin mountains, you might stumble across a network of schools unlike the standard educational institutions of central Myanmar. They were designed in the early 1990s for a particular purpose: to serve as laboratories for the cultivation among students of a commitment to the Three Main National Causes established by the State Law and Order Restoration Council when it took power in 1988: "Non-disintegration of the Union; Non-disintegration of national solidarity; Perpetuation of sovereignty."

The students targeted for these schools were not Muslim, but Christian. American missionaries had begun to arrive in the Chin Hills just before the turn of the nineteenth century, and the word of the Bible quickly spread among Chin communities, thereby extending the reach of Christianity beyond the already evangelised eastern and northern regions of Myanmar. The foreign missionary schools had been numerous in Chin State, and even though Ne Win had expelled all overseas missionaries from the country and nationalised Christian schools and hospitals in the mid-1960s, little had then been done to counter their influence. Upon the arrival of the State Law and Order Restoration Council, this began to change.

While the Na Ta La villages were being built in northern Rakhine, officials from the same ministry began to develop a network of Na Ta La schools, mostly in ethnic minority states. Where the Christian missionary schools had once provided the locus of village life in the hills, so now would Buddhist institutions of learning. The first was opened in 1994,[10] hailed by the government as a way to bring disparate communities closer together through a curriculum that was aimed at building trust between, and understanding of, the different cultures that inhabited Myanmar. The co-mingling of students, both Buddhist and Christian, under the same roof – for they were boarding schools – was "needed to avoid making habits and behaviours that could lead to racism [or] religiosity," a government minister later said.[11] Those who passed through the Na Ta La schools would then be guaranteed a position in the local government.

By 2011, 29 schools had been built across the country, a third of which were in Chin State. But reports quickly began to surface of the forced conversion to Buddhism of the Christian students who were induced to enrol by the incentives offered – cheap or free education, food and board in a region of Myanmar where nearly three-quarters of the population live below the poverty line[12] and where hunger is endemic. In a particularly cruel expression of nature's freakish ways, a famine strikes Chin State every 50 years when armies of forest rats, plumped and energised after gorging on the flowering bamboo plant, attack crop fields and grain stocks. The cyclical food crisis that results from this phenomenon drives families deeper into poverty, and makes the prospect of free education, bed and board all the more alluring.

Stories abound of army trucks turning up at villages in the Chin Hills that had been struck particularly hard by the famine and coaxing children to go with them to the schools to enrol, only for the children to be forced to shave their heads, wear monks' robes and learn Buddhist scriptures. "We had to wear robes for nuns; the boys had to wear monks' robes," one Christian girl who spent several years at a Na Ta La school in Mindat in southern Chin State told the Chin Human Rights Organisation in 2011.[13] Those who resisted conversion were threatened with forced army recruitment.

> We Christian students received worse treatment than the Buddhists. We were accused of not following the rules and regulations properly. Besides the usual subjects, we had to recite Pali and other Buddhist scriptures. If we couldn't get it exactly we were beaten by the monks. They slapped me about the face, or beat me with sacks on my legs and back.

Monks and Buddhist laymen had been drafted in to teach at the schools under the auspices of the Hill Regions Buddhist Mission. The programme was launched in 1991 when the Ministry of Religious Affairs, having formed its own Department for the Promotion and Propagation of the Sāsana – the term used by Buddhists to refer to their faith – began sending teams of Bamar monks loyal to the regime to villages and towns in Chin State. Often accompanied by armed soldiers, they would oversee conversion ceremonies for Christians and help enlist children in the Na Ta La schools, where they also taught. Like the recruits to the Na Ta La village scheme in Rakhine State, agents of the Hill Regions Buddhist Mission would induce mainly the poor and needy into the schools – sons and daughters of parents who, blighted by food shortages, could not provide for their children.

One weekend towards the end of 2013 I had taken a night bus from Mandalay to the town of Mindat in southern Chin State. The bus left the city around 6pm, on a journey scheduled to take eight hours. But as it approached the foothills in the early hours of the morning, the road seemed to run out and waterways crisscrossed our passage. We eventually made it to Mindat, only 150 kilometres from Mandalay as the crow flies, 16 hours later. It seemed the "advancement" of the communities in Myanmar's periphery, pledged by the Ministry for the Development of Border Areas and National Races years before, wasn't all encompassing. Except for the soldiers it deployed to battle insurgents and its project to convert Christians to Buddhism, Chin State remained off the radar of the regime, its roads, like its people, entirely neglected.

A man had agreed to meet me one afternoon at a point on the road between Mindat and a village to the town's northwest. By late 2013, agents of the Hill Regions Buddhist Mission had been recruiting children to Na Ta La schools for more than two decades, and upwards of a thousand were enrolled in Chin State alone at any one time.[14] I wanted to know whether there had been wider stigmatisation of Christians as a result of this conversion drive, and if that had filtered into everyday communal interactions in those hills.

A dense blanket of cloud hung low over the valleys that day. Elevated above it in the clear December air we could look out from where we sat over an endless horizon of white, beneath which lay his village. On occasions when the cloud broke it appeared far below, a cluster of 28 houses accessible only by the winding, barely paved track that had brought him up here. Mindat was the closest town, but on his motorbike it was still three hours ride away.

Naing Ki lived in the village with his wife and four children. Ten years before he had become a Baptist. After years of struggling to find peace of mind – he didn't say what exactly – he had been convinced that Christianity would bring the serenity he so wanted. But other villagers, all of them Buddhist, reacted fiercely to his conversion. His father, a "strong Buddhist," had founded the village in 1989, but died in 2004. So the son built a new house and, in March 2005, brought a pastor in to pray with his family.

> Then the village leader threw bricks at my house and villagers beat me and my wife. They said you have no right to stay here. A monk told me that if I converted back to Buddhism then I would be accepted; if not I would never be accepted. But I had already decided to become a Baptist.

The monk, he said, was from a "Buddhist missionary group," most likely the Hill Regions Buddhist Mission, that had been sent there to counter the work done by Christian missionaries long before. In 1980, Ne Win had created the State Sangha Maha Nayaka Committee, a body comprising monks handpicked by the regime to govern the Sangha in Myanmar. There are an estimated 500,000 monks in Myanmar, and the monastic community is perhaps greater than the size of the country's colossal army. Their increasing involvement in oppositional politics during the course of the general's reign required close attention, so Ne Win felt, for the reverence they held could sway huge numbers of people. Shadowy agents of the regime were dressed in robes and planted in monasteries across the country, while monastic committees were organised right from the village level to the state level to monitor "misbehaviour" among their fellow monks. It is likely from this committee and its ancillary networks that the missionary monks sent to Chin State were chosen, for their loyalty to the regime had already been certified.

Naing Ki's decision to convert would have far-reaching consequences. The village headman soon struck him off the household registration list, the only means by which someone in Myanmar can prove ownership of their home. He then complained to the township administrator, who ordered the village leader, the same one who had thrown bricks at Naing Ki's house, to reinstate him. The leader did so, but later showed up on his doorstep. "I can't take responsibility for any violence that happens to you," he warned. A subsequent complaint Naing Ki made to the township religious affairs minister was met with similar hostility. "If you do not convert to Buddhism again you will have no future," he was told. "I will send a letter to higher authorities who will come and remove you from the village."

That may have been an empty threat, for eight years on he remained in the same house he had built on his father's death. But the local dynamic had changed dramatically, and he and his family had become pariahs. Neighbours blocked him from using the communal water pipes and the vendor in the only shop in the village refused to serve him. Instead he was forced to lean on a nearby household for water, and every few weeks, he drove the three hours up that arterial track and along the road to Mindat, from where he carried goods home on his overladen bike.

Those were the arrangements that came to be in Naing Ki's village. I thought about what collective mindset had evolved among his neighbours after his conversion to bring about such hostility. Save for the Bamar monks and laymen sent from central Myanmar to roam the countryside and monitor villages like his, people here were exclusively ethnic Chin. But they evidently considered the preservation of their religious community to surpass concerns about shared ethnicity, that other sphere within which notions of belonging in Myanmar were being contested. The drive to convert Chin to Buddhism had further accentuated the idea that Christians like Naing Ki were unwelcome guests. Yet he arguably had a right over and above his neighbours to be in the village, for it was his father who founded it. And he belonged in a deeper sense too, for he was a Chin in a village of fellow Chin with whom he had grown up, whose language was his and many of whose customs he too practised. But by leaving Buddhism, he had in their eyes left the community – not physically, for he chose to remain there, unwanted and outcast, but spiritually, ideologically. That appeared enough to break the contract of belonging and sever whatever linkages should have otherwise remained intact through his conversion – shared kinship, longstanding friendships, a known family tie to the village.

These were the sorts of slow-burning effects that post-independence statecraft in Myanmar created. Resentment towards the regime would not reduce; with each push into the ethnic regions, it boiled further. But at the same time communal tensions were triangulated so that even within close-knit villages, in-groups and out-groups formed. Neighbours suddenly became unknown quantities – "foreign" in their own particular way, to be treated with suspicion. Civilians, such as the Chin of Naing Ki's village whose own ethnic identity had long before put them in the crosshairs of the military, began to pursue in their own ways the objectives of a state of whose methods of manipulation they too had been victims.

* * *

General Ne Win's fall in 1988 appeared to have marked a change in how the strategies of Burmanisation would be carried forth. As the model villages were being built in the countryside around Buthidaung and Maungdaw they made space for Bamar as well as Rakhine Buddhists, who were often transplanted into the same villages. Rakhine thus became agents of Bamar expansionism – a curious digression from the methods of statecraft pursued by the regime until then, which had largely been along ethnic lines and not religious lines, but one that reflected the ability of the military to play on multiple axes of difference. For the Rakhine participants, their fears of Muslim dominance in the state appeared to overwhelm any concern about increasing regime influence there. Conversely, by using Rakhine to further the interests of the Bamar, the regime showed how the salience of religion could be raised to a point at which it superseded the ethnic dilemma inherent in the project – that Rakhine, another of these treacherous minorities, could act in the service of the Bamar because they had that common ground in the form of Buddhism. But it also indicated a perception among the generals that the centuries of conquest, first by the kings of the pre-colonial era and then by the regime, had led to a partial colonisation by the majority Bamar ethnicity of Rakhine themselves. Coupled with their own resentment of the Rohingya, this meant the Rakhine could prove to be useful tools in the nation-building project.

For the Rohingya, life in the north of the state grew ever more perilous as Ne Win's reign ended and the State Law and Order Restoration Council regime took power. Their claims to an indigenous ethnic status had grown in volume as the subject of ethnicity became increasingly salient under the military. But this only inflamed Rakhine further, and emboldened their support for efforts to weaken the Muslim population.

While Colonel Tha Kyaw's plan for taking control of northern Rakhine State was discussed at length by Military Intelligence after it was submitted in 1988, it was never formally passed, and he faded from view as the State Law and Order Restoration Council consolidated control in the 1990s and later morphed into its successor, the State Peace and Development Council. But the proposals were not altogether forgotten. In that wedge of land between the Bangladesh border and the Rakhine Yoma mountain range, Rohingya were increasingly singled out as subjects of close surveillance and tight controls.

They had already been the target of a major pogrom in 1978, under the name Operation Nagamin, or King Dragon. Ne Win had ordered immigration officials and soldiers to scrutinise all those living in the border regions of Myanmar to determine who were citizens and who were "foreigners who have filtered into the country illegally."[15] But it mainly focused on Rakhine State, and its principal target was the Rohingya. As the operation got underway in March 1978, word began to spread from one Rohingya village to another that troops had raped and murdered their way through the communities they were meant to be conducting censuses of. Upwards of 200,000 fled to Bangladesh and set up in villages and makeshift camps. In the first eight months of the exodus, some 10,000 people died.[16] Then in 1991, long after the majority had returned, reports began to emerge of a heavy deployment of troops to Maungdaw and Buthidaung townships. Tensions had been building with Bangladesh, prompting the military to reinforce the border, yet it coincided with a bid by the State Law and Order Restoration Council to again check the status of Rohingya there, and the carnage was repeated.

"Before the rains started in May 1991, some 10,000 refugees had already arrived in Bangladesh," Human Rights Watch reported of the movement of Rohingya that followed.

> At the end of the rainy season, in November 1991, the trickle became a flood, and by March 1992 there were over 270,000 refugees scattered in camps along the Cox's Bazaar – Teknaf road in Bangladesh. The refugees told of summary execution, rape and other forms of torture which they had witnessed or personally endured at the hands of the military.[17]

Many who fled this time would also later return, moving back across the border and reestablishing their communities in northern Rakhine State. But, as they would find out, the environment they returned to had become increasingly hostile towards them. Bit by bit, Colonel Tha Kyaw's vision for the control of this pariah population had begun to be realised.

The restrictions on movement began in Sittwe in 1997, and then rippled out across the state. Along the east–west road between Maungdaw and Buthidaung in the north are a series of checkpoints where police inspect the identity papers and travel documents of passing Rohingya. On the side of the road, for all to see, they are pulled from their buses and ordered inside police booths. Should a Rohingya want to leave their village in northern Maungdaw township and visit a relative in Buthidaung, thereby crossing the township line, they must apply at the local immigration office for the permit, paying a fee of anywhere up to $8 each time. The form would state the name of the house in Buthidaung they wanted to stay in, and the date they would return home. But permit or not, each checkpoint could be the final point of travel, for failure to pay an additional bribe might see them returned to wherever they came from. They call this "tea money" in Myanmar, the kind that doesn't make it into the books, and which forms a micro-economy unto itself, offering an additional incentive for the restrictions to remain in place. If for whatever reason they were unable to make it back across the township line by their stated date, another trip to immigration would be required, and the possibility of a larger fine loomed. More tea money, more uncertainty.

In 2005, authorities in Maungdaw released an order, approved at the state level, that read: "Starting the date of this regional order, those who have permission to marry must limit the number of children, in order to control the birth rate so that there is enough food and shelter."[18] The Rohingya had long been accused of producing disproportionately high numbers of children and the ruling would stem the supposed threat their reproduction posed to the Buddhist population in the north. But it also provided a pretext for authorities, particularly the Na Sa Ka personnel who by that point had become the most prominent, and feared, authority in the area, to further invade the private space of Rohingya – to enter their houses and to count their young; to humiliate them inside their own homes. If there was suspicion that a child in a household belonged to another family, perhaps because that family had "swapped" him or her in to make it appear as if they had fewer children, then the mother would be forced to breastfeed the child in front of the visiting authorities.[19]

Yet the limits on reproductive rates may not have been needed. The regime's abject, if not wilful, neglect of healthcare in northern Rakhine State in particular seemed to be doing the job for Na Sa Ka. So absent was the state that residents of Maungdaw and Buthidaung, where Rohingya are predominant, were forced to share two doctors between 158,000 people. Down in Sittwe, where Buddhists outnumbered Muslims, the figure was 681.[20] In Buthidaung, 224 out of 1,000 children, nearly a quarter, were dying before they reached the age of five; in Sittwe, it was 77.[21] One only had to travel 85 kilometres to record a three-fold increase in infant mortality rates. The country was the same, but the community was different.

In the aftermath of the 2012 violence, the Na Ta La project was given a new breath of life. The violence had rippled into Bangladesh, pitting Muslim communities there against Buddhist, many of whom descended from those Rakhine who fled to the Chittagong Hills and settled there upon the annexation of the kingdom in 1784. It was they who, in the years after 2012, began to receive visits from monks and community leaders who had crossed in to Bangladesh to coax their ethnic brethren back to the plains surrounding Maungdaw and Buthidaung. There, new Na Ta La villages had been built to accommodate this community. Despite having been absent from the nation for two centuries, and of having no lived history in the state, these communities were "reintroduced" to Rakhine State in a bid to further the Buddhist colonisation process.

Colonel Tha Kyaw sealed another victory after the violence. As Rohingya became increasingly contained in their villages further south, so too were they denied leave from the north. The only university in a state long neglected by the central government is in Sittwe, and before the violence the two communities studied there side by side. But with Rohingya blocked from leaving the camps around Sittwe and the ghettos inside of it, and forbidden to board the boat at Buthidaung jetty that once ferried them down to the state capital, their access to higher education was completely severed and another zone of cultural and intellectual exchange eliminated.

It was only the Rohingya who suffered this fate. The singling out of one community as the target of far-reaching controls – on their movement, their ability to reproduce, their access to vital services – began to beg the question of whether there was an intent on the part of the state towards Rohingya beyond mere containment; that it might be embarking on a strategy to make life so untenable for them that they would have no choice but to flee Myanmar altogether, thereby removing that group from the country once and for all. This suspicion heightened after 2012, as their isolation grew more acute and the dehumanising speech directed at them increased in volume, free of any censorship by the government. This altered the framework within which persecution of the group was being analysed. Scholars of state crime began to argue after 2012 that precursors to historic instances of genocide elsewhere in the world – the isolation and restricting of a target group, their dehumanisation, sporadic fits of violence against them and the denial of state protections – were now evident in Myanmar.[22]

The control measures on the Rohingya expanded and tightened as time went on, and by 2016, 86 checkpoints had been set up in northern Rakhine State.[23] The routine stop-and-search of vehicles to check for Rohingya passengers greatly amplified the perception of the group as a security threat. This in turn fed the narrative, made so explicit by their denial of citizenship in 1982, that they were a lesser people. The process of distinguishing them so drastically from other groups in Rakhine State, not only in a religious or ethnic sense, but now legally, criminally, would provide more robust grounds for the violence that eventually erupted in 2012. They weren't worthy of the same protections afforded to Rakhine, limited as those were, and they became, in the eyes of those who either participated in attacks or supported them from afar, subhuman. They were animals, stripped of the qualities that normally inhibit the use of violence against a fellow human being.

It wasn't that the killings of 2012 were merely a speedily crafted response to the rape and murder of Ma Thida Htwe in late May that year. Participants would often point to that incident, remembering the images circulated of the twisted body of the young seamstress lying beneath the tree near her village, violated so brazenly. But the mental processes that allowed for the turn to violence among Rakhine, born of a perception so thoroughly cultivated by the state that the existence of the Rohingya mattered little, had been in the making long before that spark finally brought them to life.

6

2012: season of violence

Nine months before the discovery of Ma Thida Htwe's body and all that followed, a seminar was held at the Arakan State Religious Hall in Yangon. There, Rakhine historians, political leaders and intellectuals gathered to discuss what they claimed was the appropriation of Rakhine heritage by Rohingya. "We have found that the so-called Rohingya widely misuse the term 'Arakan' for their own associations and when they are making up their histories of land, culture, religion and literature," an organiser said afterwards.[1] "They have even claimed that the kings of the Arakan Kingdom are the kings of their clan, and that ancient artifacts such as coins are evidence of their historical Arakanese heritage."

The following month, in October 2011, the Rakhine Nationalities Development Party (RNDP), the precursor to today's Arakan National Party, held three seminars on the same topic. One took place in Sittwe at the beginning of October, and two more in Buthidaung and Maungdaw later that month. Attendants had left the Buthidaung talks "embittered with the feelings that their land and valued heritages are being insulted by those groups of Chittagonian Bengali Muslims with their made up histories of Rohingya," said one participant.[2]

The seminars marked the start of an increase in communal tensions in Rakhine State. Then in November, seven months before the mobs struck, a map was circulated online that depicted Rakhine State as the home of the Rohingya. It was precisely the claim that had so angered attendants of the Buthidaung seminar the previous month. The map had been published a year before by the BBC in an article detailing ethnic conflict in Myanmar, but was somehow picked up in the days following the seminars and posted to social media. It sparked outrage among many Rakhine, who called for boycotts of the BBC and threatened protests at the British consulate in Yangon. The source of the anger was clear: the Rohingya simply must not be portrayed as indigenous to Myanmar.

The content of the seminars spoke to the perception, so pervasive among Rakhine and many others in Myanmar, that Rohingya were a newly created ethnic group whose claims to a longstanding presence there were not only bogus, but part of a master plan to wrest control of the region from Buddhists. By no means were these sentiments new. Right around the time the Na Ta La village plan was being formulated in the late 1980s, a so-called Rakhine National Defence and Protection Organisation had written to Saw Maung, Ne Win's successor and first leader of the State Law and Order Restoration Council, demanding that Rohingya be subject to a range of restrictions. These included population control, limited access to education and curbs on the construction of mosques. The 30-page document, sent to the general in October 1988, warned that the threat posed by these "Chittagong Bengalis" was not limited to Myanmar, but extended well beyond her borders.

> As long as they are allowed to live legally here, they will pursue their grand strategic goal of building the bridge

between Bangladesh and Malaysia via Burma and Thailand, and the two countries will be Islamised. If the state is unable to meet [our] demands the western gate of Burma will be broken and the fate of Maungdaw will fall into the hands of the Bengalis, and the danger of Bengalis entering into Burma proper will increase.[3]

These had been the same sentiments that prompted Colonel Tha Kyaw to draw up his list of methods to control the Rohingya population in northern Rakhine State. And in the aftermath of the June 2012 violence, after mobs had wrecked Muslim quarters in Sittwe and sent tens of thousands fleeing into camps, Rakhine monastic groups offered similarly alarming solutions for the "Muslim problem," further raising fears that a bid to purify the land was underway.

★ ★ ★

In his book, *Fear of Small Numbers: An Essay on the Geography of Anger*, the anthropologist Arjun Appadurai writes that for extreme violence to occur against ethnically different, but nonetheless neighbouring, groups, there must be a confused mixture of high certainty and grave uncertainty within the in-group about the intentions of their neighbours. Who really are these people, they ask, and what do they want with us?

The worry this produces is that the ordinary faces of everyday life (with names, practices, and faiths different from one's own) are in fact masks of everydayness behind which lurk the real identities not of ethnic others but of traitors to the nation conceived as an ethnos.[4]

This interpretation of the supposedly real intentions of these neighbours, whose seemingly familiar faces hide a deeply hostile rivalry, so often provides the driving force for mass violence, and helps to construe that violence as defensive. Amid the unsettling swirl of messages circulated about those neighbours, "ethnically different groups cumulate little doubts, small grudges, and humble suspicions. With the arrival of larger scripts, of both certainty and uncertainty, these little stories feed into a narrative with an ethnocidal momentum."[5]

After the seminars were held across Rakhine State in late 2011, a gradual increase began to occur in material that cast Rohingya in a sinister, subhuman light. In February 2012, a magazine, *Piccima Ratwan*, was circulated. On its editorial board sat Rakhine monks, police chiefs and government administrators – figures of high authority in the region. The magazine repeatedly referred to Rohingya as terrorists, and warned that the threat they posed was an existential one. It wouldn't be just Rakhine living close to Rohingya who would feel the wrath of "The Black Tsunami in humble disguise," as the magazine depicted the group, but the entire Rakhine ethnicity. In one piece, titled "What the Rohingya Is," the author wrote: "The Bengalis are very deceptive – if necessary, they'd even cut their own body and flesh with knives to exaggerate their stories."[6]

Rakhine were not the only source of disparaging material. In early June, soon after the rape and murder of Ma Thida Htwe became public, popular comedian Min Maw Kun branded Rohingya "black-skinned, big-belly, and hairy *kalar* who marry many Burmese women" in a sitcom directed by one of Myanmar's best-known directors, Maung Myo Min.[7] *Kalar*, a refrain that would come to be used again and again in the subsequent months and years, referred disparagingly to anyone of dark skin or South Asian features.

Around the same time the magazine began to be circulated, the National League for Democracy (NLD) was campaigning for by-elections to fill seats that had been vacated by a government reshuffle in early 2012. Their eventual victory in April 2012 allowed Myanmar's main opposition to enter parliament for the first time. The party had won the vote in 1990, nearly two years after it had formed amid the 1988 uprising, but the military quickly annulled the results. Myanmar wasn't ready for democracy, it had decided, and another two decades of acutely authoritarian rule followed in which dissidents were jailed in their thousands and armed conflict continued to eat away at populations in the border regions. But the April 2012 by-election victory, which went some way towards diluting the political power of a military that still had a quarter of seats constitutionally reserved for it in the parliament, appeared to many a surefire sign that Myanmar was gradually moving away from outright military rule to one that allowed the opposition a role in the country's political affairs.

As the transition moved forward, the vice-like grip the military had kept on media was loosened. In the days of old, publications would require careful vetting by the censor board prior to hitting the shops. Any newspaper articles considered a threat to national security were often simply cut out of the publication, and whatever was left would be sent straight to the newsstand. Yet while many applauded the freeing up of the media, less visible was any strengthening, or indeed creation, of institutions that could monitor and act upon hateful content. So often with

political transitions, progress within one area outpaces
another, often to damaging effect, and as the reports of the
rape and murder of Ma Thida Htwe began to leak out of
Rakhine State, the media was whipped up into a frenzy of
anger directed predominantly at the Rohingya. Yet there
was no one either willing or able to rein it in.

On 8 June, mobs of Rohingya attacked Rakhine houses
in the villages outside of Maungdaw. There had been a
prayer ceremony at a mosque in downtown Maungdaw
that morning for the victims of the bus attack on 3 June,
when ten Muslims were beaten to death by Buddhist mobs
apparently avenging Ma Thida Htwe's murder. Following
heated exchanges with nearby groups of Rakhine on the
street outside the Maungdaw mosque, a brawl broke out.
Police allegedly shot at Rohingya, who then began stoning
Rakhine shops. They moved into the outlying Na Ta La
villages, many of which had been built on land confiscated
from Rohingya. Hundreds of houses were torched by
Rohingya. Amid the chaos, the popular *Weekly Eleven*
journal, run largely by Bamar out of an office in downtown
Yangon, reported that Rakhine were killed as a result of
"Rohingya terrorist attacks."[8] Later it claimed that the "risk
and danger of ethnic cleansing or genocide was possible,"[9]
referring to the potential for Rohingya to eliminate
Rakhine. In the months after that attack, material evidently
engineered to mobilise more Rakhine against Rohingya was
distributed in greater frequency, produced by local political
parties, community groups and monk organisations. At no
point did the government condemn the messages being
circulated, either on the leaflets or in national media, and
the effect they had on transforming a floating sense of fear
and resentment of Rohingya into something more concrete

and deserving of action soon became clear. In justifying their support for the violence, Rakhine I later spoke with used epithets strikingly similar to those printed beforehand.

★ ★ ★

Adul Shukur remembers 12 June 2012 well. It was the day Ko Myat had waited on the road running through Nasi, machete in hand, while Rakhine picked their way around the quarter with flaming torches. It was the worst of those two days of violence, yet somehow his house had been spared. In the days before, as violence had spread from Maungdaw down to the villages outside Sittwe, and then into the town itself, Rohingya in Nasi had stopped venturing far from their quarter. Reports were circulating with greater frequency of attacks by both sides. As Rohingya neighbourhoods were being swamped by Rakhine, so too was the converse happening, with Rohingya mobs entering the predominantly Buddhist Min Kan quarter on 10 June and torching several houses.

As the days passed the atmosphere in Sittwe grew increasingly sinister. Normally come evening, people would be sitting on the roadside, talking and playing guitar, but by the evening of 10 June, the streets feeding into Nasi had emptied and the lights in houses were off. Many inside the quarter thought better than to leave their neighbourhood, where people had lived among one another all their lives and where surely they wouldn't turn against each other. Adul thought that the fighting being reported elsewhere would be quickly resolved. But it wasn't. On 11 June it hit Nasi, and again the following day. "Then Nasi burned, and that was the final day of violence. The government then put us into camps."

When I met him three and a half years later, the 45-year-old was still in a camp. In the wake of the violence, numbers of Rohingya had fled to the village of Thet Kae Pyin, northwest of Sittwe. As they arrived in greater numbers in the months after, a camp grew up around the village for more than 5,000 displaced Rohingya who came to live inside cramped wooden huts and tarpaulin shelters built by international aid agencies. It was outside one hut, in which he lived with his extended family, that we had spoken. Most of the Rohingya who had escaped their homes had remained in camps such as this, but growing numbers were leaving on boats, or via overland smuggling routes. For a fee that could reach $2,000, more than double the average annual income in Myanmar, they would buy passage to Thailand or Malaysia, sometimes via traffickers' camps on the border separating the two countries. In early 2014, dozens of bodies of deceased Rohingya were dug up from shallow forest graves on either side of that border, where they had been held until families could pay a ransom fee.

Rakhine residents of Nasi had initially taken refuge in two factories close to the quarter, before also being sent to camps separated from Rohingya. Adul ran a small business in Thet Kae Pyin camp drying and selling fish, and lived among other Rohingya from Nasi who had fled there. On 13 June 2012, once the mobs had cleared out and the arson and machete attacks ceased, he and his neighbours had asked police to take them to safety. "There were thousands of us leaving, but we didn't have enough protection. The police only came with us for a bit of the journey," Adul had said. He and the remaining inhabitants departed the quarter that morning. The roads they took led them to camps that had quickly sprung up along the coastline, and they were

choked with people carrying their belongings out from
Sittwe. They went first to another camp and stayed for
two days before moving on to Thet Kae Pyin, where they
would settle indefinitely.

Mohammed Ismail had also grown up in Nasi quarter
and knew Adul. The two were now neighbours in Thet
Kae Pyin. As a student at the high school in Nasi, he had
friends from among all the different ethnic and religious
communities that inhabited the quarter. No evidence of
that school now exists, nor is there anything to indicate the
once plural makeup of the neighbourhood. That was wiped
clean by the violence.

Like Adul, the young teacher had felt that unfamiliar
atmosphere settle upon Sittwe in the days before the mobs
arrived at Nasi. Cycling home on the evening of 10 June,
Mohammed Ismail saw the empty streets and dark windows
of houses, and told friends of the sense of foreboding that had
come over him. Only days before, there had been people
milling around long past sundown, in the restaurants and
teashops of the town. But not anymore. There was a heavy
stillness, a sense of apprehension, and it was altogether new
to him.

He wasn't the only person to fear the worst. The
following morning, on 11 June, the then Rakhine chief
minister, Hla Maung Tin, brought community leaders from
both sides together in the school and warned of the potential
for violence in Nasi. At the same time, another meeting was
taking place across the quarter, and Mohammed Ismail was
present. Twenty or so Rakhine and Rohingya leaders had
met and pledged that neither side would attack the other.
But before the meeting was over, groups of armed men
had arrived at the fringes of the quarter, and began to move

in. Mohammad Ismail recognised some of the men. They had come from a nearby ward. Dozens if not hundreds of others like Ko Myat had been bussed in from further afield. Whether or not community leaders had kept their promise that neither side would engage in violence ultimately mattered little. Mobs from outside who knew no more of their targets than their ethnicity and religion were already primed to attack.

★ ★ ★

So often in the wake of ethnic violence, any preexisting divisions are dramatically sharpened, making the prospect of further violence build with each attack. As communities withdraw into their collective shells, stories begin to circulate about the exact meaning of the violence that just occurred – who attacked and who defended, and what would happen if the battle was lost. In Rakhine State these began to circulate with an increased urgency and venom. With Rohingya and Rakhine no longer interacting, there was no countervailing information to correct them.

By 13 June, the violence had largely ceased. It had lasted only for four days, but even in that short space of time, it had completely transformed the social dynamics of the town. As the dust settled on Sittwe and the two communities moved further apart, government officials began to add their own input. Hmuu Zaw, the then director of the President's Office, was one of these. "It is heard that Rohingya Terrorists of the so-called Rohingya Solidarity Organisation are crossing the border and getting into the country with the weapons," he warned on his Facebook page, referencing the armed group that had been active in the 1990s but was now widely considered to be defunct. "That is, Rohingyas from other countries are coming into the country. Since our Military has got the news in advance, we will eradicate them until the end!"[10]

There was indeed violence committed by the Rohingya, and it left numbers of Rakhine dead and many more sent fleeing from their burning homes. It was often executed with the same brutality as Rakhine themselves experienced – close-quarter machete attacks, the torching of houses. But only their violence was construed as terrorism. That charge spoke to the enduring perception that they were outsiders intent on violently usurping the position of Rakhine. That fear of a reversal in status has been a principal driving factor in instances of mass violence along ethno-religious or racial lines the world over, and it had now come to bear on western Myanmar.

Rakhine Buddhists regularly spoke to this fear that a much larger Muslim campaign was underway in Myanmar, connected to events elsewhere. This interpretation gave the "terrorist" label great salience among the community there. Both sides had committed horrendous acts, but perhaps the use of that label by Rakhine was a defensive mechanism, a way to assign evil to the acts of the rival, and in doing so paint equivalent actions as morally justified.

I once met a Rakhine man by the side of a road just north of Sittwe that connected a string of Rakhine villages to a Rohingya village, Thandawli. During the violence of June 2012, as rumours had passed from one Rakhine village to another that Rohingya were mobilising inside Thandawli, the fields that separated the two communities were transformed into a battleground. Rakhine in their hundreds armed themselves and, via the mobile phones of the administrators of each village in that tract, coordinated to march en masse across the fields. At a midpoint between the villages they met with Rohingya, and there the two communities engaged one another in a frenzied battle. The man, who was in his fifties, had joined the hordes of Rakhine that crossed the field, accompanied by his teenage boys. But as the crowds up ahead came into view he understood that the fight would be a bloody one, and so he took his sons and he turned back in the direction of his home.

Until that day, he explained, relations between Buddhists and Muslims here had been very different. "Before the conflict, when we knew each other, we were good. We often went there and they also came here," he said, referring to Thandawli. But as he spoke he became more animated. "What happened to our country?" he exclaimed. "They are trying to swallow the world! They are animals, they are not human beings." The conversation had clearly stirred something inside him, and as it proceeded he became increasingly agitated, for the most part looking not at me but out across the road as we talked. "The problem is with the Muslims of Rakhine state. When they declare Jihad, they help each other. And when they meet Rakhine, they cut their neck and kill them. It was their God that ordered this."

This persistent framing of the violence as terrorism driven by religious zealotry took on a new force after June 2012. These were the "larger scripts" that Appadurai spoke of, and they would be incorporated into local understandings of the conflict. They would begin, in the minds of Rakhine, to significantly reshape its character and implications. By raising the spectre of terrorism, opponents of the Rohingya could connect the events playing out on home soil to a broader conspiracy at play beyond Myanmar's borders, one fuelled by images that began to circulate on social media of the September 2001 attacks on New York and the destruction by the Taliban of the Buddhas of Bamiyan in Afghanistan the same year. Unless checked, so it went, there was the potential for similar carnage to be wreaked on Myanmar. This changed the parameters of the conflict, elevating it above the local level on which it was playing out to a global one. And in doing so, the ramifications for Rakhine of any loss of their territory were greatly heightened, thereby inviting a response proportionate to that threat.

★ ★ ★

"We will take care of our own ethnic nationalities," President Thein Sein had said exactly one month after Nasi burned. "But Rohingyas who came to Burma illegally are not of our ethnic nationalities and we cannot accept them here." The solution, he said, would be for the UN to settle them in camps that they would then manage, relieving the government of any responsibility. "If there are countries that would accept them, they could be sent there."[11]

If a campaign was indeed underway to drive Rohingya out of Myanmar, then it increased in momentum after June that year. A monk's association in Mrauk U released a statement soon after Thein Sein's that offered a stark solution to the problem.

> The Arakanese people must understand that Bengalis want to destroy the land of Arakan, are eating Arakan rice and plan to exterminate Arakanese people and use their money to buy weapons to kill Arakanese people. For this reason and from today, no Arakanese should sell any goods to Bengalis, hire

Bengalis as workers, provide any food to Bengalis and have any dealings with them, as they are cruel by nature.[12]

Three months later, as the threat was amplified louder and louder across Rakhine, violence once again swept the state. I arrived in Sittwe at the end of October that year, a week or so after attacks had taken place in nine townships spread across 250 kilometres of the state. The first wave occurred early on the morning of 22 October in the towns of Mrauk U and Minbya, and grew in intensity in the days after. In and around Mrauk U, groups of Rakhine had descended on six villages carrying spears and machetes and flaming torches, and they spared few houses. In Kyaukphyu, they had arrived in fleets of boats, as they had done in Pauktaw. In the days after 23 October they set about razing the Muslim quarters of both towns, home to Rohingya and, more predominantly, Kaman Muslims. Those who escaped from Pauktaw were brought in longtail boats down the 30-kilometre stretch of river to Sittwe. They alighted on the shoreline west of the state capital and walked inland, carrying their belongings across the low ground to a spot within view of the beach. The place was named Ohne Daw Gyi, or Coconut Garden, and in better times one might have sat looking out to sea as that big orange ball of a sun sank below the Bay of Bengal horizon, cutting through the clusters of palm trees that earned the area its name and bathing the landscape in a rich glow. But Ohne Daw Gyi became a refugee camp, and its population swelled as the days passed. By the time I and two colleagues had arrived there in late October 2012, having walked from downtown Sittwe to a still-inhabited Rohingya village where we hitched rides on motorbikes, some 80 makeshift shelters had been set up.

The structures were flimsy – wooden poles loosely bound together with twine, over which rags of fabric were draped for cover. Families of ten and more huddled beneath, and as the evening set in, large pots for cooking rice were placed over open fires.

By October Sittwe had become entirely segregated. Nasi had long since been emptied, and the only Rohingya communities still in the town were confined to two quarters, Bumay and Aung Mingalar. Armed police manned the barricades that had been erected at the entrances to both quarters after the June violence, and it was with them that I had needed to negotiate access. Families in Aung Mingalar were struggling to bring food and medicine in. No one could walk to the market in Sittwe any longer. Police allowed limited provisions to pass through the checkpoints, but it had to all intents and purposes become a barricaded ghetto. If you go to Sittwe now and find yourself at one of the entrances to these quarters, it won't be long before a policeman approaches and asks to see your documents. Whoever enters and leaves is closely monitored, and that heavy pall that hung over the neighbourhood in 2012 is still there. When I visited for a second time in late 2015, three and a half years on from the violence, a man in his twenties explained that the only occasions on which he had left the quarter since June 2012 were to go to the refugee camps, usually for medical treatment. There were many more like him – prisoners inside their own neighbourhood.

Rakhine mobs had entered Aung Mingalar in June 2012, the day before the violence had taken hold in Nasi. Inhabitants I spoke with described how they had been accompanied by riot police, and fanned out as they moved inside the quarter. By the time I got there in October that year, there was little sign of the destruction they had reportedly left in their wake. It was puzzling, for even if structures had been levelled in the way they had been elsewhere, there would still be clear indications they had once existed – building foundations, damaged walls and the stumps of supporting pillars. A man took me to a spot where the concrete base of a building remained, rubble scattered nearby. Here, he said, the police had opened fire on Rohingya, and bullet holes had peppered the wall of the building. But soon after the violence, bulldozers had been sent in to erase all traces.

Other accounts of police violence emerged from the June 2012 attacks, fuelling speculation of official complicity in what unfolded in Rakhine State that year. They would also circulate in the violence that came the following year, in towns in central Myanmar where security forces were caught on camera standing and watching inert as Buddhist mobs attacked Muslims. By then it was clear that both Rakhine political parties and the government had little intention of safeguarding the lives of Rohingya, for they had long been denied even the meagre protections afforded to others. But the accounts of police actually participating in attacks further raised suspicions of a higher hand in the violence. No smoking gun ever materialised that directly linked the mobs on the ground to whatever ambitions the government held towards Rohingya. Yet beyond just the disdain that the state in Myanmar held towards the Muslim group, there seemed to be a rationale that leant support to the idea that the unrest was strategically useful amid the changing political landscape. This I began to consider more closely when violence erupted in central Myanmar the following year.

★ ★ ★

Sittwe was by and large spared the second wave of violence in October. But it did become a thoroughfare for victims of attacks elsewhere in the state who would pass through the town *en route* to hospital or the camps along the coast. News of the violence that engulfed towns and villages up or downriver passed from community to community and, preempting the arrival of mobs, families would gather their belongings and leave their homes, later converging on safer ground outside of the state capital.

One afternoon in early November 2012, I had stood at the jetty on the Sakrokeya Creek, to the north of downtown Sittwe. In towns and villages to the north and east, fits of violence were continuing. As I waited, a clunking two-tiered public boat, one that would normally be laden with groceries and commuters travelling between Sittwe and elsewhere in the state, came into view further down the creek and slowly made its way towards the jetty. On the lower deck was a Rakhine man whose arms and lower abdomen were covered in burns. The 45-year-old had been brought in from the town of Myebon. His house had been torched by Rohingya the day before, and he wasn't able to escape the flames in time. His burns had been covered only in cling film and a local ointment, and he was carried off the boat and into a waiting taxi that took him to Sittwe hospital, his face contorted in agony.

The violence of October 2012 had been particularly acute in Mrauk U, 60 kilometres upriver, and unconfirmed reports were coming through that bodies of Rohingya had been dumped in mass graves outside the town. Authorities in Rakhine State were reluctant to permit journalists to travel to the sites of violence, and it took a week of petitioning before the Rakhine chief minister's office allowed us to hire a speedboat and travel there. We left early one morning, riding down the Sakrokeya Creek and into the mouth of the Kaladan River. Three hours later, towards the end of the journey as we closed in on the ancient kingdom, the waterway narrowed and the flat rice fields either side began to rise. Through the tall grass that ran the length of the banks, the hundreds of ancient pagodas that dot the tree-covered hillsides slowly came into view. The panorama that gradually opened up would have been the same that greeted the traders who plied that river eight centuries before.

It was an eerie sensation – the quiet and beautiful approach to a scene of great turmoil. We disembarked at the jetty and walked into Mrauk U. A stillness hung over the town that day and the streets had more or less emptied. A rickshaw took us to one of the many monasteries that over the days before had become refuges for Rakhine who had fled their outlying villages. They slept side by side on the floors, next to whatever belongings they were able to carry. One monastery held Rakhine families from a cluster of villages south of Mrauk U who had escaped the violence that began there on 23 October. One teenage boy recounted how, as he and his family had left their village upon the arrival of armed Rohingya, he had caught sight of his 15-year-old friend lying on the ground, blood running from a machete wound just below the neckline.

But it was from inhabitants of one these villages, Yan Thei, that word had spread of a massacre of around 70 Rohingya on that same day in October. A small number of riot police had been deployed to the village the day before, evidently privy to information that it might be targeted. Soon after dawn that morning, mobs of Rakhine armed with spears, machetes and Molotov cocktails gathered outside the village. Witnesses later told how riot police had disarmed the Rohingya villagers as the mobs approached.[13] They then fired into the air in an attempt to disperse the crowds, but that failed. The armed Rakhine breached the thin police line and set about attacking homes and those who tried to flee. The riot police retreated to a safe distance as flames engulfed the houses of Yan Thei, and returned two hours later. According to a number of the villagers that were able to escape and later met with investigators, police then opened fire on the Rohingya that remained.[14]

Similar stories were to emerge from across the nine townships targeted in that wave of violence in late October, and they created a ripple effect that uprooted communities and pushed them further towards the camps along the coastline. By November, more than 100,000 people, the vast majority Rohingya, but also Rakhine and to a lesser extent Kaman, had been displaced. It seemed natural that the camps would form along ethno-religious lines – Rakhine Buddhists were given their own sites, at a safe distance from where Rohingya and Kaman were placed. The communities would remain apart until tensions had eased, and they could once again live side by side. Or so it went.

At the time the talk from the government centred on the need to stabilise the region. President Thein Sein had announced a state of emergency on 10 June, but that hadn't stopped the October violence. If anything, the conflict of June 2012 had torn open divides even further, driving a far deeper antagonism between the two communities and raising levels of distrust to a point at which the slightest spark could mobilise groups to attack. Segregation appeared to be the sole guarantor that communities could not reach one another in the event of another trigger.

But the measure also sought to placate Rakhine who had come to view the camps and ghettos as the rightful place for Rohingya – confined spaces where they could be watched over for signs of mobilisation, and from where they might eventually decide to leave the country altogether, their lives in Myanmar no longer worth the added burden they now carried. The effort to limit the movement of Rohingya, or even rid the state of them entirely, was enthusiastically backed by high-level political powers in the state. The Rakhine Nationalities Development Party had said in late June, prior to President Thein Sein's statement requesting UN help in resettling the community, that Rohingya should be deported to a third country and that all other ethnic groups should collaborate to prevent "Bengali trespassing."[15] This position continued long afterwards. Dr Aye Maung, head of the party, later told me that he was happy with the current situation, of Rakhine remaining in Sittwe town and Rohingya in the camps. Inside those perimeters they had freedom to move around, he said. "It's good. There have been terrorist attacks, and if people live together they will be afraid."

Back in 2012, he had looked to another country for a model of how Myanmar should respond to the Rohingya. "We need to have a policy; an exclusive one, for these people and figure out how to defend this region – they will be repeatedly invading our territory ... We need to be like Israel."[16] Three years on, the likelihood that Rakhine would accept Rohingya as neighbours once again was slim. It could take 20 or 30 years before the two groups could live together again, he believed.

High walls, both real and figurative, were being built between the two groups, and these would rise as the months

passed and increasingly sinister "solutions" to the problem
were issued by Rakhine nationalists. Several weeks into the
state of emergency in the middle of 2012, a group of Rakhine
monks met at the Myo Ma Pavilion in Rathedaung, due
north of Sittwe. It was early in the afternoon of 5 July,
three and a half months before the October violence, and
they spoke for several hours. At the meeting's close later
that day, a statement had been drawn up commanding
Rakhine to cease all contact with the "Bengali *kalar*." They
were no longer to be employed as they had been in the
ports and harbours of the state, on the farms and in the rice
mills and brick kilns. They would not be allowed on boats,
ferries and motorbikes, and nor should Rakhine trade with
them.[17] Several days later, a letter was circulated, signed by
the "Group of Wuntharnu Ethnic People," warning that
international NGOs supplying aid to displaced Rohingya
had "watered poisonous plants."[18]

These were the calls that had presaged the events
of October 2012. The force of the propaganda, and its
unremitting circulation – not just in leaflets and statements,
but in domestic media of all stripes, state-owned and private
– left little mental space within the Buddhist communities
of Rakhine State to consider the Rohingya as anything but
menacing. That image had become a staple of the Rakhine
imagination and, it soon became evident, the Buddhist
population of Myanmar more broadly.

Four days before violence again swept the state, another
group of monks convened at the Dakaung Monastery in
Sittwe, under the banner of the All-Arakanese Monks'
Solidarity Conference. In a statement, they reaffirmed their
commitment to keeping Rakhine and Rohingya separate,
but added an additional point: "To expose sympathisers of

Bengali *Kalars* as national traitors along with photos and spread the information to every township."[19]

The "sympathisers" would be those Rakhine who continued to assist, even interact with, Rohingya. This had continued on a small scale after June, with numbers of Rakhine discreetly helping to get food and medicine into Aung Mingalar quarter. But they were now considered disloyal, and would need weeding out. There were echoes of Rwanda in 1994, when Hutu "moderates" were targeted by Hutu Power fanatics solely on the grounds that they had aided Tutsis to flee to safety, and in doing so, betrayed their own people. Frightening similarities were beginning to show between Rakhine State and other sites of mass violence elsewhere in the world – the ghettos, the witch-hunts, the Othering and the isolating of rival groups.

The tensions continued to mount, and on 21 October 2012, a Rakhine man in Mrauk U was caught selling rice to a Muslim customer. A group of fellow Rakhine descended on his stall with clubs and beat him to death. The following day, a Rohingya husband in a nearby village struck his wife on the face after an argument inside their home. Rakhine neighbours got wind of the news and quickly surrounded the house. Soon after, Mrauk U erupted.

But far away on the other side of the country, something ominous had begun to stir. On the banks of the Thanlyin River, which courses through Kayin State between lime-stone mountains whose walls rise up in steep verticals from the river plain, lies the town of Hpa-an. Kayin State is pre-dominantly Buddhist, but has a sizeable Christian population. Less significant, population-wise, is the Muslim community. But four days before the call had gone out in Rakhine State to expose any moderates aiding the Rohingya, Ashin

Kawi Daza, the head abbot of the Mae Baung Monastery in Hpa-an, circulated a statement that carried a similar warning: Buddhists should not lease land or property to Muslims, and neither should they shop in Muslim stores nor marry Muslim men.[20] There were no Rohingya here in Hpa-an – only Bamar and Kayin Muslims. But, so it seemed, what had begun several months earlier as a localised conflict between two ethnic groups in the westernmost state of Myanmar was beginning to be echoed hundreds of miles away.

Several weeks after the abbot released his statement, four men climbed on their motorbikes in Kyondo, a sub-township of Kawkareik in Kayin State and, shortly before midnight, rode past a mosque. They threw two grenades. One landed inside, and the other hit an outside wall and fell to the ground before exploding. Within an hour, two more grenades were thrown at another mosque elsewhere in the township. It was the first time mosques had been attacked there, residents later said.

★ ★ ★

As the communities moved further apart in Rakhine State, instances of violence lessened. By the end of October, the situation had become "almost normal," the President's Office said.[21] But that normality was a state in which communities were segregated along religious lines, for Kaman now populated the same camps that Rohingya did, and where checkpoints ensured that Muslims in and around Sittwe could not leave their camp or neighbourhood limits. It had indeed calmed, but what kind of calm was this?

It would be another eight months before violence again hit the state. On 30 June 2013, reports of the rape of a

Buddhist woman by two Kaman Muslim men in Thandwe, south of Sittwe, led to the destruction of four Muslim houses. And it struck the town again in October that year. A Kaman man argued with a Buddhist taxi driver over parking spaces. Word then spread that a Muslim had insulted a Buddhist, and the attacks resumed. In a village outside of Thandwe, men burst into a house where a 94-year-old Kaman woman was resting in her bed. With machetes, they hacked her to death. Her daughter had managed to flee, but returned to find the elderly woman with fatal wounds to her stomach, neck and head. In the following days, mobs razed more than 70 Muslim houses across Thandwe and in nearby villages before the army moved in. The houses belonged to Kaman. There were no Rohingya involved, indicating that the rationale behind the violence had moved on from one of defending the country against illegal invaders, and towards a general assault on the Muslim community. Kaman were citizens of Myanmar, and accepted as indigenous to Rakhine State. But they were Muslims, and had quickly become as reviled as the Rohingya. Among those arrested in the following weeks for participation in the Thandwe violence was the local chairman of the Rakhine Nationalities Development Party.

But in the meantime, the violence had moved beyond Rakhine State to towns in central Myanmar, many of which hadn't before known such communal hostility. First there were small incidents, like the mosque attack in Kawkareik, but these grew bigger. In March 2013, three Muslim quarters in Meikhtila, just south of Mandalay, were entirely levelled. Hundreds of armed men, many unrecognisable to residents, flooded the town and sent upwards of 12,000 people, the majority Muslim, fleeing to makeshift camps on the outskirts. There they would remain for months, if not years. Then in April, Muslim houses in and around Okkan, two hours north of Yangon, were torched, and the following month, mobs struck Lashio, over in the west of the country. The village of Htangone, 100 or so kilometres north of Mandalay in Myanmar's dry zone, descended into violence in August 2013, when Buddhist monks led crowds of men towards Muslim houses and the local mosque, turning them to rubble. From a localised conflict in Rakhine State, violence between Buddhists and Muslims had gone nationwide.

7

At first light the darkness fell: Myanmar's democratic experiment falters

What shocked almost as much as the violence of 2012 was the public response to it. Crowds of Rakhine that had stood on the roadside as Mohammed Ismail and hundreds of others carried their belongings from the ruins of Nasi quarter towards the coastline jeered as they passed by, but noises soon began to come from further afield, and from unexpected quarters. Rakhine nationalists evidently hadn't been alone in their resentment of the Rohingya; prominent voices within the pro-democracy movement appeared to be so too.

For so long it had seemed that the major unifying force among the Myanmar public had been opposition to the military. It was the glue that bound together in a show of virtuous accord all who did not benefit from its rule. There were the monks, the student activists, Aung San Suu Kyi and her party comrades. There were the victims of the military's campaigns in the borderlands and of its extensive surveillance apparatus in the centre, which sent thousands to jail for interminably long periods of their lives. They all seemed to sing in chorus, and in their mostly peaceful, dignified defiance of the state, it often felt as if the public was as good as the military was bad. Of course that was a superficial reading. Ethnic armies fighting the military took the lives of civilians and often turned against one another, making enemies of one-time allies, while the pro-democracy movement was far from a single cohesive unit. But the veil that dictatorial rule casts over a country often obscures nuance.

With the junta supposedly in retreat by the middle of 2012, however, it appeared that a new common enemy had arisen. Volatile fault lines came into view that cut across Myanmar society, and at particular moments in 2012 and thereafter it felt as if the constellation of solidarities and enmities that once had seemed so clear and rational was being dramatically reconfigured.

The National League for Democracy entered parliament for the first time in April 2012. The first day of that month was, for the thousands gathered outside the party headquarters and elsewhere as the by-election results came in, a magical one. As the sun dipped in the sky and that familiar pink evening light wrapped itself around the buildings of Yangon, seat after seat fell to the opposition – 43 out of the 44 it contested by the close of play. Each time they won a seat, a screen erected in front of the building on Shwegondaing Road flashed up a new constituency and the crowds roared. It had been 50 years since Ne Win's coup, giving Myanmar the unhealthy distinction of having one of the twentieth century's longest running dictatorships. Although the NLD was still a minority in parliament, that seemed about to change.

But it wasn't clear exactly why. The regime hadn't crumbled in the face of mass protest, as seemed to be the trend of that period – in Tunisia, in Libya, in Egypt, and not so long before, in Indonesia. It was a gradual transfer of power, in line with the "seven-step roadmap to democracy" unfurled in 2003 that would ostensibly see the military reduce its political role and pass the reins to a civilian government. No one outside of the junta's inner circle really knew the reasons for the shift – perhaps it feared regime change, knowing that a deeply unpopular leadership had a limited shelf life. Its increasing reliance on China for economic and political support had also chafed with the nationalistic ambitions of the military, which had given China an almost free run of the country's resources. A choreographed transition was a deft way for it to lock in its interests and rid itself of the dependence it had on its neighbour, thereby finally allowing the country to rejoin a world from which it had retreated half a century before. How it would pan out exactly was difficult to say, but standing outside the NLD headquarters that evening it was impossible, even for the sceptics, to resist the feeling that a significant break in the historical continuum of Myanmar was occurring – the beginnings of a government brought about by popular vote.

Yet democracy is in the eye of the beholder. Between the act of freely casting a ballot and the fuller manifestation of equal rights to all, there is a long process of negotiation and compromise that so often becomes the site of battles over what version of the democratic ideal should take hold. In Myanmar, where for half a century political contestation was considered a criminal act, this period was always going to be fraught with conflict. Not only would old forces want to limit the authority of new ones, but the public understood that new avenues for the expression of different desires had begun to open – a freer media and a freer space for protest, and a parliament with a semblance of an opposition through which different visions for the country's future might be turned into legislation.

When the reactions to the violence of June 2012 began to be aired, it wasn't merely the extent of anti-Rohingya hostility that surprised at first, but rather that hostility towards the group wasn't locked to a particular political orientation. There is often a tendency to associate xenophobic sentiment with a far right mentality, but that didn't seem to hold true for Myanmar in those years. There were people like Ko Ko Gyi, a leading figure in the 1988 uprising against military rule who, for his opposition to the junta, spent more than 17 years behind bars. He had never drawn the same international attention as Suu Kyi, but inside Myanmar he was known and revered by many as the stoical young man who had been willing to sacrifice so much to bring about a change to the leadership of the country. But as Sittwe was convulsed by violence, he seemed to undergo a transformation of sorts. He explained to a journalist that international pressure on Myanmar to accept Rohingya had reached a point at which "if powerful countries are to keep pressuring us, then us, the democratic forces of Burma, will view this as a national affair and will resolve this issue by joining hands with the Tatmadaw," the Myanmar army. The Rohingya were "absolutely not an ethnic race of Burma," and those who said otherwise were infringing on its sovereignty.[1]

His reaction, and that of others who instead of condemning the violence used it as an opportunity to call for the expulsion of Rohingya, seemed so out of sync with what the pro-democracy movement in Myanmar had once seemed to represent. Ko Ko Gyi's talk had been of a "democratic" effort to deny Rohingya the rights that other groups in the country were asserting, born of a fear that if this Muslim minority was to be empowered, then all others would suffer. All of a sudden, human rights in Myanmar didn't appear to be a public good, accessible or applicable to all.[2] Instead they were open to select groups whose position would be greatly weakened if additional constituencies were enfranchised. The anxieties that drove this sentiment had become so overwhelming that the military, for so long holders of the monopoly on violence against civilians – and the institution that put Ko Ko Gyi away for 17 years – might become protector of those same civilians against a new, even more nefarious force. It seemed to matter little that the restrictions placed on Rohingya in the decades after their denial of citizenship had effectively quarantined them in Rakhine State, subjected to a degree of control that no other group in Myanmar faced. Despite this, they had still become a source of national hysteria.

The National League for Democracy too remained conspicuously quiet on the violence towards the Rohingya. Suu Kyi would often take an ambivalent line, arguing that both sides were to blame and thus that singling out the Rakhine mobs would give the impression that they had been chief protagonists. During a trip to India in November 2012, soon after the second wave of violence had ceased, she spoke of a "huge international tragedy" playing out in western Myanmar. "But don't forget that violence has been committed by both sides," she continued. "This is why I prefer not to take sides. And, also I want to work toward reconciliation between these two communities. I am not going to be able to do that if I take sides."[3]

By that point 115,000 people were living in refugee camps, the vast majority Rohingya. Displaced Rakhine could move freely between their camps and nearby towns; Rohingya on the other had were forbidden from leaving theirs by armed police stationed at entry points who warned of likely attacks by Rakhine should they venture out. There had been atrocities committed by both sides, and in that, Suu Kyi was correct. Yet her reluctance to call out the widely held racism towards Rohingya that had helped to feed the violence hid a more significant problem. As 2012 wore on and the segregation became firmly entrenched, it grew increasingly apparent that no one in a position of influence was willing to counter the prejudices towards Rohingya, and indeed Muslims more broadly, that were either activated or reinforced by the events of that year. The silence of Suu Kyi, known internationally for her non-violent resistance towards a military that had kept her under house arrest for 15 years, did seem out of character, and for that she drew sharp criticism. Yet at the same time, there was a certain continuity to it. Never had the decades-long suffering of the Rohingya featured on the radar of the pro-democracy movement in Myanmar, and nor was the group included in the calls for equality between ethnicities in a post-junta society. Prior to 2012, theirs had always been a peripheral issue that made headlines only when it became an international point of contention – when Rohingya fled the country on boats, prompting warnings from neighbouring nations that Myanmar's domestic crises were becoming regional ones. They were never incorporated into the narrative of the wider struggle of persecuted minorities there. They had no voice, and no presence. It seemed as if they were ghosts – people who lived in Myanmar, but who didn't quite exist.

I grew to wonder after 2012 whether, if left long enough, these prejudices could grow even more entrenched, particularly given the absence of any countervailing narratives that might de-stigmatise the identity of the Rohingya. Suu Kyi was often accused of harbouring a possible bias of her own, for she was an elite Bamar and thus a beneficiary of the ethnic hierarchy that had formed in Myanmar. But regardless of her own feelings towards the Rohingya and the reasons for her silence, the neutral line she had taken in a situation that greatly favoured one side over another was deeply problematic. Unless the country's most revered figure gave the crisis a true reading – acknowledging the decades of state-sanctioned debasement of the Rohingya and the effect that this had on the turn to violence among Rakhine – then she and her party were complicit in fuelling the mentality that gave rise to it.

Over and again, when questioned on the matter, Suu Kyi pointedly refused to be drawn. She was evasive, never using the name "Rohingya," lest hardline nationalists viewed that as recognition of the group. After entering parliament following the by-election victory, she quickly developed a reputation for avoiding media, and I was never able to secure an interview with her. When journalists did get the opportunity to press her, she urged the government, at that point run by the military-aligned Union Solidarity and Development Party (USDP), to grant all ethnic minorities equal rights. She knew however that Rohingya were not considered an official ethnic minority, and thus was able to project to the international community a sense that she was engaging in the issue while still avoiding the wrath of the sizeable anti-Rohingya lobby in Myanmar. Citizenship laws needed to be "clarified," she would say. At no point did she call out the prejudicial basis of the citizenship framework in Myanmar, in which entire groups were rendered stateless regardless of the individual histories of those within the group.

Given the weight of hostility towards the Rohingya across Myanmar society, her approach might have been a coldly pragmatic one. Defending this despised community ran the risk of casting their indigenous Buddhist rivals, the Rakhine, as the evildoers, and this might prove political suicide for someone eyeing office. The next elections were set for 2015, three years after the violence, and Suu Kyi needed to keep her support base onside. There was talk of her playing the long game, waiting until the transition had moved along to a point at which she felt secure enough to begin to tackle more substantially the ingrained resentment shared by too many people in Myanmar. But this seemed dangerous. With the communities of Rakhine State so fissured by the violence, time might only deepen the divides beyond the point of mending.

She, along with many of the activists that had suffered as a result of their resistance to military rule, began, as the transition progressed, to move further into mainstream politics. But as the responses to the 2012 violence were aired, it became evident that the particular democratic quality many of these figures held to had never really been tested. They had stood against military rule, and had used "democracy" as a powerful sign around which to mobilise a movement, but what exactly they stood for was less clear. I had unthinkingly equated the concept of democracy with the principle of tolerance for all, but in the harsh light of 2012, this seemed woefully misinformed. And the surprise wasn't reserved only for that movement. When monk groups began to fan the flames of violent chauvinism in Rakhine State, and in time elsewhere in the country, the narrative of Buddhism as inherently peaceful began to stretch at the seams. Foreign commentators who criticised the apartheid system that was developing in Rakhine State, who questioned these appeals to the military and who called out the seeming hypocrisy of this exclusionary strain in the pro-democracy movement were branded neo-colonialists or terrorist sympathisers, and told that this was no business of theirs.

★ ★ ★

It was perhaps the fate of Myanmar that the democratic opening would bring forth division. So violently had notions of identity and belonging been manipulated and thrust to the centre of life under the military that, as it began to step back, those contestations formed a core part of the search for a new Myanmar. While the public had always seemed to reject the regime's propaganda, the discourse on belonging and the "truths" peddled by the military about the intentions of certain ethnic minorities in Myanmar seemed to carry such force that they were incorporated into present-day understandings of the dynamics between communities. Regardless of whatever paeans to solidarity between different ethnic and religious groups had been voiced in opposition to the military, the more subtle day-to-day prejudices that Hla Hla and many others experienced from their peers persisted.

So the kindling for the violence may have already been in place. But what the transition did was to allow an opportunity for it to be lit. In Rakhine State, it seemed at first glance that animosities deeply rooted in history but long contained were bursting to the surface, spontaneous and uncontrollable. But soon it became apparent that they were also being stoked, whether overtly or quietly. The seminars held by the Rakhine Nationalities Development Party were designed specifically to warn of this Muslim threat, and the leaflets circulated in the aftermath, by monk groups and other activist networks, raised that threat level even further. There were appeals being made to the greatest fears of the Rakhine, yet the remedies offered ran counter to the direction Myanmar appeared to be heading: away from the military's divisive politics and towards an embrace of the ideals of a democratic state. Rather than entering an age of national healing, deeper divisions were being sown.

The Rakhine Nationalities Development Party was like ethnic-oriented parties the world over who, in seeking to consolidate support during a transition, played the ethno-nationalist card. It had formed six months before the first elections in November 2010 and knew that future elections lay ahead. It needed relevance, always the first mission of any new political party, and in Rakhine State the whipping up of local nationalist sentiment seemed an obvious way to direct support to a party that modelled itself as the only viable defender of the ethnicity, particularly when that group had for so long been denied a political voice. Ethnic Rakhine rightly wanted greater involvement and greater returns from the democratic shift. They had been forced to watch as the state they held strong claims to became a feeding ground for predatory economic interests, local and foreign, whose gains went almost anywhere other than back to its people. By the time of the 2010 elections, poverty levels there were nearly twice that of the national average,[4] a position that belied the abundance of gas and other natural resources that lay under the ground and out to sea but which, at the behest of the junta, had been feasted upon by companies from China, Korea and elsewhere.

The transition would be an opportunity to correct this – to bring Rakhine to the table and to begin to rectify some of the damage wrought by state interests in the previous decades. Yet the processes that might allow this to happen would involve a certain levelling of the political playing field, and here the danger lay, for any democratic opening could also empower Rohingya to assert their own claims to the state.

Those fears had played out before. As preparations for the 2010 vote had gotten underway, the junta's Electoral Commission announced that anyone holding the Temporary Registration Cards, or "white cards," could vote. The Rakhine Nationalities Development Party accused it of political trickery, for Rohingya had these and would surely vote for the Union Solidarity and Development Party (USDP) – that which represented the generals who had just enfranchised Rohingya. Prior to the vote, USDP members toured Rohingya villages in the north of the state, encouraging inhabitants to sign up to the electoral roll. The RNDP's fears were confirmed when several Rohingya politicians won seats in parliament as representatives of the USDP, which had received strong support from their ethnic constituents. Although the RNDP still came out strong in Rakhine State, taking 18 seats in the state parliament against the USDP's 16, the transaction between the Rohingya and the ruling party that had taken place beforehand warned of what might lie ahead were Rohingya to be further empowered.

In November 2012, a month after the second wave of violence hit Rakhine State, the RNDP ran an editorial in its magazine, the *Development Journal*. It read:

> Hitler and Eichmann were the enemy of the Jews, but
> they were probably heroes to the Germans … In order for
> a country's survival, the survival of a race, or in defense of
> national sovereignty, crimes against humanity or in-human
> acts may justifiably be committed … So, if that survival
> principle or justification is applied or permitted equally (in
> our Myanmar case) our endeavors to protect our Rakhine
> race and defend the sovereignty and longevity of the Union
> of Myanmar cannot be labeled as "crimes against humanity,"
> or "inhuman" or "in-humane."[5]

The passage illuminated the venom that Rakhine State's largest political party – no longer fringe, but with seats in parliament – held towards Rohingya, and the alarming measures it considered necessary to deal with this community. But its publication also spoke to another problem, one that was becoming increasingly difficult to negotiate. The magazine had gone out without a whimper – there was no redaction of its content, and no recriminations for the hand that authored it. The government censor board had been done away with several months before its release, meaning that magazines no longer required vetting prior to publication. Although restrictions were being eased across the board as authoritarian rule waned in 2012, there were no functioning institutions in place to contain the rise of hate speech and to manage the conflicts that followed it. Rather, as the focus of national rage homed in on the Rohingya in the aftermath of the 2012 violence, the rhetoric was allowed to run free – in party magazines, on online blogs and social media platforms, and in protests that called for international aid groups assisting Rohingya to be ejected from the country.

In April that year, Suu Kyi had hosted the first Irrawaddy Literary Festival on the shores of Inya Lake in Yangon, an event that stood as a totem of the progress made over the previous year. Big name international journalists and authors were flown in, some of whom had spent years on the junta's blacklist, and although tempered by the knowledge that all this was very new and unpredictable, there was a sense of jubilation at Myanmar's final emergence from the darkness. Yet it seemed that no one really knew how to manage the space for free expression, or whether it should even be managed. This cut to the core of the democratisation problem: should the forces that inevitably result from liberalisation, and which can aid the opening of a country as much as they can imperil it, be constrained, or should they be allowed to run free? That desire to own one's destiny, to have a stake in decisions that affect one, to spread ideas freely and to enjoy the freedom to support or resist the ideas of others – these are what authoritarianism denies, and what democracy promises. But as much as they engender an openness and tolerance, they can also have the opposite effect. And as 2012 drew on, the divisive ideologies that had taken hold and played such a pivotal role in the mobilisation of Rakhine mobs seemed to pass over the mountains and find expression among Buddhists in central Myanmar.

★ ★ ★

One evening in early 2013 I boarded a bus in Yangon and rode through the night to Mawlamyine, the sleepy riverside capital of Mon State. There is a monastery in the town I'd wanted to visit, and an abbot there I hoped to meet. In the months between October 2012 and my visit to Mawlamyine, U Wimala had become a household name among those watching the spread of anti-Muslim sentiment beyond Rakhine State. Soon after the second wave of violence the year before, he had ordered a printing company in Mawlamyine to produce a batch of stickers, and it was these that had begun to appear on shop fronts and taxi windows not just in this town, but across Myanmar. They provided the most visible indicator of the extent to which the target of anti-Muslim sentiment had broadened beyond just the Rohingya, and had coalesced into something approaching an organised movement. The stickers appeared on stalls in Mawlamyine market, as they did in Yangon, in Mandalay, and in far flung towns in the border regions. In Myanmar numerals, they bore the numbers 969, set against the backdrop of a chakra wheel and the Buddhist flag, and floating above a podium on which four lions were seated.

U Wimala had also grown fearful that Myanmar would follow the same fate as its neighbours in the region and see Buddhism displaced by Islam. The stickers were printed in order to protect Buddhism, he had explained, for the numerals signified the nine attributes of Buddha, the six attributes of his teachings, and the nine attributes of the Sangha. It counteracted a similar practice among Muslims, whose shop fronts had long bore the numbers 786 – a sequence that corresponds to the opening phrase of the Qur'an, "Bismillah ir-Rahman ir-Rahim," or "In the name of Allah, the most Merciful, the most Beneficent."

The stickers were distributed freely around the country, and as hard as it was to sympathise with them, it was at first equally difficult to reject them outright. Muslims had theirs too, so the argument went. And there were many for whom the underlying message of the 969 campaign represented not a wild fantasy but a deeply personal anxiety. Not for every bearer of the sign were Muslims evildoers, but for all who sported them, Buddhism was evidently vulnerable enough to warrant protection. Religion had been that most precious of sanctuaries for many in Myanmar before and during military rule, and families invested in it heavily – perhaps more so at certain points than they did healthcare and education.[6] Long before it had been imperilled by the British, and the impact of that had been enough to spur monks into taking up arms. The campaigns of the 1920s and 1930s may have melded neatly with a more politically focused desire for self-rule, but the religious element wasn't a petty misgiving: for many in Myanmar, their nation stood as that increasingly rare thing in the world – a place where Buddhism had a chance of survival against hostile forces. The monks of the modern age, like U Wimala, would do as their predecessors had done more than a century before, and provide the vanguard of a movement to protect the faith.

Five months after the second wave of violence in Rakhine, attacks on Muslims erupted in towns across central Myanmar. They took a similar course: a small trigger incident followed quickly by the arrival of mobs that levelled neighbourhoods and sent Muslims fleeing to camps. Other similarities also emerged: the circulation of leaflets beforehand warning of the Muslim threat, except that this threat wasn't now limited to Rakhine State but to Myanmar more broadly. The narrative that underpinned the violence in the west of Myanmar, which had been geographically contained, seemed to have spread to the centre, indicating perhaps that the fate of Myanmar hinged to a large extent on events in Rakhine State. The Rakhine Yoma mountain range may have once buffered central Myanmar from its vulnerable western flank, providing a barrier against the

further encroachment of Islamic cultures into the country.
Perhaps the hills would no longer hold.

★ ★ ★

Meikhtila was the first to go in 2013. A busy trading hub, the
town sits at the centre of a web of highways that run north
to south and east to west, linking Mandalay to Yangon and
connecting the people and markets of far eastern Shan State
to those near the Indian border.

Early in the morning of 21 March that year, Sandar had
boarded a public bus near her home in Mandalay and rode
the two hours to Meikhtila. The young journalist, then a staff
reporter for an exiled Myanmar media organisation, carried a
bag with a few clothes inside and her video camera – a small
handheld device she had owned for several years. The bus she
took stopped regularly to pick up passengers and goods bound
for Meikhtila. But 30 minutes outside town it had stopped for
a final time, and refused to continue. At the side of the road,
she and the other passengers were ordered off. Normally it
would have taken her direct to the station in the centre of
Meikhtila, but that day she and the others disembarked well
before the town limits and looked for any waiting motorbike
taxis. She found one, bargained a price, and climbed on the
back. The bike took off, but after a few minutes pulled over.
The driver told her to pick up a bamboo pole and carry it
with her. You have dark skin, she heard him say, and you
might be mistaken for a Muslim. The pole would indicate
that she was Buddhist. In the other hand she had the camera,
and her bag was slung over her back. She climbed back on
and the bike wove through the backstreets of outer Meikhtila
and eventually into the centre.

Once inside the town, she understood the driver's fears. Beginning from the outskirts and carrying through to the town centre, dozens of shop fronts were destroyed. They were owned by Muslims: the Arabic inscriptions on the signage outside that gave away the identity of their owners had, that morning and the day before, sealed their fate.

The damage was an early, but wholly inadequate, indicator of what lay further down the road: the debris, human and structural, of a bout of violence between Buddhists and Muslims on a scale that hadn't been seen in Myanmar since the carnage of October the previous year in Rakhine State. From behind the row of buildings that lined the main street running into the centre of town from the west, smoke rose up into the sky. It came from Thiri Mingalar quarter. The night before it had been visited by hundreds of men armed with sticks, machetes and flaming torches. Many had been brought into town from outside, residents later said. Few recognised the groups of men that had appeared that evening – they seemed drunk or high, and were unsure of their coordinates, asking directions to neighbourhoods that, hours later, would be burning. A few blocks north of Thiri Mingalar, Mingalar Zayone had also been razed, and further to the west of town, across the large lake around which Meikhtila grew up, lay another neighbourhood now in ashes. Inside the three quarters, the panorama of destruction was staggering – in the space of an evening's work, the mobs had turned hundreds of buildings to rubble and sent their inhabitants fleeing to camps on the outskirts of town.

Sandar had been to Meikhtila before. There a roundabout in the busy heart of town, and the streets that radiate out from it are always choked with cars and people.

The marketplace to the south that comes alive with the rising of the sun each morning was shuttered on that day, and the crowds were no longer there. Instead, the only people she saw stalked the streets in groups of four or five, carrying sticks and machetes.

She and her driver parked by the side of the road near the roundabout. It was shortly after midday on 21 March and Sandar's camera had been rolling for most of the morning. She kept it going as she climbed off the bike, and panned over the street in front of her.

"A group of people were just standing at the junction and some guys came along on motorbikes," she recalled. "Two of the men who were standing there had knives and the rest had sticks. The people on the motorbike stopped next to one of the guys and they spoke for about five or ten minutes." Their voices didn't carry far, and she was unable to hear what was being said. But still, she kept the camera rolling.

Two days earlier, on 19 March, an argument had broken out in a Muslim-owned jewellery store in downtown Meikhtila. It was over a golden hairpin, bought by a Buddhist couple that had come to the shop from a village outside Meikhtila. The hairpin turned out to be a fake, so they claimed. The couple accused the Muslim owner of defrauding them. Amid heated exchanges, the owner grew angry and struck out. A fight broke out, and then word began to spread that the Buddhist lady had been killed. Outside the shop, crowds of Buddhists quickly gathered. Among them there were monks. Within hours the gold shop, and several other Muslim shops either side of it, had been destroyed. Footage that later emerged showed police watching inert as the shops were attacked and as a Muslim person lay injured in the street, onlookers discussing whether to leave him to die.[7] Later that day, a group of Muslim men knocked a monk off his bike and beat him as he lay on the road. His body was then set ablaze. He was hospitalised, but later died. The carnage began the following morning.

Sandar had been working for six years as a video reporter, and as reports of the violence on 20 March began to circulate, her editor telephoned and asked if she would go to Meikhtila. Even before she had made it into the centre of town the following day, she had seen from afar the plumes of smoke rising high, mapping the sites of destruction onto the sky.

The conversation between the men on the other side of the road came to a sudden end. As she watched, the group moved in. "They started to kill that guy. They just beheaded him, or tried to." Those holding knives sawed at his throat and he dropped to the ground. He was still moving when they poured gasoline on him and burned the body.

One of the group then spotted her filming and ran across the road. He ordered her to delete the footage. She refused, and he threatened to kill her. She and the driver leapt on the bike and sped off, but they were followed. For ten minutes they raced through the streets before eventually managing to shake them off. Sandar made it to a friend's house and waited there for several hours, and as evening set in, she and her friend rode back into town. They went past the roundabout and the street where the body had been. It was still there, a blackened figure lying on the edge of the pavement. The flames had died but smoke still rose from it, and people made narrow detours as they walked past.

The body on the street was one of 43 victims that were counted after the butchery in Meikhtila had ceased. And butchery it was. When we speak of a fit of violence, we imagine a sudden convulsion of the collective body, one short-lived but so powerful that the scale of devastation it leaves seems far greater than the window of time in which it was achieved. By the afternoon of 22 March 2013, when a state of emergency had been announced, nearly 830 buildings in Meikhtila had been destroyed. A little over two weeks later I walked around the remains of Thiri Mingalar and Mingalar Zayone and understood that the devastation was more or less total. Row upon row of houses lay in ruins, and cooking pots, shoes and clothing were left among the rubble. There were pillars and walls still standing, but save for small groups of people who picked among the ruins and cast long stares at any visitor, there was no life in those quarters.

There was talk of how the violence had "spread" from Rakhine State to Meikhtila, like a contagion that moved from one locale to another, emptying Muslim neighbourhoods of their inhabitants. But it wasn't quite as simple as that, for the dynamic between Buddhist and Muslim communities here was different. Meikhtila hadn't seen this before, in any form, and there wasn't the violent cleavage of ethnicity that, alongside religion, had provided another powerful marker of difference between Rakhine and Rohingya in the west of the country. Here, the Buddhist and Muslim communities were both largely Bamar. Meikhtila, as a key centre of trade, thrived on interaction between all who lived in and depended on the town and its busy commerce.

★ ★ ★

The violence had been particularly brutal in Meikhtila, and it drew in a surprising cast of characters. In one video clip

taken of the attack on Mingalar Zayone on 20 March, a
Muslim man is seen being brought out of his hiding place in
the tall grass that rings the neighbourhood and pushed into
a clearing. Once there, he is quickly set upon by two men
holding long poles. The first blow is a powerful horizontal
one to the back of the neck that sends the man straight to
ground. Other attackers run towards him and rain more
blows down, one after the other, his legs jerking up into
the air with each contact made. It is a vicious scene, more
redolent of the actions of the military than of civilians. But
then a monk – or at least a man, shaven-headed, dressed in
monks' robes – appears at the right-hand side of the melee.
He lands one blow with a pole he is clutching, then two,
three, four, five.

That scene, and the rhetoric of the monk groups in
Rakhine State the previous year, contrasted starkly with the
prevailing idea of Buddhism as not just pacifistic, but actively
against the use of violence; that its highest authorities had,
in their passage from layman to monk, sworn a doctrinal
commitment to non-violence. Perhaps to divert from the
unthinkable, people questioned whether the man had been
a thug dressed in monks' garb, brought in to give the attack
a veneer of "justness" and to mobilise more Buddhists to
participate. Yet in the wake of the Rakhine State violence
of 2012, the position of a number of vocal monks – not
just in Myanmar's west, but across the country – on the
issue of Muslims had become increasingly aggressive. This
monk in Meikhtila may have been an extreme example, but
he nevertheless reinforced a perception that a prominent
cross-section of Myanmar's monastic community had
adopted a militant stance towards Muslims that provided
fertile grounds for violence. The robed figureheads of the

969 movement had used their sermons not to preach peace but to open religious divisions even wider, a process that had intensified in the build up to the Meikhtila attacks.

Although U Wimala had led the early charge, another monk increasingly came to dominate the spotlight. U Wirathu was abbot of the Masoyein Monastery in Mandalay. He had travelled to Meikhtila in December, several months before the violence began, and delivered a sermon in which he implored Buddhists in the town to cut ties with Muslims. "Buy only from our shops. If our money goes to enemies' hands, it will destroy our whole nationality and religion." The 969 stickers would indicate which stores were Buddhist-owned, and it soon became apparent that they were being used not as a mere emblem of Buddhism, as a Christian might display a crucifix, but as part of a boycott campaign of Muslim businesses. "They will use that money to manipulate women, forcefully convert those women into their religion, and the children of them will become enemies of the state," he continued. "They will destroy the whole nation and religion. When their population grows, they will do the same thing as they did in Rakhine state: invade. They will take over the whole country."[8]

In the aftermath of his visit to Meikhtila, leaflets began to be circulated around the town. "We are writing to report you that the Burmese Buddhists have been living under the threat," began one. It was signed only by "Buddhists who feel helpless," and addressed to the head of the local Sangha committee there. "According to the above situation, Muslims in Meikhtila, those tiger *kalar* are wearing their *kalar* mosque clothes and going around in the town more than before. In that group, there are some stranger *kalars* who we haven't seen before."[9]

Meikhtila had been the bloodiest instance of mass religious violence in central Myanmar in living memory. But the phenomenon wasn't altogether new. It had occurred sporadically over the three decades before, at times seeming to correlate with periods of unease for the junta. In July 1988, as resentment towards Ne Win's rule simmered, attacks on Muslims occurred in Pyay and Taunggyi, with claims that the junta at the time had orchestrated them to divert attention from protests breaking out across the country. There had been similar claims following anti-Chinese riots in the late 1960s and 1970s that coincided with soaring inflation and growing public disquiet. There seemed to be a logic to the claims: splitting communities perceived to be united in their opposition to the military allowed the focus of anger to be redirected horizontally, rather than towards the oppressive military apparatus that had brought these communities close to economic ruin.

Confidential government material that was leaked in the aftermath of the Meikhtila violence leant support to the idea that this strategic fomentation of violence had continued into the present era. A letter dated 13 September 2013 that was sent from the General Administration Department to township authorities across the country explained how Muslims from a particular mosque in Yangon had "discussed to strive for the creation of a countrywide communal violence" between Buddhists and Muslims in September and October that year.[10] According to the letter, Muslims would provoke Buddhists into violence and then burn their own homes, before circulating videos of the violence worldwide. Townships authorities should therefore be on high alert and make "necessary preparations ... in advance." The violence never materialised, and the imams of the mosque in Yangon that was mentioned in the letter claimed to know nothing of these plans. Yet it showed how the military might seek to manufacture communal tensions and encourage Buddhists to preemptively defend themselves against a threat that wasn't real.

There were other episodes in which the hand of the military was less certain. In 2001, Muslim neighbourhoods in towns across Myanmar, from Rakhine State to Bago Division to Ayeyarwady Division, were struck by mobs. The Taliban in March that year dynamited the Buddhas of Bamiyan, the huge stone figures carved into a cliff face in central Afghanistan 1,500 years ago, and it sent ripples across the Asian continent and into Myanmar. Groups of armed men led by monks that attacked Muslim properties in the town of Taungoo in May 2001 claimed to have done so in response to the destruction of those sacred figures 3,000 kilometres to the west.[11] From one angle it seemed that the fear of Islam that arose so sharply after the September 2001 attacks in New York knew no borders, and provided a basis for acute suspicions towards Muslims to develop in countries unaffected by the events. But again, eyewitnesses in Taungoo and elsewhere reported that police and army had stood by and watched, drawing suspicions of a higher hand in the violence.[12] That year had seen inflation soar and food shortages increase. According to a US State Department Report on religious freedom, it also saw a "sharp increase in the level of anti-Muslim violence" in Myanmar, "some of which the Government may have tacitly supported, contributed to, or even instigated."[13] Perhaps the violence was a way to distract from the growing public disquiet of that year.

And there was Kyaukse, U Wirathu's hometown. In October 2003, at the end of Buddhist Lent, a stone was thrown into a monastery compound where young monks were reciting sutras. Next door to the compound was a mosque, and the finger pointing that followed quickly became violent. Buddhist monks led a mob that attacked the mosque and nearby Muslim homes. Reports of the violence then spread to Mandalay and caught the ear of a number of politically active monks there. They travelled down to Kyaukse and goaded similar attacks on Muslims, some fatal. The junta arrested and de-robed 44 of them, U Wirathu among them. He was to spend the next eight years behind bars.

The suspicion among residents of Meikhtila that the violence had been planned in advance was heightened by the arrival of mobs composed of people unfamiliar to locals there. "When I saw them they seemed totally drunk – they had lost their senses," Sandar said of the men that stalked the streets of the town. Despite their condition, they had still managed to destroy more than 800 houses in less than 72 hours, and without inviting intervention from security forces. Vijay Nambiar, UN Special Envoy to Myanmar at the time of the Meikhtila violence, had spoken of a "brutal efficiency" to the killings[14] – that these weren't the work of blind rage alone, but something more organised. And it wasn't until the third day of the violence that a state of emergency was announced and police began to take action. Over the two days before then, Sandar had seen only a handful of police on the streets of Meikhtila as the mobs ran amok and the butchery began, and they had done nothing. Groups of men were free to roam the town with sticks and machetes, while the agents of the state tasked with ensuring security stood and watched. In past episodes of unrest – the nationwide anti-junta protests of 1988 and 2007 in particular

– police hadn't been so nonchalant. They fired into crowds, and protestors dropped like flies. But, of course, this wave of unrest hadn't been directed at the junta.

It hadn't only been the residents of Meikhtila that became the target of mob intimidation. Five months after the attacks there, the UN Special Rapporteur for Myanmar, Tomas Quintana, visited the town. It was late in the evening of 19 August, and the Argentine lawyer was travelling with a representative of the Ministry of Foreign Affairs. He had scheduled visits the following day to Muslim displacement camps on the edge of Meikhtila. That evening he approached the town from the east, in a convoy of vehicles. His vehicle wasn't marked with the UN logo, but the others were, and authorities there had been warned in advance of his arrival. But as the convoy entered Meikhtila, he grew apprehensive.

> Something strange started to happen. The representative
> said there was a problem and we would have to change our
> schedule. They started to give me unclear information about
> what the problem was, but it was obvious that at some point
> they were receiving information that something was wrong.

The representative told him that there had been a demonstration, and the convoy would need to take another route. The details were vague, only adding to his sense of foreboding. "I started to feel somehow nervous because I knew from the reports I'd read what had happened in Meikhtila. I knew how violent it had been."

After the violence in Rakhine State the year before, he had become the target of protests by Rakhine nationalists calling for the UN to cease providing aid to the Rohingya, and his photograph was printed on placards held aloft at demonstrations in Yangon and elsewhere. By the time he made the visit to Meikhtila in August 2013, his face was well known.

"We were reaching the entrance to Meikhtila and suddenly the convoy stopped and I started to see people around the convoy, very agitated." There were 200 of them, he estimated, and they were heading to the van marked with the UN logo.

> My guess, and something that was confirmed later, was that they thought I was in that van. They started to look inside it – to open and punch doors. Once they realised I wasn't in there they started to look in other vans. Fortunately when they came to my van and started to punch the doors the convoy began to move slowly.

He remembers seeing one policeman nearby who stood and watched as the mob went from van to van. The government later released a statement claiming that the men who surrounded his vehicle had wanted to hand him a letter, but he wasn't convinced.

> When we reached the township office we went into a room, and we started to hear the mob reaching the building. Again I couldn't see any police so we were really in a very tense situation, with authorities not clear as to what was going on.

That morning Quintana had been in Lashio, in northern Shan State, where attacks on Muslims had taken place in May that year, two months on from Meikhtila. Houses, shops and a Muslim orphanage were torched by mobs that had arrived out of nowhere, again unfamiliar to residents of the town. Among the targets they attacked were local journalists who were attempting to report on the violence.

Quintana was granted access to the prison where the Buddhist participants arrested in the aftermath were being held.

"Those Buddhists in jail I spoke with were hired; they were not from Lashio," he explained. "They were just workers going from one township to another. People approached them from outside the township, saying 'Come with me, we will do this and this'. But they wouldn't say who these people were. They were silent and of course they were frightened."

There had been similar ambiguity about the forces organising the violence in Rakhine State in 2012. When I had asked Ko Myat for more information on the men aboard his bus who had divided the two teams up once they reached Nasi quarter and who had ordered him to attack any fleeing Muslims, he was equally sparing with the detail. He referred to them only as "the organisers," and said little else. Perhaps he didn't know their identity, or perhaps he feared retribution were Rakhine participants to implicate others. This seemed to be the case in Lashio too.

Quintana was forced to cancel the meetings he had arranged for the following day with victims of the Meikhtila attacks. That night, after the mob that followed him to the township office had dispersed, he drove on to Mandalay. "The outcome was that I couldn't get firsthand information on what happened in Meikhtila and then report it to the UN, and that for me was very important because the reports and the allegations were very serious," he said. "I needed to hear from the Muslims and from the authorities what happened, but I couldn't do anything like that. If the purpose was to avoid a UN investigator reaching the victims, then it was accomplished."

He never was able to determine how the mob knew of his arrival, and why the policeman had watched from afar as the men encircled his vehicle. But there evidently had been an organised effort to block information about the violence from reaching the UN, and the nearby policeman who did nothing to intervene was culpable in that. Why exactly it wasn't clear, but theories began to circulate that perhaps civilian-on-civilian violence could prove beneficial for the military, which controls the police via the Home Affairs Ministry. One supposition that gained traction among those watching the events of 2012 and 2013 went that factions of the regime that were nervous about the potential for the transition to eat away at their influence might either manufacture, or allow to take hold, violence that appeared communal in nature. Greater political bargaining rights could be dangerous in a society with such deep fissures, so it went, for the populace was apparently already prone to conflict and this would only drive violent competition for the spoils of a democratic state. The scenes that emerged from Meikhtila and elsewhere would show that Myanmar was not ready for the military to step back. As a result, it could remain in a position that allowed it to protect its substantial political and economic interests.

The violence also placed Suu Kyi and the National League for Democracy in a significant bind. The party had taken seats in the by-elections the previous year, and all knew that unless significantly challenged, her next election run would be a landslide and the military's centrality could further weaken. But were Suu Kyi to condemn violence committed by Buddhists in a conflict increasingly demarcated along religious lines, then amid the heightened tensions of 2013, she might be seen as siding with Muslims and their suspected project to Islamise the nation. Wanting to secure a substantial political stake in the transition, she would be forced to choose sides: either take the moral high-ground, from where she would defend Muslim victims but lose Buddhist supporters, or maintain an ambivalence that, while not angering her chief constituency, would see her international reputation as a human rights defender weakened.

The degree of organisation of the Meikhtila violence never became clear, and the lines of communication down which the directions to mobs were passed remained obscured. To what degree the state was complicit purely on account of its agents having either participated, or not intervened, was similarly uncertain. Perhaps those police harboured deep prejudices of their own towards Muslims, and had in fact acted independently from their superiors; perhaps they saw the arrival of outsider mobs as evidence that authorities higher than them were executing a plan that they were not to interfere in. Or indeed they may have received orders to do nothing.

Police Captain Htay Lwin was on the ground in Meikhtila when the violence erupted. He had seen the mobs wrecking Muslim properties, and from him I tried to get an idea of why police had been so inert. He, like all figures of authority in Myanmar concerned with the violence, was reluctant to speak.

"There were orders from above to intervene, and it is our duty to do so," the captain said. "We tried to intervene. But, for instance, there was only one policeman for 10 or 20 people." He seemed to suggest that there had been insufficient numbers of personnel for the enormity of the event. Some of the videos showed police trying to negotiate with the hundreds-strong mobs that swarmed around them, but others had shown officers just standing by as Muslim property was destroyed. It seemed odd, even suspicious, that there was such a weak security presence. "I don't think that kind of conclusion can be drawn," was all the police captain would say. "We tried to stop it as much as we could."

Whatever the truth behind the behaviour of the police, the state had clearly failed in its responsibility to protect victims of attacks, both in Meikhtila and in Rakhine State, and on that reading it was culpable in what unfolded over 2012 and 2013. But although there seemed to be a logic, a method in the madness that struck Meikhtila, there was never a smoking gun linking the violence to figures in the government or the military that it was aligned to at the time. There had been people unfamiliar to locals participating in the attacks, but so too had residents of the town been mobilised by the slaying of the monk by Muslims, and who then proceeded to participate as fiercely as anyone else.

What did become clear, however, was that the government under President Thein Sein had allowed much of the groundwork for the violence to be laid. His administration had done nothing to counter the hate speech that circulated around Rakhine State in the lead up to attacks there, and had given its blessing to the 969 monks. The President's office released a statement in June 2013, three months after Meikhtila, that lauded 969 as "a symbol of peace," and its spiritual figurehead, U Wirathu, as a "son of Buddha." Despite the invective the monk continually levelled at Muslims, and which often appeared to presage violence towards them, the abbot was able to tour the country unhindered by higher authorities, and the material he and other ultra-nationalist groups circulated was never condemned. A decade before he had been placed in prison for goading attacks on Muslims; now he was free to roam.

In the months after the Rakhine State violence, which came a year after his release, U Wirathu had adorned the entrance to his monastery in Mandalay with images of Buddhists allegedly killed by Muslims. By March 2013 he had grown in prominence, and I went with two other journalists to visit him. He asked for the interview to take place in front of a wall covered floor to ceiling in self-portraits. Intermittently during the conversation his stony face would suddenly break into a huge smile, eyes ablaze, that disappeared as quickly as it came on.

As we sat in a room of the Masoyein Monastery he ran through what would become a common refrain for him and other monks of the 969 movement: that every single rape recorded in the country was carried out by Muslims, and that Muslim husbands would torture their wives until they converted. There was evidence that Islam had "broken" Christianity and Buddhism in Malaysia, Indonesia and elsewhere. Myanmar would soon meet the same end, for entire villages were becoming Muslim and their men were trying to marry and reproduce at a high rate.

U Wirathu had ended his sermon in Meikhtila in December 2012 with a declaration to his followers: "That is why by looking long term, use only places with the sign 969." That would ensure that no Buddhists shopped at Muslim stores, and no Buddhist money would go towards strengthening their rivals. The 969 leaders wanted that distinction made clear. And just as the Star of David was painted on the doors of Jewish properties by the Nazis to brand their inhabitants, so too were the numbers 786 scrawled on Muslim houses in Meikhtila as the mobs pushed through the town, evidently marking them out for attack.[15]

After Meikhtila there was more violence, and it moved in mysterious ways. There is a highway that runs north from Yangon towards Pyay, and if you were to plot on a map the sites of unrest that occurred along that route in the eight days during and after Meikhtila then a neat line would form, starting in the small town of Thegon and ending in Tharawaddy. Somehow it travelled along that road, striking 11 towns, each roughly five kilometres from one another, in little over a week.

There seemed to be a contagious element to the violence. How it was being transmitted from one location to the next wasn't clear, but a pattern seemed to be playing out whereby an increase in material designed to stoke fear among Buddhists was soon followed by attacks on Muslims. There would usually be a trigger, something isolated and, on occasions, seemingly insignificant – the young Muslim girl who bumped into a monk while riding her bike in a marketplace in Okkan at the end of April that year, knocking his alms bowl to the ground and launching a day of attacks that left close to 70 Muslim homes damaged, and one person dead. Again the mobs seemed to form quickly, but no one knew where they came from.

A second effect of the violence of Meikhtila and afterwards was to put the question of Muslim belonging back into the public consciousness – not only Rohingya, but Muslims from the majority Bamar ethnicity whose citizenship hadn't before been questioned. After the brawl in the gold shop, the *Myanmar Post* newspaper explained that the owners were a "Husband and wife from non-indigenous people group who beat a person who came to sell gold."[16] In the years after the violence I spoke with numbers of Muslims, and even Buddhists with Muslim relatives, who said that obtaining an ID card had become increasingly difficult. Officials at the immigration offices where they went to renew their IDs were refusing to register them as Bamar Muslims, as they had done before. Even the offer of a bribe no longer worked, and new nationalities were being forcibly added to the cards: Indian, Bangladeshi or Pakistan, for surely no Muslim could be purely Bamar. The violence had further Othered the Muslims of Myanmar in a legal sense too, for it was authorities who were questioning with greater intensity the claims to belonging of people who before had been recognised as indigenous.

The men in robes moved from town to town in late 2012 and 2013: in December 2012 it had been U Wirathu in Meikhtila; in late February the following year it was U Wimala who spoke to crowds of Buddhists in Minhla, one of the 11 towns along that volatile stretch of road north of Yangon. Several weeks later, mosques and Muslim houses were burned. The same happened in Thandwe in September 2013 – U Wirathu addressed crowds of Rakhine in villages close to the homes of Kaman Muslims, the same ones that became targets of attacks the following month. U Wirathu would say that he visited these places to ease tensions, but it was hard to believe. The sermon he gave in Meikhtila explicitly called on Buddhists to disassociate themselves entirely from Muslims, thereby solidifying the religious divide and making it clear that they were two very different groups of people, one to be trusted, the other not.

As I was leaving U Wirathu's monastery in Mandalay in April 2013, he handed over a bundle of DVDs and books. On the cover of one book was a painting of a young girl, her face contorted with fear as a huge wolf-like animal bared its teeth. It wasn't difficult to figure out who was being represented.

Accompanying us that day at the monastery was an English teacher from a local school who acted as translator, and a man in his late twenties who had arranged the meeting with U Wirathu. He was a former monk, and although he had known U Wirathu for some time, he was wary of the abbot's position on Muslims. The language was too extreme, he thought, and he worried about the effect it would have on relations between the two communities.

Our conversation with U Wirathu lasted around two hours. Once it had wrapped up we emerged back into the compound and walked past the images of slain Buddhists. The heat in Mandalay in April is particularly fierce, and we made a beeline for the road outside where we could flag down a taxi and escape to cooler sanctuary. But as we went, the translator exclaimed that she had been impressed with the wealth of information the monk had. I was surprised. My thoughts had been moving in the opposite direction. Many of the statements U Wirathu made appeared so obviously baseless that it felt almost pointless to question them. Did she believe the claim that Muslims were responsible for all rapes in the country? She wasn't sure, but had come to understand the significance of the threat facing Buddhism in Myanmar.

We reached the road and parted ways. I returned to Yangon several days later. Soon afterwards a message came through on my phone. "I watched Wirathu CD. I feel very angry – they take our air, water, land; they make terrorism!"

It had come from the young man who had organised our meeting. Only days before he had thought the monk to be a dangerously provocative figure. All it had taken was a DVD to flip him and to bring to his attention the supposed enemies in his midst. It gave an inkling of the power of the propaganda being circulated, which linked together in a simple chain of causation the fate of Buddhism to the fate of the nation, and thus the fate of the individual. Unless checked, it warned, events happening elsewhere in the country would soon come to bear on the security of people hundreds of miles away. Was it that linkage that allowed the fear to jump from Rakhine State into towns in the country's centre, to transform neighbours into enemies and to turn supposed democrats into militant nationalists, espousing beliefs that otherwise seemed at odds with their political direction? Or was it that each eruption offered a fresh reminder that old problems hadn't been addressed? Perhaps the violence and the information that followed it brought to the attention of Buddhists the irresolvable differences between them and Muslims, prompting a recall of past conflagrations whose revised meanings were brought into the present.

The young man had said nothing to indicate support for the attacks, but his epiphanic message illuminated how those mental processes might begin to work. If violence was an act of defence against those who threaten the air, the water and the land then the cost of not engaging in violence could be enormous. U Wirathu would always emphasise that he never encouraged attacks, and nowhere in his sermons does he implore followers to take up the sword. But he did lay down tinder that could easily catch flame.

By no means were all affected by the fear-mongering, and as the violence began to spread further, small grassroots movements formed to push back against the misinformation.

Buddhists in Meikhtila who watched their community descend into bloodletting also spoke of their disgust at the attacks. One family whose home I visited in the weeks after the violence, when the sense of apprehension was still heavy in the town, had kept a metal pole with a blade attached inside their doorway in case Muslims visited. Yet they expressed no prejudice. They just knew that amid a frenzy of killing like this, anyone within the rival group was a potential target.

★ ★ ★

In the days after the Meikhtila violence, displacement camps outside of town began to swell. One school had doubled up as a place of refuge for Muslims, and there in early April 2013 I had met the mother of a young man who was killed in the single worst massacre to befall the town, or indeed any other in central Myanmar that year. He had been 26 at the time, and taught in the Himayathol Islamic boarding school for boys in Mingalar Zayone quarter. On the morning of 20 March 2013 the madrasa was filled with 120 students. The youngest was 11 years old. They had learnt of the attack on the gold shop and the large mobs of armed Buddhists that were roaming the streets, and locked the doors of the building.

At the western edge of Mingalar Zayone, the ground rises and a bank forms, along which runs a road. On the other side lies the northernmost point of the lake. By the evening of 20 March, the mobs began to appear on that road. They moved down into the quarter and the students could hear them working their way from house to house searching for Muslims. The students then fled and hid in small groups in the thickets of tall grass nearby. There they spent the night, standing in water up to their knees.[17]

Shortly before sunrise more groups began to gather on the bank. Elevated above the quarter, the road offers a vantage point to survey the ground below. Using the light from car headlamps, the people gathered there served as guides for the armed men down in the quarter, calling out the places where they could spot Muslims hiding. As the shouts rang out, those who had been in the grass all night ran back in the direction of the madrasa. They hid in a building inside a compound near to the school and stayed there until dawn broke. Groups of men then surrounded the compound and began to throw bricks and flaming wooden sticks. The group remained inside. Soon after eight o'clock on the morning of 21 March 2013, police arrived at the quarter and encircled the compound. They told those inside to come out.

The woman I'd met in the camp had heard of her son's final moments from other students at the school. She recounted how they were marched out of the compound by the police, hands held behind their heads. The officers had told them to walk towards the nearby Oat Kyune quarter, around 150 metres from the madrasa. "They said they would be safe," the mother had said. "Some of the students tried to run but were caught by the mob."

They were beaten and hacked, with motorcycle chains, clubs and machetes. It was during this march out of the quarter that the man had been pulled from the tall grass into a clearing, where the monk had struck him repeatedly with a long pole. The attack was filmed by an onlooker, and shortly after the monk delivers his final blow, the camera pans to the right and the line of Muslims being led by police comes into view.[18] Testimony later given to investigators detailed how people at the end of the line were being picked off and beaten to death, and how monks had goaded attacks and had forced the Muslims to kneel on the ground and worship them.[19] The video footage shows that police were armed with rifles, yet they had done nothing to intervene.

As he was marched through the quarter, the woman's son confronted one group of attackers. They struck back. "The students told me that they saw him fall to the ground and then they cut him with a sword."

U Win Htein had been on the elevated road that morning. At the time he was the National League for Democracy's member of parliament for Meikhtila, having taken the seat in the by-elections the year before. He had grown up in the town and knew its people well. On the morning of 21 March he walked the 20 minutes from the NLD office to Mingalar Zayone as news had spread that mobs were descending on the quarter.

"That day was the worst. A house where the Muslim youths were hiding was surrounded by the Burmese crowd, and also monks," he said. This was the compound where those from the madrasa had ended up.

Between the Muslim youth and the Burmese mob there were police standing. It was about 8am. I asked the district official and district police commissioner whether they had a loudspeaker. They said yes. So why don't you shout to the people, I asked? But they didn't do that. And some people passed through the police line and dragged some of the young Muslims out and beat and killed them in front of me. I tried to stop them, but the boss of the group said, "You don't interfere!" The police came to me and told me to move back, otherwise I would be harmed.

He then went to see the chief minister for Mandalay Division, who had just arrived in town. They were together for half an hour, and their conversation quickly became heated. He was told by the chief minister that orders had been issued to "limit the damage to people." But, said U Win Htein, in the time in which the conversation took place, "more than 20 or 30 people were killed in the same area."

U Win Htein had also grown suspicious of the reasons for police inaction. The officers deployed to Mingalar Zayone that morning appeared to have allowed armed men to pass between them and pick out Muslims hiding in the house, before taking them outside and beating them to death. There may have been a number of motives, he thought.

> One is that the police were ordered not to do anything. The second is that they were not given any specific instructions. I don't know which. Why might the first possibility have happened? Because the government wanted the problem to get bigger and bigger. The MPs, especially me, represent the people from Meikhtila, and they want those people to think that I didn't do enough to solve the problem. They want to blame me.

Later on the day of 21 March 2013, Sandar also arrived at Mingalar Zayone. By the time she got there, the police had gone. She also stood on the road, among crowds that were still directing the killers below. "I could see Muslim people hiding in their homes. Some were throwing stones at Buddhists, but the Buddhists had knives and they kept burning everything they saw." She could see the remains of the madrasa and the skeletal structures that had been houses. And from up on the bank she saw a pile of bodies. "It was around my height. The biggest pile in the city," she said. As she looked down she saw one person dragging the body of a man across the earth and throwing it onto the mound of other slain Muslims. Amid this stacked pile, rising up to the height of a human, would have been the students and teachers of the madrasa. And perhaps somewhere in there was the son of the woman I'd met. She knew that he had been "cremated," but wasn't sure exactly how.

After waiting for some time, Sandar went away. She returned to the spot two hours later. The sun had already gone down, leaving only a dull glow over the neighbourhood, and flames leapt from the pile.

"At night they burned it, while I was there."

8

"We came down from the sky": the Buddhist preachers of hate

Three years on from U Win Htein's remonstration with the chief minister in Meikhtila, I went to visit him in his small, spartan one-room apartment in the capital, Naypyidaw. It was late March 2016, and much had changed since the day the mobs levelled Mingalar Zayone. The National League for Democracy had won a resounding victory in nationwide elections in November the previous year and was preparing to take over government. U Win Htein, still a close aide of Suu Kyi, had been appointed spokesperson for the party.

The nature of the movements agitating against the country's Muslim population had also evolved. In the aftermath of the Meikhtila bloodshed, the 969 movement had faded. In August 2013, the State Sangha Maha Nayaka Committee, the government-appointed body charged with regulating the monkhood, issued a directive stating that it was illegal for monastic networks to organise around the principles of 969, and told its leaders that they were forbidden to use the 969 emblem as a symbol for Buddhism. The stickers began to disappear from the shop fronts and taxi windows they once adorned, and its followers melted back into anonymity. No longer were they so evident among the everyday public.

But in the meantime, another equally divisive monk-led movement arose. It displayed a high capacity for organisation, with millions of supporters and an ability to wield influence at the highest rungs of government. Its leaders, some of whom came from the ranks of 969 – U Wirathu, U Wimala, Ashin Kawi Daza, the abbot in Kayin State that circulated the boycott order in October 2012, and others – preached a similarly exclusionary brand of nationalism that fixed on Islam as the overarching threat to the health of the nation. But like 969, these leaders also appeared immune to criticism from politicians – even Aung San Suu Kyi and the NLD had refused to condemn the sermons of the men in robes that so often appeared to precipitate attacks on Muslims.

The party seemed to have cowered in the face of this new movement that formed in June 2013, as 969 began to wind down. Its official name, the Organisation for Protection of Race, Religion, and Sāsana echoed the mantra of the nationalists of the 1930s. Those were the three pivots around which the discourse on belonging revolved. In time it had come to be known by its acronym, Ma Ba Tha, and its leaders spoke of it as a deity.

"We are a two-year-old boy," U Wirathu once said,[1] "but we came down from the sky, not like a normal person. We are brilliant people."

In comprising both monks and laypeople it was able to circumvent the restrictions that had been the downfall of 969. With its own Education and Propagation Department, led by U Wirathu, a Legal Affairs wing, an accounting department and a clutch of savvy media officers, it had become a well-resourced organisation with a nationwide presence. It included more considered monks alongside the firebrand figures in the leadership. Even more so than its former incarnation, however, this group had displayed an alarming ability to intimidate the political leadership in Myanmar.

I told U Win Htein that the international media were portraying the NLD as cowardly, given the party's reluctance to challenge the messages being circulated by Ma Ba Tha. The order given to 969 evidently hadn't been all-encompassing, for the same monks continued to sermonise on the perils of Islam, free from any condemnation by the NLD. The charge irked him. "You understand our reasoning!" he fired back.

> The monks are quite respectable – they keep their eight precepts: celibacy, no eating after 12 o'clock; that thou shall not steal, thou shall not kill, thou shall not commit adultery. We regard them with a high standard. If we argue politically we feel we commit a misdeed, to them and to us. It is not cowardliness, it's abstaining from unnecessary argument. It is self-preservation.

The National League for Democracy was endowed with a reverence that often seemed as much a curse as a blessing. After its founding in 1988, there had never been any question of who would take over government if and when the military fell, and in that sense the party had almost become a byword for democracy. Having seen its victory in the 1990 elections annulled and Suu Kyi placed under house arrest, it hadn't needed to play the difficult political game – to bargain and compromise with competing powers, yet avoid alienating its support base. In the eyes of its legions of followers it became something approaching an ideal, a representation of everything the military was not. Its party base was vast, and cut across ethnic, religious and class lines. But that carried a particular burden, and upon entering parliament in 2012 and taking up ministerial roles that put it in direct confrontation with its diverse constituency, it became evident that the party could not please everyone. In 2013 Suu Kyi was made head of a commission to investigate a crackdown on demonstrators at a copper mine in Myanmar's north, when security forces fired incendiary devices into a protest camp. The white phosphorous that sprayed out from the devices left more than 100 people, including monks, with extensive chemical burns. The commission criticised the use of force and the underlying bases for the protests – the duping of villagers into vacating their land, the lack of revenue returned to the displaced communities. But the protestors' demands that it be closed would not be met, Suu Kyi said. Doing so would upset the delicate relationship with China, the commission argued, and hurt Myanmar's domestic economy.

Suu Kyi, for so long a seemingly inviolable figure, drew sharp criticism from communities around the mine. "Sometimes politicians have to do things that people dislike," she told them. But placing her at the head of the commission seemed an astute move by the administration of President Thein Sein. Although it was the security forces, controlled by the military, that inflicted the damage, it was she who became the scapegoat.

The idea that Suu Kyi might hold an ulterior value for the military seemed to be substantiated by the NLD's position towards 969 and Ma Ba Tha whom, it would gradually become clearer, shared an ideological affinity with the military. Were she to condemn movements that pitched themselves as defenders of the country's Buddhists, then she would be depicted as pro-Muslim and lose support; continued silence, and her international reputation as a stalwart of democracy would suffer. Both scenarios could work against the standing of the NLD.

I asked U Win Htein whether there wasn't a need for deeper engagement with the messages being put forth by Ma Ba Tha. Among the key objectives set out in the organisation's founding charter was the prevention of violence related to race and religion, yet it had undertaken a number of campaigns that appeared to be aimed at furthering the religious divide and planting the seeds of conflict. Monks like U Wirathu and U Wimala continued to tour the country and disseminate anti-Muslim propaganda through Facebook and other social media websites, meaning the potential for violence remained present. And not only had it grown to become perhaps the country's most expansive social movement, with offices in the majority of townships, but it had set a precedent for other groups to emerge, some with an even more exclusionary stance towards Muslims. It was a reality he seemed reluctant to address.

"We have thousands of problems, and Muslim problems are one of a thousand. We will deal with each and every problem according to the priority we choose."

That evasiveness reflected the NLD's broader approach to an issue that had rapidly become a serious threat to its standing. Shifting the blame elsewhere seemed to be the party's preferred strategy.

"You media! You enlarge the problem, and say that we don't have any problem other than that," he finished.

★ ★ ★

When the NLD took power it inherited a country of far-reaching institutional and infrastructural ruin. On nearly every index of development, Myanmar lagged behind all other countries in the region. Only Afghanistan seemed a realistic challenger to its crown for Asia's most moribund state, so corroded and corrupted had it been by decades of authoritarian rule and economic mismanagement. In the years prior to 2011 and the coming to government of the Union Solidarity and Development Party, combined spending on healthcare and education was less than 3 per cent of the total budget. As the USDP settled into office in 2011, the army launched repeated offensives against ethnic rebels in the north and east of the country, greatly widening the longstanding conflicts at a time when the military was supposed to be in retreat. Responsibility for ending these was placed in the portfolio of the NLD when it came to power in 2016, as were the more quotidian problems – persistent power shortages, an acute lack of resources for vital sectors – that resulted from decades of neglect. The economy remained dominated by military-aligned consortiums and tycoons that had made their wealth through close ties to the old guard, ones they were reluctant to relinquish.

It would be up to the NLD to correct all this, and it understood both the burden it had taken on and the weight of expectation it carried. The party's historically antagonistic relationship with the military provided an additional problem, for several key ministries were still under its control: Home Affairs, Defence and Border Affairs – those tasked with managing the country's security and administration, but which instead seemed to perpetuate instability. These myriad problems would need to be fixed if the government of the NLD was to really make a break with military rule.

Yet the rise of groups like Ma Ba Tha and the unabated mass antipathy towards Rohingya did seem like priority issues, and not only for the threat it posed to the security of Muslims. Groups like Ma Ba Tha were manipulating the religious divide to weaken Suu Kyi's party. As the NLD campaigned for the November 2015 vote, senior figures in Ma Ba Tha began to implore followers to support the military-aligned USDP. Despite its past wrongdoings, their argument went, that was the party that would best safeguard Buddhism. "Do not look at the party. We only need to care about who will take care of our religion, who will care about the development of our community," U Bhaddamta Vimala, a monk and prominent Ma Ba Tha member, told more than 1,000 monks at a Ma Ba Tha conference in June 2015, five months before the elections.[2]

The NLD on the other hand had opposed a package of four laws submitted to parliament in December 2014 that were written and heavily promoted by Ma Ba Tha, and that smacked of discrimination, both along faith and gender lines. The "Protection of Race and Religion Laws," as they came to be known, criminalised polygamy and required those who wished to convert to another religion to seek official permission beforehand. Local governments were also given the power to limit reproductive rates of women if they considered their particular region to be suffering as a result of overpopulation. Given the popular narrative of Rohingya as rapacious breeders bent on overwhelming the Rakhine Buddhist population, it appeared this law might have a particular community in mind. Finally, marriages between Buddhists and non-Buddhists were to be subjected to public opinion, with the couple required to publicise their union and await whatever objections might come forth. It seemed a clear attempt to curb interfaith marriages, for there remained a perception that Buddhist women must convert to Islam if they wanted to marry a Muslim man, thereby diluting the religious line further.

Once again, history appeared to be repeating itself. An article in the now defunct *Seq-Than Journal* from 1938, several months on from the early wave of anti-Indian violence, had warned any Buddhist woman marrying an Indian that "You Burmese women who fail to safeguard your own race ... are responsible for the ruination of the race."[3] It seemed that strain of patriarchy hadn't diminished over time. The marriage law promoted by Ma Ba Tha hinged on the belief that in order for women's freedoms to be protected, women should be denied the freedom of choice over whom they marry. "Our Buddhist women are not intelligent enough to protect themselves," the head of one Buddhist group, the Theravada Dharma Network, had said in June 2013, soon after the laws were first mooted by Ma Ba Tha.[4]

There was pushback, but it came at a cost. Grassroots networks coordinated to petition the government, but very quickly, those who opposed the laws came to understand that the movement they were squaring up against was an altogether new beast. May Sabe Phyu had been among a number of activists that put her name to a joint public statement and letter sent to parliament that called for the laws to be dropped. The women's rights campaigner, known widely across Myanmar for her efforts to end gender-based violence, decried the laws during public addresses, and told inquiring media that they were discriminatory and regressive. A day after the statement was released, Ma Ba Tha published an article in its journal describing the signatories to the letter as national traitors. Posters began to appear in monasteries bearing May Sabe Phyu and others' faces and personal details, and branding them once again as traitorous. Then her phone began to ring.

"If you're against the race and religion law you will be killed," a voice on the other end would say. Photos of the naked bodies of women who had been assaulted and killed were messaged through. "They told me that if I continued to oppose the laws I would be killed like this."

Her phone number started appearing on adult websites identifying her as a call girl. Men began to ring through asking for her services, sometimes more than 100 times in a night. Explicit photos and videos were messaged to her mobile. The house phone then began to ring, and her children would pick up. "Why does your mother dare to oppose the laws? Tell her to take care," the voice warned.

In more than a decade of campaigning against military abuses in Myanmar's ethnic regions, May Sabe Phyu hadn't known anything quite like this. The content of the threats was both sinister and debasing, and they came at her again and again. Her children hadn't before been targeted. She and the colleagues who co-signed the letter had decided early on not to speak face to face with Ma Ba Tha. They feared that were they to travel to the organisation's headquarters in northern Yangon, their conversation would be videotaped and then possibly manipulated and circulated to discredit them. But monks did visit her to discuss her objection, and when she spoke with them she was courteous. Still the threats arrived, however, and members of her civil society network began to worry about the public statements she continued to make. Perhaps the warnings would be extended to all associated with her, they feared. Once again, the campaign of intimidation had a chilling effect that stretched far beyond its primary targets.

Despite the no-vote from the NLD, the laws were passed. Ma Ba Tha had been able to dictate policy at the highest level of government. Only four years before, the military leadership had been utterly impervious to popular will, and criminalised any expression of it. But much had changed in Myanmar in a short space of time, and this monk-led movement, feeding off the rise of xenophobic nationalism that had accompanied the transition, was now able to set the political agenda.

Ma Ba Tha's success with the laws reinforced a feeling of symbiosis between the nationalist monks and the military-aligned Union Solidarity and Development Party. The party had voted overwhelmingly in favour of the laws, and in return it received the backing of the monks as it campaigned for the 2015 elections. The fact that electoral laws in Myanmar explicitly ban the use of religion in politics seemed to matter little – complaints from competing parties about this close relationship between Ma Ba Tha and the ruling party were consistently ignored by the Union Election Commission. At other times, Ma Ba Tha clashed head on with the USDP and won, thereby reinforcing a growing sense that a major political force had materialised that threatened the longtime predominance of the central state in Myanmar. In the middle of 2015, the government of President Thein Sein cancelled a planned development of high-rises, one worth $300 million, in downtown Yangon. In the months before, Ma Ba Tha had protested the project on the grounds that the construction of the buildings might damage the revered Shwedagon Pagoda. It won popular support, and threatened to take the protests nationwide. The government was forced to compensate the developers.

For the NLD, its lack of support for the Race and Religion laws intensified a campaign of vilification of the party
in the lead up to the 2015 polls. Doctored photos of Aung
San Suu Kyi wearing a hijab were circulated online and the
NLD was accused of being too strong on universal human
rights and weak on protecting those of a select group, the
country's Buddhists. Ma Ba Tha encouraged voters to ask
six questions of each candidate, including whether they are
Buddhist, whether they support the four laws, and whether
they would try to change the 1982 Citizenship Law that
had excluded the Rohingya.[5] So hounded was the party in
the run-up to the elections that it rejected the candidacy
of more than a dozen of its Muslim members, as did other
parties. It never said why, but all understood it to be a way
to appease Ma Ba Tha and its legion of supporters at a time
when the NLD was rallying support among its vital Buddhist
constituency. Ma Ba Tha and its prior incarnation had made
the subject of religion so toxic that it was reshaping not
just the orientation and make-up of a party that proclaimed
inclusivity, but the entire political landscape in Myanmar.
And the irony that arose from the decision by the NLD
and other parties to block Muslim candidates wasn't lost
on anyone. To ensure a victory in the elections by civilian
forces over the USDP, one that would mark a substantial
step on the road to democratic governance, the country's
two-million-strong Muslim population, recognised as citizens, would have no representatives in parliament.

What became increasingly apparent around this time was
that the pro-democracy movement had begun to turn in on
itself. Prior to the 2012 violence, Suu Kyi and the NLD had
been a force so sacrosanct that criticism of it felt treacherous,
even for foreign journalists writing on the country. Its only

obvious nemesis had been the military, but now the party, as well as the activists who sought to bridge the religious divide after 2012, were coming under sustained attack from figures once allied to it. Exiled media organisations, once a key pillar of the pro-democracy movement, soon came to be targeted too. Their shortwave radio and television broadcasts that were beamed into the country from outside had comprised the only independent, uncensored source of information during military rule, but they came to be slandered as "pro-Bengali" for reporting on atrocities committed by Buddhists in Rakhine State. Very quickly, the importance of the nationalist cause had outflanked that of the democratic cause among a sizeable portion of the Buddhist population. Not only that, but the nationalist movement had become a chief threat to the transition, for its hostility towards calls for inclusivity played so neatly into the hands of regressive forces that had no desire to see the democratic opening come to fruition. The propaganda spun by Ma Ba Tha, in particular the way it framed democracy as antithetical to sovereignty and stability – and, along the way, Buddhism – had dramatically shaken up what once appeared to be a fairly coherent and unified movement for democratic change.

In its denial of Muslim candidates and its capitulation to Ma Ba Tha, the NLD indicated that within the country was a political force more powerful than the one soon to lead the government. I put it to U Win Htein that unless challenged, Ma Ba Tha might take confidence from its success in intimidating the NLD to press the party even more. Was the Muslim issue really being over-exaggerated, I asked, or did it stand to threaten the NLD's popularity among the electorate, not to mention imperil the several million Muslims in Myanmar?

"No," he replied. "It is because the Muslim lobby is much greater and much richer and much more influential. That is why the issue gets spread across the world."

Suu Kyi had come under criticism in late 2013 for making a similarly contentious claim. Asked by a BBC reporter about the underlying reasons for the violence, she replied: "You, I think, will accept that there is a perception that Muslim power, global Muslim power, is very great."[6] It seemed to be a riff on the fear that global events were coming to bear on Myanmar, as if the violence inside the country wasn't localised but instead part of a wider pattern playing out beyond its borders. And it put Suu Kyi's own stance towards Islam in Myanmar under scrutiny. Earlier in the same interview she had said, "There are many moderate Muslims in Burma who have been well integrated into our society." It suggested that she might also perceive them to be outsiders, and thus that Buddhists held the sole claim to indigeneity in the country – a claim that had been a primary basis for the conflict.

At one point in my conversation with U Win Htein he had mentioned self-preservation as a reason for not criticising the monks. It seemed a strange subject to raise in a debate that appeared, from the outside at least, predominantly political, and not one to be reduced to the individual or party level.

"We believe in reincarnation," he explained. "We might suffer by crossing those high-ranking monks. They may not have followed the teaching of Buddha, but that is up to them. We don't cross them because we don't want to lower ourselves for the next life."

That reply had felt inadequate, not because I dismissed the hold that karmic fears can have on the pious, but because it appeared self-centred. He and his colleagues may lose support for speaking out, but wasn't there a greater common good at stake that trumped the fears of a few who, in coming to government, had sworn an oath to act in the common interest? I put that thought to him. "Yes," he replied. "That's in our hearts."

But there it appeared to stay. Suu Kyi and the NLD's decision to refrain from criticising the monks and from calling for greater protections for Muslims may have been a politically astute calculation in the sense that it might shield her government from further attacks, but it was sorely lacking from a moral perspective. Perhaps it was even short-sighted, for wasn't there a chance that as this strain of bigotry became increasingly entrenched, it would grow ever more combustible and eat away at whatever stability a civilian government might bring to the country? Ma Ba Tha had already been able to codify prejudices in the form of the four Race and Religion Laws, and with time it could do more. It seemed at points as if the organisation served as a powerful lobby group. The petition in support of the package of laws eventually gained close to five million signatures, but the organisation was also able to supersede the role of local authorities. In the middle of 2015, as flooding submerged large parts of Myanmar's north, Ma Ba Tha took it upon themselves to expel a local aid group in the town of Kawlin on the grounds that it hadn't coordinated its efforts with Ma Ba Tha. It then took over responsibility for providing assistance to victims, unchallenged by township government officials. It had become both a mass nationwide pressure group, able to steer legislation in parliament, and one that took on local-level duties of the state. When accused of divisiveness it could point to its philanthropic work: the provider of welfare to communities that knew only neglect. When I went to the Ma Ba Tha headquarters in northern Yangon, a stone's throw from where I had listened to the young man in the teashop explaining with such urgency what a Myanmar without Buddhism might look like, I asked how it could generate the kind of finance it seemed to have. Its magazines were disseminated en masse around the country, and it could buy up stocks of food and medicine to distribute to flood victims and other Buddhist poor. But it could also book out vast public spaces for rallies, like the 30,000-seat Thuwanna stadium in Yangon, packed to capacity in October 2015 to celebrate the passing of the Race and Religion Laws. In response, I was told of the public donations that devoted Buddhists poured into temples and monasteries. These were part of the "Charities and Ceremonies" expenditure that Myanmar households invested hugely in, hoping to "make merit" and improve their chances in the next life. Ma Ba Tha had that all-important monastic leadership that held sway over its audience, and it pitched itself as the only body willing and capable of protecting Buddhism. It was a powerful platform.

"We have many donors," a man in the headquarters, who asked only to be identified as a Ma Ba Tha project manager, had explained. "Monks ask people to donate and they do – both rich and poor." He held up his arm, pointing to his wrist. "Even the poor can still donate a watch." Not long before, a gold company had donated a lump of gold worth close to $70,000. "If they do good things they believe they will get advantage," he continued.

The rapid rise of Ma Ba Tha and 969 had caught many in Myanmar off guard. But it was not altogether surprising. Nationalist movements like those that arose during the transition are direct products of democratisation. They seek to exploit the insecurities of a population undergoing rapid change by pointing to the consequences of that change: upheaval, the decline of tradition, the introduction of unfamiliar norms that threaten the cohesion of society; of conflict and breakdown. The sudden explosion in new information channels that occurs as authoritarian rule winds down – and this was particularly key for Myanmar, given the soaring use of social media as Internet penetration expanded after 2011 – can be captured by these movements and used to spread fears of how newly enfranchised constituencies threaten the standing of the traditional order. There was a continuity in Myanmar that had been broken by the British, so it went, and now it would be broken again by Islam, with a bit of help from Suu Kyi and her party. The vision of a harmonious society that the monks of Ma Ba Tha articulated, one of religious or ethnic uniformity, isn't read by its supporters as regressive. Instead it is a return to a supposedly ideal past of familiarity and security, where Buddhism reigned supreme, and gains traction during times of great change precisely because it counters the momentum towards openness, and all the dangers that brings. This reimagining of the past helps sell to the population a deep conservatism because it ties security to exclusivity, and promises a stable, purified order like that of old. The kind of mass ideologies that the monks of 969 and Ma Ba Tha began to spread from 2013 onwards took hold and proliferated because they tapped into those latent anxieties, and at no time were they better able to than in the early stages of democratisation, when the objectives of a nervous political elite eager to retain power aligned with a grassroots nationalist base. These movements shackled the fate of Myanmar to the fate of Buddhism. Anyone not supportive of Buddhism, whether they be Muslims or dissenting Buddhists, didn't support the national project, and therefore threatened Myanmar and those within it. It was for this reason that those who began to organise to counter that message found themselves in the crosshairs of the movement, derided as enemies of Buddhism and subjected to threats to their lives.

★ ★ ★

One of these was Myo, a soft-spoken young Muslim interfaith activist in Mandalay. He had held a workshop there in late July 2015 in which he brought monks and nuns together to discuss what pathways to harmony might exist. A year before, in July 2014, violence between Buddhists and Muslims had struck the city. But perhaps more than any other episode over the two years prior, this one appeared to bear the mark of higher organising powers. Once again it was triggered by reports of the rape of a Buddhist girl by two Muslim teashop owners. The allegations were first published on a Myanmar-language news aggregation website, Thit Htoo Lwin, but with the help of U Wirathu's by then prominent social media presence, the report circulated quickly. On his Facebook page, the abbot named the teashop, and the next day a mob gathered outside. But the allegations had been cooked up, authorities later stated – the girl had been paid by two local men to fabricate the story.

Who the men were and what interests they represented was never made clear. Suu Kyi had been due in the town two weeks after the violence to rally for changes to the constitution that would allow her to become president.

Perhaps this had been an attempt to derail her campaign. Either way, the rumours catalysed four days of attacks that left two people dead – one Buddhist and one Muslim. Sandar, the same journalist that had witnessed the horrors of Meikhtila a year before, had seen the final moments of the Buddhist man. U Tun Tun was killed close to midnight on 2 July, the second day of the violence, when a group of Muslims emerged onto the road from a mosque in downtown Mandalay armed with sticks and knives. They pulled him from his motorbike and beat him to death. U Soe Min, a 51-year-old Muslim, followed the next day, also knocked off his bike and set upon by a group of men, this time Buddhist. The mobs that had attacked Muslim property in the meantime were unfamiliar to residents, as many had been in Meikhtila. After witnessing the death of U Tun Tun, Sandar had gone to the Masoyein Monastery where U Wirathu resided. It was midnight, and there she found a crowd of monks and lay Buddhists gathered outside, holding sticks and knives, preparing to march through the streets. Again she began filming, and one of the monks approached. "Don't film," he told her. "If you film I will kill you." She noticed that he was wearing jeans under his saffron robe.

At the workshop a year later, Myo began a discussion on the Buddhist concept of Right Speech, which commands followers to abstain from lying, divisive and abusive speech, and "idle chatter." This seemed a topical point of conversation, given the continued provocative rhetoric of Ma Ba Tha monks and the rumours of Muslim misdeeds that had caused such strife in the city the year before. He knew one of the nuns was an assistant to U Wirathu. Most attendees at the workshop willingly partook in the discussion, but as it went on the nun became withdrawn. He thought little of it until a series of messages came through on his phone several days later.

"Fucking *kalar*," the first read, using that same derogatory term that had been levelled at Rohingya so persistently. "Why don't you stop your work?" The following day another arrived. "You want to die? Why are you pressuring our monks?" Myo responded to neither, but grew agitated. A third then came through. "Who the hell are you to teach our monks? Motherfucker *kalar*, you're going to die." After a fourth message, he skipped Mandalay and went into hiding. "We will see you tomorrow," it warned.

Whoever was behind the messages believed his workshops to be an attempt to turn monks and nuns against Ma Ba Tha. In hiding in Yangon, he began to receive anonymous phone calls. The voice on the end of the line would curse him repeatedly and mock him for running away. He often thought he was being trailed by plain-clothed officers of the feared Military Intelligence, or MI. Unfamiliar men would follow him in the street, or loiter outside his office. "When Ma Ba Tha find out something wrong that you've done, they tell MI," he said. He never did warn police of the threats. If he made that call, he knew they would tell him that it was too dangerous to continue with his interfaith work, and pressure him to stop. So he continued alone, believing that Ma Ba Tha and Myanmar's security agencies somehow seemed to be acting in unison.

I met with Myo in his office in Mandalay several months after the text messages came through. Sitting next to him as we spoke was a young monk. As Myo outlined the dangers that accompanied any attempt to bring the two communities back together, the monk had waited quietly.

He was also engaged in interfaith work, Myo explained. The monastic order in Myanmar wasn't the monolithic entity it sometimes appeared from afar; there were many monks within it who, as the violence spread, began to articulate Buddhist responses to the posturing of the ultra-nationalist monks, drawing on those same concepts of Right Speech that Myo had tried to illuminate.

As I began to direct questions at the monk he told of how his work had isolated him from old friends, both inside and outside the monkhood. Any call for peace amid such sharp religious divisions was taken as a signal of support for Muslims, he said. The young monk had marched in September 2007, as did tens of thousands of other monks, when soaring fuel costs unleashed a wave of agitation against the regime that came to be known as the Saffron Revolution. But he was sceptical of the goals of many of the monks back then.

"The monks didn't understand much about democracy – they were concerned with petrol prices," he said. "Most people who fight for democracy don't understand it. They think it means that you can change the government and then do whatever you want. The monks didn't like the military, but they didn't have any alternative answer."

There may have been truth in that. Democracy was by and large articulated as an end to military rule and the conflicts it brought, and the election to government of the NLD. What happened beyond that, and how the process of reconciling different versions of democracy would play out, hadn't appeared to figure much. But it seemed like a somewhat harsh statement. Monks had died in the crackdown that followed the uprising and they were integral to the mobilisation of tens of thousands of people of all creeds. The word in Myanmar language for "boycott" is *thabeik hmauk*. It means to turn the alms bowl upside down. At the front of the protests in September 2007 were lines of monks doing exactly that, their lacquer-coated bowls inverted, signifying their refusal to take merit from the generals that had overseen the ruination of the country. They had chanted the *metta sutta*, invoking the desire of the Buddha to see all beings free from suffering. They had used Buddhist symbols for the purposes of effecting change, and for that were gunned down.

But it was true that vocal monks were now preaching an entirely contrary message, one that ate away at the momentum of forces pushing for that democratic quality of inclusivity. Myo hadn't been the only critic of Ma Ba Tha to be hounded. In Mandalay, not long after the text messages came through on Myo's phone, another Muslim interfaith activist began to be stalked by police. One day in the middle of July 2015, Zaw Zaw Latt received a phone call from a policeman telling him to head to a café in downtown Mandalay where he would be met by officers from the Criminal Investigation Department. Once there, the then 31-year-old was questioned about a photo that appeared on Facebook of him holding a rifle. It had been taken in 2013 during a delegation of interfaith activists to Kachin State to meet with Christians displaced by the conflict between the army and Kachin rebels there, but somehow it was picked up two years later and circulated online. Police detained him on charges of "unlawful association" with an illegal group, the Kachin Independence Army, and another charge related to illegal border crossing from a trip to the India–Myanmar border the same year. A colleague of his, Pwint Phyu Latt, had also been on the delegation. She was arrested the following week.

But it quickly became apparent that it hadn't only been police pushing for their arrest. A month beforehand, the same photo had been printed in an article in *Atu Mashi* magazine, one of Ma Ba Tha's two main publications that devote considerable column space to deriding alleged enemies of Buddhism. The article, written by a so-called "Scholar of Masoyein," the monastery to which U Wirathu was abbot, was titled "Photo evidence of threat to Buddhism." The author had scoured Zaw Zaw Latt's Facebook page and published 11 images that supposedly proved his intent to damage Buddhism. Next to one photo of the interfaith activist sitting on a chair at a Buddhist temple, shoes still on, was written: "This is evidently an act of trespass, disgracing Buddhist artefacts to hurt the feelings of Buddhists with an intention to incite religious riots and insurrection against the state." Not long after his arrest, a relative of Zaw Zaw Latt explained to me that at every court appearance, members of Ma Ba Tha had been present. "They put pressure on the mother of Pwint Phyu Latt and told them they could be in prison for seven years," she recounted. After a nine-month trial ending in April 2016, they were both sentenced to four years in prison.

It wasn't the first time Ma Ba Tha had been able to influence a legal case so effectively. In October 2014, Htin Lin Oo, an information officer in the NLD, had given a speech in which he decried the fusion of violent nationalism and Buddhism. A video of the speech circulated on social media, and two months later he was arrested and charged with "outraging religious feelings." He underwent a seven-month trial, and from time to time when he was taken from his cell to face the judge there would be monks outside the courthouse demanding the strongest sentence possible.

That was eventually realised. In June the following year he was given a two-year prison term with hard labour. Ma Ba Tha appeared to have become so influential that it could sway judges. And amid all this, the NLD was nowhere to be heard. So chilling an effect did Ma Ba Tha seem to have on the party that upon his arrest, Htin Lin Oo was ejected from its ranks and left to fend for himself.

★ ★ ★

Ma Ba Tha rose to heights that could only be reached with the backing of elements within the state, but exactly what connection existed wasn't clear. There were politicians and military men who donated large sums to monks within the movement – $7,800 from an army colonel to the organisation's chairman, Ashin Tiloka Bhivunsa, in the middle of 2015;[7] $31,000 from a USDP candidate to U Wirathu in August that year, and who published photos of the handover of the money on Facebook.[8] Local authorities would regularly allow Ma Ba Tha rallies to take place while refusing permits for other activist groups, including those marching for religious harmony. Yet none of this provided clear evidence to determine what interests the ruling party was funnelling through Ma Ba Tha.

In the absence of facts, speculation began to mount that mirrored the kind that followed the Meikhtila violence. One line went that hardline factions within the military-political elite needed a force like Ma Ba Tha to warn of the dangers of a democratic opening led by the NLD. There were figures like the late Aung Thaung, industry minister under the junta and a close associate of former junta leader Than Shwe, who was known to have met U Wirathu shortly after his release from prison in 2012. It was Aung Thaung who was rumoured to have played an organising role in the attack on a convoy carrying Aung San Suu Kyi through the town of Depayin in 2003, when 70 NLD supporters were killed by a mob made up of Swan Arr Shin, or Masters of Force, vigilantes – young, poor men who were paid with money or food for a day's violence. This force was supposedly the brainchild of Aung Thaung. Suu Kyi once likened them to the Brown Shirts, the paramilitary unit tasked by Hitler with protecting Nazi rallies and attacking German opposition parties.[9] Perhaps the mobs that suddenly appeared in Meikhtila, in Mandalay and elsewhere were also Swan Arr Shin, or a newer incarnation, working in the service of those who wanted to thwart, or at least slow, the transition.

So much of politics in Myanmar operates in the dark, leaving observers with only briefly illuminated clues about the interests being fought over. Exactly which forces were driving the violence never became clear, yet a picture did begin to form of how Ma Ba Tha had become so powerful, so quickly. Not only was the organisation tacitly sanctioned by the political leadership under the USDP, and used by it to undermine support for the opposition, but because of the influence it held over a large cross-section of the population, and the risks that came with criticising the clergy, it was then tolerated by the opposition. This created a vacuum in which it could grow and grow, unchallenged by parties either side of the political spectrum. Despite its campaigning prior to the 2015 elections, it didn't succeed in re-electing the USDP to power, and the NLD won a resounding victory. But as the new leadership assumed office in early 2016, the monks brought their full pressure to bear. The party that in 2015 had staunchly opposed the four Race and Religion Laws told a UN convention the following year, soon after coming to office, that it would not seek to repeal them. At some point in its shift from opposition to leadership, it had been pressed into flipping its position. Those four laws were evidently off-limits.

Whereas 969 had lacked coherence, Ma Ba Tha showed adeptness at making its presence known in the villages, in the classrooms, in the media and in parliament. It began Sunday Schools where students would learn the virtues of Buddhism and the importance of protecting race and religion. These soon expanded into fully fledged private high schools aimed at creating devoted Buddhists out of the country's young. It seemed as if Ma Ba Tha was taking over where the Na Ta La schools in Christian-dominated border regions had left off – the cultivation of a dedicated youth that understood the national project of Myanmar. There were echoes of the school curricula under military rule, when textbooks would be prefaced with exhortations to the young to promote "patriotism, union spirit and the spirit of protecting independence."[10] Other ultra-nationalist groups that formed around the same time took the education initiative a step further. The Myanmar National Network toured schools in rural areas of the country, and in front of audiences of young children explained the horrors committed by Muslims elsewhere in the world. At one gathering that was caught on film, a teacher holds up a banner showing images of the bloodshed in Syria and asks, "Who is committing these violent murders?" In unison, the children shout "Islam!"[11]

Time and again people in Myanmar who were critical of the message of Ma Ba Tha explained that the group found most support among the poorly educated. Measures of nationwide literacy fail to illuminate the problem they were getting at, for close to 90 per cent of the country can read. It was how and what children were taught. A group of students in their late teens whom I met in Yangon had all spent time in government schools. They recalled that a typical lesson consisted of the teacher reading page after page from a textbook. Pupils were required to commit this to memory, and then regurgitate it word for word in exams. The asking of questions was frowned upon, even punished, so they would be compelled to pay for afterschool tuition where they could safely probe the material they were being taught. If authoritarian rule relies on a certain measure of submission, then perhaps the regime thought that the stifling early on in life of critical thinking faculties would help pacify the population. So often it was proven wrong. Throughout military rule, Myanmar's rich culture of defiance and its critical analysis of the ways in which power functions were displayed again and again, in public protest, in the mobilisation of underground activist and civil society networks, and in the quiet resistance to the military of farmers and rural villagers. But there were factors outside of this that seemed to work in Ma Ba Tha's favour. The students I met with showed a diversity that wasn't reflected in the school curriculum. Among them was a Chin Christian, a Shan Buddhist, a Bamar Buddhist and a Bamar Muslim, but the latter said that at her government school in Yangon all children were required to attend Buddhist ceremonies. The curriculum didn't allocate much space to develop an understanding of religion, save for mentions of Buddhism's growth in the country during Anawratha's rein, but it did replicate the ethnic hierarchy in Myanmar. Bamar were often presented in textbooks as businesspeople engaged in commerce, while the other distinct minorities were folded into one, depicted loosely as farmers and peasants.[12] Apart from tokenistic references to heroic figures from ethnic minorities who joined the battle for independence, thus assisting what was a Bamar-centric movement, the students said they learnt little about their compatriots, and virtually nothing of other religious communities.

"We just thought they were insignificant, until we began to read the news," one of the girls had said of the minority groups that formed 40 per cent of the country's population, whose insignificance in the curriculum might well be read by students as a marker of their inferiority.

The growth of the Sunday Schools seemed particularly concerning. The infusion of fear-laden propaganda into the minds of a youth already oriented towards an understanding of Buddhist Bamar superiority could provide a powerful foundation for the further spread of a xenophobic nationalism. The monks who preached division had a status level that for many meant their words were taken as gospel. U Win Htein was proof of this, for even a senior politician in the country's ruling party saw criticism of the clergy as a high-risk enterprise, fraught with both material and otherworldly concerns. Whatever message the monks delivered couldn't be easily corrected, publicly at least, and this shield allowed Ma Ba Tha to continue its campaign against the country's Muslims.

★ ★ ★

Still missing from my broader understanding of the conflict was a sense of how monks, the supposed practitioners of non-violence, could rationalise such provocative rhetoric. U Wirathu had said when we met in 2013 that he would never encourage violence against Muslims; rather, that he used his sermons to "strengthen Buddhism." But was there not a connection between his Othering of Muslims, one that would be doubly influential because it was undertaken by someone in a position of such reverence, and the mobs who over the years since Ma Thida Htwe's rape and murder had attacked Muslim communities in the name of defending Buddhism against that Other?

It was a question I put to U Parmoukkha. The monk had grown up in a village in central Myanmar "where only Buddhists live and where we didn't know much about other religions," and had become a prominent figure within Ma Ba Tha's highest circle, the Central Committee. He appeared to have cultivated close connections to authorities, with images circulating online of him meeting with police over cases in which Muslims were accused of doing harm to Buddhists.[13] He took to the podium at Ma Ba Tha rallies and spoke to crowds that gathered before him in their thousands. But he was often critical of Ma Ba Tha's closeness to the USDP, and that seemed to provide a counterweight to characterisations of the movement as solely a vehicle for conservative political forces in the country to exercise their will among the populace.

Like so many others, it had been the killing of the young seamstress in Rakhine State that had spurred a need for a closer inspection of Islamic teachings. "Only then," he said, "did I start to learn the history of Islam and how the Buddhist nations had been converted to Islamic states."

I had gone to meet him one day in high summer at the Magwe Pariyatti Monastery on the northern fringes of

Yangon, where he was abbot. It was a vast site, its buildings set back from a straight road lined with fences and gates that had doubled up as drying racks for dozens of saffron robes. U Parmoukkha had begun to read up on Islam after the chaos of June 2012, and from those books, he said, he had come to understand it as a religion of crusaders.

> Let's take Indonesia as an example. Buddhism arrived in Indonesia in the second century, and from the seventh to the thirteenth century it was a glorious period for Buddhism in Asia. But after that, Islam arrived, and within a few hundred years Buddhism had fallen. The same is happening in Rakhine State, in Buthidaung.

I asked him what he made of the success of Christian missionaries in converting communities in the far north and east of the country two centuries ago. Why hadn't this nationalist rage also fixed on that population? He had concerns about this too, he said, but Christians didn't possess the capability for violence that Muslims had. He spoke of it as something innate – to be a Muslim was to be aggressive.

"They don't have the idea to dominate the whole world and to make it Christian," he had said of those missionaries. "But Muslims have been trained since they are young in the mosque about these kinds of extreme ideas. Most of the Muslims are touched in this way."

From under his bench he pulled out a bundle of posters. On one was a photograph of a young Buddhist woman with bruises and dried blood on her face. U Parmoukkha knew the woman; she had been attacked by two Muslim men in the Botataung area of Yangon one evening not long before. She was too poor to attend court, and he had helped her file a case against the men. I asked why he was showing me the photo. "The woman has suffered violence. There's no affiliation between the attacker and the attacked; the innocent woman has been attacked by a person she doesn't know."

It had sounded like a random assault, but in that climate of heightened suspicion, nothing was random anymore. What actually happened, and how those involved were connected, wasn't clear. And for me, it mattered little. How he interpreted it seemed more important, for it revealed the ways in which, in the swirl of anxieties provoked by Myanmar's transition, new "truths" had come to displace facts, thereby creating a new mode of understanding events like these. U Parmoukkha leant forward, speaking slowly, each word clearly enunciated: "That is radicalism." I paused. But what about cases when Buddhists attack Buddhists on the street?

> In Buddhist teaching it is taught that you cannot harm other people. So the person who harms is not someone who follows Buddhist teaching. There cannot be radical Buddhists. I don't know whether the people who say they are Buddhist and then attack only temporarily follow Buddhism, or whether they do not follow it at all.

He seemed to be suggesting there was an on–off switch available to Buddhists; that for the time taken to commit an act that violated the sanctity of their belief, they could step outside of their faith. It was in stark contrast to narratives of violence committed by Muslims, which were underpinned by a sense that theirs was an inborn evil, a constant – something core to their very being, and thus ineradicable. This partly explained why those pushing the idea of Muslims as a threat were unable to disaggregate individual acts from the group, because those acts were seen as being carried out in the service of the group. The killing of Ma Thida Htwe and the interpretations of it that were distributed en masse in its wake appeared bent on making this linkage explicit.

Always when people unfamiliar with the conflict in Myanmar begin to learn of it, it is the notion of Buddhist-as-perpetrator that confounds the most, for it goes against constructions of Buddhism as the ideal religion, doctrinally committed to peace. Just as Islam is so often associated with violence, Buddhism has been stereotyped as its polar opposite, and so we profess shock at the fiery language of the monks and the actions of their followers. That shock isn't matched when we learn of similar acts being carried out by Muslims, and it spotlights a habit of which we are regularly guilty: that of essentialising the belief systems and cultures of faraway places, and bracketing people into static units of analysis to which we pin select attributes – good or bad. The way we better interpret and understand the exotic is to radically simplify it, but in the process, all nuance and objectivity is lost. This has greatly muddled our understanding of the actions carried out by Buddhists – sometimes in the name of Buddhism, sometimes not – and we temper our surprise with a false rationale: that these people have broken with their teachings and chosen to now chart a different course. But Buddhist history carries the same tales of blood-soaked conquest as do all other religions, from the Zen masters of Japan to the Sangha in Myanmar today. In contemporary Sri Lanka, monks have also goaded attacks on Muslims in recent years using strikingly similar calls for protection of the faith. Like all other religions, when Buddhism deploys violence it does so with a powerful sense of righteousness, of a "just" battle being fought to ensure its longevity.

But were the events of 2012 and after acts of "Buddhist violence," or were they expressions of nationalism, of which

Buddhism was one pillar? It was difficult to say, for in the minds of those trying to rationalise their support for attacks on Muslims, the nation had become so deeply entwined with the faith that one could not be distinguished from the other. Even so, I wanted to ask U Parmoukkha whether violence committed by a Buddhist could ever be justified, or indeed whether the actions of a Buddhist who contravened the Buddha's message of peace and goodwill were not a greater threat to their religion than Islam. It was a question the abbot evidently felt uncomfortable answering. There was nothing in the scriptures that rationalised violence, he said. But after some hesitation, he began to speak.

"When Buddhism is on the verge of extinction, violence could probably be used. If there is no Buddhism, there will be more violence, and the situation will be even worse."

Buddhism wasn't yet on the verge of extinction in Myanmar, he said, but it was under threat. Impermanence is a fundamental part of Buddhist belief: nothing lasts forever, and the Buddha had predicted that his teachings would one day disappear, thus pitching the world into a state of chaos before the next Buddha arose and the cycle began again. This period, which many Buddhists believe will begin 5,000 years on from his passing in 544 BCE – meaning that we are now into the period of decline – is the source of an acute anxiety among traditional followers, and needs forestalling. Just like the young man from Ma Ba Tha whom I'd met in the teashop in northern Yangon, U Parmoukkha painted a doomsday scenario for what might follow its fall.

"In Buddhism, all the robbery, all the killings are seen as bad deeds. So if there is no Buddhism, ideas might come about that these acts are not sinful. There would be no one to teach that they are bad."

If that were the case, and the values contained in the teachings were to perish, then those robberies and killings might no longer seem so bad, and society would spiral into a state of anarchy. Violence thus prevents further violence, he explained, and followers of an ideology can justify actions that deviate from, or go explicitly against, their teachings in order that those teachings are maintained. In Myanmar, the symbiosis between religious identity and national identity meant that a threat to one became a threat to the other, thereby greatly exaggerating the survival imperative and seemingly justifying more radical ways to defend it. It was the same reasoning that drove the bands of monks to attack British forces in the late nineteenth century. Theirs was a quest to reinstate Buddhism to its core place in Myanmar society, because doing so would restore the qualities of harmony that were central to it.

That too seemed to be the message of Ma Ba Tha. But like the mobs that in the years past had delivered violence in the name of protecting the master religion and ethnicity, these monks seemed to be pursuing the same project begun by the military decades before, one of national uniformity masquerading as unity. The risk that, under circumstances particular to such a fragile socio-political context as Myanmar, history might repeat itself, as it seemed to be doing now, had been prophesised long before by the same figure Ma Ba Tha had sought over and again to undermine. "Without a revolution of the spirit," Aung San Suu Kyi had warned in 1990, "the forces which produced the iniquities of the old order would continue to be operative, posing a constant threat to the process of reform and regeneration."[14]

★ ★ ★

Ma Ba Tha went from strength to strength as 2013 became 2014. But in Mandalay, in the middle of its second year of life, an interesting development occurred. The mobs that moved through the city on the evening of 31 June 2014, goaded on by the provocations of U Wirathu and others, garnered little support from locals, unlike in Meikhtila and elsewhere the year before. They went to the Moe Kaung Taik Monastery and gathered outside the gates, urging the monks to come out and join them. U Dama, the abbot, was inside the monastery that day. He told me the building of the sprawling complex was financed by a Muslim man, married to a Buddhist woman, who had moved to Mandalay from Ava soon after King Mindon Min established the seat of the royal throne there in the middle of the nineteenth century. There were Muslims in the king's court and he gave land for mosques to be built on. Mandalay hadn't seen this kind of violence before, and there was little kindling there to be lit; no backstories of communal hatreds that could be dredged up to mobilise locals.

"They shouted that there were Muslims killing monks in the mosque and they called out for help," U Dama said of the group that gathered. And he refused. A number of monks from the monastery had gone out earlier that day, after the violence had begun, and saw a group of people approaching both Buddhists and Muslims to warn that attacks were being plotted by the other side. The monks returned and told U Dama, so that by the time the men arrived outside the gate, his suspicion was already heightened.

> There were about 20 or 30 people and they were all drunk or on drugs. Only one person spoke – the rest were hanging their heads. They told me Muslims were killing Buddhist

monks, and I said I don't trust you because you are all drunk and you are not from this area.

The manufactured nature of the violence in Mandalay seemed too obvious for it to take hold en masse among residents there. Religious leaders from both sides called snap meetings to prevent its further spread, and U Wirathu, who had warned in the wake of the attacks that a jihad was underway, later acknowledged that he hadn't verified the claims of rape of the young Buddhist woman that he echoed to tens of thousands of followers on Facebook.

But in a sense the forces behind the violence did achieve a measure of success. In villages outside Mandalay, members of the two religious groups became suspicious of one another, and a distance grew between them. Even though it was clear the trigger for the violence had been fabricated, the fears it awakened rippled out to communities living side by side on the edge of the city that hadn't had direct exposure to it, injecting into them a distrust that hadn't been so present before. Rumours began to spread, and that same old process was activated, whereby violence elsewhere forced individuals to retreat within their own group. There, they would find security amid uncertain times, but the effect once again was to turn religious differences into a divide. It was in these villages that, soon after the violence of July 2014 in Mandalay, interfaith activists like Myo began their attempts to mend the fissures that had opened, and they became small laboratories in which different methods of communal healing could be tested.

9

Apartheid state: camps, ghettos and the new architecture of control

One effect of the violence of 2012 in Rakhine State was lost amid the tales of bloodletting and the growth of displacement camps along the Sittwe coast. Further north in the state, Rohingya were banished from towns in which they once lived and worked. The market in Kyauktaw, 70 kilometres north of the state capital, had been a place where the two communities interacted, and the town's hospital once treated patients of all creeds who would travel there from homes nearby or in the surrounding countryside. But the reconfiguration of the security landscape in the years after 2012 meant that was no longer allowed. Checkpoints along the roads leading into Kyauktaw became the final point of movement for Rohingya. Increasingly they were contained inside their villages. Any attempt to cross the invisible perimeter fence that now encircled them would, they came to discover, be considered a criminal offence.

In one village two kilometres from Kyauktaw lived a man, Aarif, who ran a small shop selling basic goods.[1] He was the father of three children – two girls and one boy, the latter born in 2011, a year before the violence. Back then, as the boy had begun to signal his desire to enter the world, Aarif called upon a village midwife to attend to his wife. With only rudimentary medical training, the midwife felt his wife's womb and knew delivery was close. She was driven the 10 minutes along the road connecting the village to Kyauktaw, and in the hospital there she gave birth. Several days later they returned to the village.

Three years later, his wife became pregnant with their fourth child. That was 2014, long after the segregation of the two communities had dramatically transformed the environment around them. She had conceived in early 2014, and by January the following year was in her final month of pregnancy. But she began to feel that all was not right. There were pains she hadn't known before, and once again Aarif called the midwife to their bedroom in the tiny wooden house in the village where his wife lay. The baby was alive in the womb, but the wrong way around. As the pains built the husband informed the village administrator, who called the health department in Kyauktaw. That was the morning of 5 January 2015. And so began the process, altogether new to Aarif, of getting his wife to hospital.

The after-effects of the violence of 2012 were multiple. What the banishing of Rohingya from Kyauktaw and towns elsewhere in the state amounted to was a purification of urban areas of Muslims. They were penned inside camps, villages and barricaded ghettos. No longer could Aarif's neighbours go to the markets; instead they were forced to develop roundabout ways of trading. They went to individual Rakhine, who at a reduced price bought from them a basket of eggs or fish to be sold at normal prices in the market, making a tidy profit for Rakhine but causing a loss in already meagre revenue for Rohingya.

But the impacts on access to healthcare were more dramatic. When the health department received word that morning in early 2015 of the complication with Aarif's wife, it organised for staff to go the village. They arrived in the evening, eight hours after the first call was made, and confirmed the midwife's fears – the baby was the wrong way round, and an operation was needed. The medics left, saying help would come. Aarif and his wife waited through the night, and by early afternoon the next day an ambulance arrived, accompanied by a police escort. The couple climbed aboard and drove out of the village onto the main road. Several years earlier, on the eve of her son's birth, she had taken a right-hand turn at this point, and in a matter of minutes had been at the hospital in Kyauktaw. This time, however, they turned left.

There are multiple strands to the story that follows, each telling in their own way of the acute condition of the Rohingya. They drove for three hours, winding their way down to Sittwe, where the only adequately equipped hospital in the state still permitted to accept Rohingya was. By the time they arrived it was late in the afternoon, more than a day and a half since Aarif had made the call to the village administrator. He remembers walking hand in hand with his wife from the ambulance to the hospital entrance. She had been shaky but could still stand, and they were taken into a room on the ground floor. She was able to explain the problem to the doctor, and after having done so she lay down on a bed. The doctor checked her over.

"We had arrived at the hospital at five o'clock in the afternoon," Aarif recalled. The doctor asked why she hadn't been brought in sooner, given that it was an emergency case. The young man, 31 at the time, explained the staggered process he had undergone to get his wife there: that he first needed permission for the two of them to travel; that he had waited a day and a half since first reporting the problem for an ambulance to arrive, and that instead of being able to take that right turn to the hospital in Kyauktaw, they had needed to drive another three hours in the opposite direction. But five minutes after arriving at the hospital, as Aarif sat in a chair in the doctor's room with his wife lying next to him, the doctor told him to leave. He had inspected the womb and, standing back from the bed, told him it was too late for his wife. The baby would die and so would she. Police were waiting outside the room to take Aarif away. Two nurses came in and lifted his wife to her feet. Still conscious and alert and able to move, she was walked out of the room and up the stairs, guided by the nurses. The police ordered Aarif back out to the ambulance. He was driven the three hours back to his village.

Whatever power differential already existed between doctor and patient was greatly amplified in that room by the particular hierarchy of status between the sick woman and the man tasked with remedying her. Aarif wasn't able to challenge the doctor, nor the police who walked him out of the hospital, because of a unique burden that Rohingya carry. Their statelessness gives them no recourse to legal action because they exist outside of the law, and all that it entitles. But that culture of forced submission bleeds into everyday interaction with figures of authority, whether legal or not, creating a culture that denies them any voice to challenge decisions that affect them. What became of his wife after she left the room Aarif never knew, save for the fact that she had died. That most final of decisions was made entirely arbitrarily – another snapshot of a much larger problem for Rohingya. The day after Aarif returned to his village he received word that his wife's body had been taken to Bumay, one of only two surviving Rohingya neighbourhoods in Sittwe. There, close to her family, she would be buried. He asked police in his village to grant him permission to travel back down for the funeral. They refused, claiming they wouldn't be able to provide security for him, and he was left alone inside his home with his three children. The $100 he paid for he and his wife to board the ambulance – $60 for the vehicle, $25 for the police and their food, and $15 for the driver – had cleaned out the savings he had stored away for his baby. But the baby was no longer, and his wife now lay in the ground in a town he would not be able to visit.

★ ★ ★

When the physical segregation began after June 2012, severing interaction between the Buddhist and Muslim communities of Rakhine State, it opened a gaping psychological divide. Several months after visiting Ko Myat in his home in Par Da Lek village and hearing of his role in the attack on Nasi quarter in Sittwe, I returned to try to meet with the village administrator. Min Oo lived not far from Ko Myat, in a stilted wooden house he shared with his wife and son. Having walked again through the winding streets of that village of less than 3,000 people we eventually found his home. On the raised wooden porch we sat and drank tea, and began to talk. He was an affable person with a lively face, but it was he who Ko Myat had said encouraged people to board the buses that took them along the road into downtown Sittwe. Min Oo shook his head, denying the charge as it was put to him. But he knew that his neighbours had gone to Nasi.

"I can't count how many from this village went to Sittwe," he said. "It wasn't only this village but people from nearby villages that went by buses too. It was a scary time. The whole village was worried that Muslims would come here. If they come we will kill them or they will kill us."

There had been no hope for protection from the military, who were stationed in barracks barely a kilometre down the road. Min Oo had been the administrator for two years before the violence; until June 2012 the toughest problem he'd faced was the confiscation of villagers' farmland, 100 acres of it, by the military as it sought to expand the barracks outwards. The army freely abused its power, he said, but it was the Muslims he feared more.

Close to an hour into our conversation his son arrived and joined us on the wooden deck. He was in his mid twenties, and had inherited the wide eyes and face-splitting grin of his father. During the violence he had been at a monastery in Yangon. Like many young Buddhists in Myanmar, he had undergone a brief spell as a monk, and returned home to find a divided state. He no longer interacted with Muslims, and spared few praises for them. "I get a fever when I see them," he said, and couldn't bear to be around them.

But he once had a Rohingya friend, a boy who came to his village to buy rice and who would, on occasions, stay over. That relationship had been broken by the violence. The friend was now in Thet Kae Pyin camp along with thousands of others, and he knew little else of his condition. But it hadn't seemed to bother him.

"I was friends with him for two years and when I think about him now I would not like to be friends. They are very stupid," he said, referring to Muslims in general. "Before the conflict he would come to stay here and all was okay. Now we have no relationship. Their religion is bad. Before 2012 I didn't think that way. After 2012 I think they're bad."

He knew his friend hadn't been involved in attacks on Rakhine Buddhists, but that mattered little. What became apparent as we spoke was that his perception of his friend had been entirely flipped by actions for which he bore no responsibility, except for his membership of that group. "His blood is different," the young man had said. "I don't think he is a bad person, but even though he's not bad, his ethnicity is bad. The group is bad."

At one point Min Oo leaned in, suggesting that I head up to the Mayu River if I wanted my questions answered. That was the boundary that marked the beginning of northern Rakhine State, where Muslims outnumbered Buddhists, and whose attempted rescue had come in the form of the Na Ta La village project decades before. The son then ducked inside the house and came out with a book. It was called "Mayu River is Crying," and he had bought it at a store in Mrauk U some time ago. It detailed the trajectory of the region in the decades after the Mujahid groups had run amok following the Second World War, and listed the death of every Rakhine person at the hands of Rohingya since the 1960s. "The book is real," the son had said. "The book is describing how Muslims come and destroy the whole village and burn it down."

I had no solid grounds to question it. The accounts of the violence that followed the war showed it to have been savage and extensive. And I had been guilty in the past of falling for the tendency to sympathise with the side that suffers most in a conflict, to a point at which the claims of brutality directed at it by the other side are viewed with scepticism. It was always the Rakhine who were depicted as the sole perpetrators, and the Rohingya as passive victims, but no conflict is that black and white, and victims too can be perpetrators. The book was a supposed corrective to that narrative, yet what in there was actually truth and what was fiction seemed secondary to another effect it had. Material like this provided a file of memories that percolated down through the generations and allowed the young man to make sense of the current situation. He had decided that his friend was now of "bad blood." What hadn't been an innate quality now was, and I wondered if that had been in part triggered by the stories told in the book and elsewhere that suddenly gave this evil a history, and made the violence of 2012 look not like an aberration, but the continuation of a norm.

If that was the case, then the likelihood of bringing the two communities back together seemed that much harder. In place of the countervailing information that normally comes with interaction, the divide that followed 2012, working its way through the towns and villages of the state, allowed whatever fears lurked beforehand to crystallise. That created a cycle, whereby physical segregation fuelled a process of mental segregation that, over time, lessened the potential for wounds to heal. "I'm afraid of going to the Muslim village," the young man's father, Min Oo, had said of the community of Rohingya six miles from Par Da Lek where mutual exchange was once a daily activity. "If I go they will kill me. I do not dare to go."

★ ★ ★

After the violence first erupted in June 2012, President Thein Sein dispatched battalions of soldiers to areas where attacks had taken place. For all the criticism of a militarised state, they appeared to have been effective in deterring more violence in those particular spots, and numbers of Rohingya welcomed them, as did Rakhine. But they were not the only security force there. After 2012 Rakhine civilians too began to police the state. Along the stretch of road running south out of Mrauk U lies a string of Rohingya villages whose inhabitants rarely leave anymore. Forbidden to enter the town, they suffered a similar fate to Aarif and his neighbours close to Kyauktaw – a trip to Sittwe hospital entailed the same drawn out processes and the same fees, and for many it was beyond the realm of possibility. But one evening in early 2015 a brawl broke out in one of the villages south of Mrauk U. A man was stabbed in the left shoulder, the blade sinking two inches into his flesh.[2] His family arranged for a trishaw to take him to a small hospital in a town further to the south that Rohingya were still allowed to access. The doctors there were unable to treat the wound, and with the man bleeding heavily, police were called and they made the decision to take him in the trishaw to the hospital in Mrauk U.

It was a rare call, one that appeared to reflect a degree of police attentiveness towards Rohingya that was otherwise absent from narratives of the violence. But as the vehicle neared the entrance to the town, a group of Rakhine armed with knives and sticks gathered in the road. There appeared to have been prior warning. They surrounded the vehicle, and the police ordered them to disperse. They refused, and so a call was made to the main police station in Mrauk U and the township chief and several other officers came down. They spoke with the group, but still they wouldn't let the injured man through. The driver turned the trishaw around in the direction of the village and gunned the motor, but the group blocked their exit. It took an hour of police persuasion to allow them to leave, and the man eventually returned to his village, his wound untreated. A year after the stabbing, the pain was still there, and it grew more acute each time he went to work in the fields next to the village. He had been forced to cut the number of hours he farmed each day, from nine to two or three, and his income dwindled.

When I'd heard before of instances in which police denied Rohingya access to towns on the grounds they might be attacked, I had been sceptical. It is easy to suspect a higher hand in everything that happens in Myanmar, so adept was the regime at manufacturing unrest that appeared, on the surface, to be random. I often found myself thinking that perhaps there was no threat at the other end, and the police who denied Rohingya freedom of movement were instead willing players in a grand design to limit their means of survival. Yet the Rakhine who blocked access to the hospital showed this wasn't always the case. They were equal participants, and although the state and Rakhine may not have coordinated their actions, their agenda was closely aligned. This illuminated the combined weight of power that was pitched against the Rohingya.

Rakhine policed the state in other ways too. The presence of international aid groups there had long been a point of contention. Rakhine believed that assistance was unfairly concentrated on Rohingya, despite the clear poverty that Rakhine too suffered. These tensions built after 2012 as the presence of aid organisations became more visible in the camps and as global attention fixed largely on Rohingya victims of the violence. Rakhine had already felt there to be an imbalance in aid distribution before 2012, and as Rohingya in the camps were increasingly cut off from basic resources, more international assistance was channelled to them. Clinics were set up, only for camp residents. It was standard protocol in light of the restrictions that limited the ability of Rohingya to seek treatment at the hospital in Sittwe, but it meant a further escalation in tensions: the access, however limited it was, that Rohingya and other confined Muslims now had to internationally provided healthcare was not so readily available to Rakhine. Aid workers could arrange for an ambulance to collect the sick, but Rakhine were left to their own devices. Through eyes clouded by bitter resentment, it may have appeared that the lot of Rohingya had in some ways improved as a result of the violence, while Rakhine were left once again to battle for whatever scraps the state provided.

In March 2014, a foreign staff member working for an international aid organisation based in Sittwe removed a Buddhist flag that had been placed near the gate outside her office. Within hours, mobs of Rakhine began attacking that office and several others in the town, and in the subsequent days they destroyed stores of food and medical aid and the cars and boats used to deliver them. They went from one location to another, appearing to know in advance the addresses of NGO offices. More than 30 properties were attacked, and suspicions mounted that it had been planned in advance. The names of Rakhine staff that worked with organisations assisting Rohingya were circulated around Sittwe and they were warned to cease their activities. Landlords that rented property to international organisations were instructed not to, and the organisations began to pull out. Staff were evacuated to Yangon, and for several months the infrastructure that supplied aid to Rohingya was reduced to its barest form.

That allowed local civil society networks in Sittwe to exert influence over the allocation of aid, and when international organisations returned to the state they discovered a new landscape for the aid industry. Rents for properties had doubled, even tripled, as a result of the pressure put on landlords leasing buildings to organisations assisting Rohnigya. And they had a new authority to answer to. The Emergency Coordination Committee (ECC) was run by U Than Tun, a prominent Rakhine elder who taught in a local school. By the time I met with him, nearly two years had passed since the ECC's founding. It quickly became clear that any talk of the Muslim community in Rakhine State greatly animated him.

> You first know that these Muslims are illegal – at least 80 per cent of them are. They are not from our country. They come from Bangladesh. They say they are Rohingya but that's never seen in history. They want citizenship and to become an ethnic group. They are liars. Their name was never seen and never heard.

The attacks of March 2014 "were a time bomb; they weren't planned in advance," he said. Rakhine had grown increasingly angry at the perceived imbalance in aid distribution and had exploded. But Rakhine staff working for international NGOs had been receiving threats since late 2013, long before the town erupted once again. Leaflets were circulated that detailed the bias of these aid organisations, and staff were visited by local Rakhine nationalists who warned them that they should stop cooperating with the international community. These NGOs weren't here for good reasons, they were told. Many staff quit as a result. A version of the ECC had been recommended years before by international aid agencies working in Rakhine State who wanted greater local input, but they had imagined something quite different to what eventually transpired. Rather than a body comprising Rohingya, Rakhine and representatives of the international community, U Than Tun's group was solely Rakhine. Other local networks became more vocal too, and began to marshal aid distribution in their own particular ways, by blocking deliveries to camps and, in some cases, blocking camp exits as ambulances tried to take Rohingya to hospital in Sittwe.

In the wake of the March 2014 attacks, the ECC appeared to grow as powerful as a government ministry, and had forced organisations to negotiate over even minor issues, like repairs to camp shelters. Moreover, the distribution of aid was now politicised. No longer was it needs-based, with aid targeted at those who required it most, but instead was reconfigured so that the balance in provision didn't reflect the imbalance in the vulnerability of the communities receiving it, but rather an artificial 50–50 split so as to appease Rakhine. I suggested to U Than Tun that, regardless of popular perceptions of Rohingya, their condition in the crowded camps where they lived in wooden shacks and tents, where one latrine was often shared among nearly 40 people,[3] and where inhabitants largely depended on outside assistance surely indicated that they required aid more than Rakhine. That was a fundamental principle of the international humanitarian system – that aid goes where it is most needed.

"You are a western journalist coming here and saying to me, 'Humanitarian, humanitarian!' But in any country, national security is more important than humanitarian aid," he replied.

The aid given to Rohingya was a national security threat because, he said, it created a pull factor for "Bengalis" to enter Myanmar. They would be coaxed over the border by the prospect of better healthcare and everything else the aid industry here offered. International NGOs were also brainwashing Rohingya, he thought.

"They are giving a political mindset to the Bengalis. 'You are Rohingya, you are not Bengali. This land is not Rakhine land, this is your Rohingya land.'"

And, of course, they weren't citizens. He asked whether my country, the United Kingdom, allows illegal immigrants the same rights as full citizens. I replied that immigrants, whether illegal or not, were still able to access healthcare. They were denied a great number of rights, but their access to hospitals wasn't curtailed in the same way it had been for Rohingya since 2012. Locals in the villages around Kyauktaw had said that an impending birth was by and large the only reason police would allow passage to Sittwe hospital. Other illnesses would only be treated locally, often by poorly trained medics with only rudimentary equipment. U Than Tun waved his hand. The healthcare situation "was not serious for the Bengalis," he said. "Their healthcare had been upgraded; they have no worries."

There were yet more effects of the violence that only gradually came into view. Colonel Tha Kyaw's list of directives had been targeted specifically at Rohingya, but the violence of 2012 functioned like a dragnet that swept up all Muslims and lumped them together as one, so that Kaman too began to experience a particular type of treatment they hadn't known of before. The violence created its own set of informal regulations about who could go where and what entitlements went to whom, and it flattened distinctions between different Muslim groups so that Kaman, who were citizens of Myanmar and whom Rakhine knew to have had a centuries-long presence there, also joined the ranks of the unwanted.

★ ★ ★

Along one road running north from Sittwe is a village called Thinganet that borders on a large military barrack, an extension of the same one that had eaten into the land belonging to the farmers of Par Da Lek village further to the west. Thinganet is like many villages in this part of the country. The walls of houses are built from latticed wooden panels that somehow withstand the heavy monsoons each year, and people gather each morning soon after dawn at a small market along a narrow street, where fish, vegetables and meats are laid out in all their colourful glory on mats on the baked ground. It is a Kaman village, and farmers here used to take their goods to the markets in Sittwe to sell for a higher price than they could get at home. Ma Win had done that for 30 years, each day taking a bus or rickshaw from outside her village into town, and each afternoon returning with the day's income to spread among her family.

"All ethnic and religious groups mixed in the market, working together," she said of the time before the violence. She was in her early fifties, and had two children. "Things were normal and we socialised. We were sister to sister; we shared snacks."

For the two weeks after Sittwe erupted the Muslim villagers of Thinganet had stopped venturing into town. Ma

Win had been there on the first day of the violence and was warned by a group of armed Rakhine to leave immediately, and so knew the dangers of returning there. But without access to the market, her income dried up, and by late June 2012 she was penniless. She left her village at around six o'clock one morning three weeks after being ordered to leave by the armed men. Other villagers needed supplies too and she was given $60 and a list of goods to buy.

> I wasn't earning any income and couldn't provide for my children so I got some vegetables from my garden and went to Sittwe to sell it. The market was very busy at that time in the morning but I didn't see any other Kaman or Rohingya. It was very early, and there were only Rakhine there.

She set up her stall, and after doing so the group of women whom she had traded alongside for the past three decades approached.

> As I was selling the vegetables they arrived and asked why I was here selling vegetables. They had come from inside the market, from the same spot we used to sell at. I said because I have difficulty earning any money. They were saying, "You are *kalar*, you are Kaman," and grabbed me. Two women held my hands, and then three or four beat me with sticks. For one hour they beat me. I could not walk. I fell down and police arrived and took me to the station. They investigated for half an hour and then sent me back to the village. My eyes and my face and my back – I needed 20 days of medication.

There had been someone nearby who tried to stop it, she said. It was a lady Ma Win knew. But when she tried to intervene the women shouted: "Why do you intervene? We will also beat you. Are you Kaman or not?"

Three years on from the attack, Ma Win still experienced pain in her shoulder and head. She was forced to work longer days now, from six in the morning until nine at night, picking vegetables and carrying them to markets in villages nearby. She made less than $2 a day, and her sons who worked in a brick factory supplemented the family income. She felt frightened and depressed. The memories of the attack still haunted her, and travel to Sittwe to see a doctor was impossible. Only one person from the village now went into town to buy goods, a girl in her early twenties who could pass herself off as Rakhine. This girl had a lighter complexion and wasn't suspected of being a *kalar*, the slur thrown at Ma Win as she was being beaten that branded people of darker skin with the "outsider" tag. It was clear from this and other developments that the violence of 2012 hadn't been strictly ethnic in nature – it was also both religious and racial, for a different appearance meant a different origin, and thus a different nature of being.

As the violence went on, the target lacked the boundedness that these categories – religion, ethnicity, race – seemed to offer. Instead a broader Otherness developed that seemed to come about in opposition to an increasingly purified notion of Rakhine-*ness*, and it was against this that the Kaman were lumped in with the Rohingya. They too became confined to their villages, unable to enter the towns and earn a viable living. They may have been citizens, on an equal legal footing to Rakhine, but a new set of rules had come into being that stripped that status of much of its meaning.

After the violence, the various smaller Buddhist ethnic groups of Rakhine State – the Dainget, the Mro, the Khami – formed associations among themselves that excluded the

Kaman. It may have been defensive, given the risks of association with any pariah community, but the effect was to push Kaman further towards the edges. U Than Tun had said that Kaman were targeted because the Rakhine "don't accept them as part of our nationality. We accept them as citizens but we don't accept them as our ethnic group." They knew they were citizens, but the laws that made them so had been written by the government, not the Rakhine. The son of the village administrator in Par Da Lek had also evinced a disdain for Kaman. "They are like a stick with each end pointed," he said, using a metaphor to illustrate how Kaman would "make friends with both Muslims and Rakhine," something that was evidently unsound.

Yet what perhaps singled out the Rohingya over and above Kaman wasn't the mere fact of their complete social isolation from society. It was that the gulf between them and the system of laws designed to protect members of a community was both codified and routinised. They had neither legal rights nor political rights, and this spoke to the particular quality that makes statelessness so cruel a punishment – the stateless exist only in their physical form; every other claim to living is denied. They had from time to time served as useful tools for the government, which in return for their support had courted Rohingya in the run-up to the 2010 elections. But after the violence, even that kind of exploitation for political gain ceased. As the 2015 elections approached, Rakhine Buddhists, flanked by monks, marched in their thousands in Sittwe to demand the Rohingya not be allowed to vote. The government then confiscated the "white cards" that five years before had been their ticket into the voting booth, thereby leaving them with no political voice whatsoever. Perhaps the incumbent

Union Solidarity and Development Party, aligned as it was with the military, knew that with the National League for Democracy running this time, as well as a number of smaller Muslim-dominated parties, votes would not go to them. The rights granted to Rohingya in 2010 had been only temporary rights, it became clear, to be traded for a vote and then discarded. When the 2015 elections came round, the Rohingya had neither any hope of securing a representative in parliament, nor of even participating in that basic act of democracy, the casting of a ballot. They crowded the camps outside of Sittwe and the towns in the north of the state, but they were essentially invisible.

It was into this divided land that enumerators had come in 2014 to carry out Myanmar's first census in more than three decades. It was supported by the UN, and the teams that fanned out across Myanmar to collect data on the country's population were to include religion and ethnicity among the list of questions asked. It had seemed foolish from the very start, for those two identifiers were already sources of great tension, and contestations over belonging – something the census was designed to establish officially – had played out so violently only two years before. The census used the list of 135 "national races," the same index that had given such a flawed rendering of who did and did not belong in Myanmar.

But there were other concerns. Included on the enumeration list was a box labelled "Other." The government had assured the UN that Rohingya would be free to write their identity as they chose. But Ma Ba Tha campaigned vigorously to have this overturned, as did Rakhine political parties. And at the final hour the government reneged. Any attempt to register as Rohingya would be refused, it said, as it would for other groups that lived in Myanmar but were excluded from the "national races" list – Indians, Chinese, Gurkha and others. It would need to be "Bengali," or otherwise nothing. Enumerators went from house to house in towns and villages across Rakhine State in March 2014. Upon arriving and being told the inhabitants were Rohingya, they turned around and walked away. The debacle only served to fuel the mass resistance towards any acceptance of the Rohingya, giving Buddhist nationalists another reason to assert their hostility towards the group. And so the Rohingya were pushed even further away, their statelessness reaffirmed.

★ ★ ★

Over the mountains in central Myanmar, the violence too had long-term effects on the makeup of communities. When displaced Muslims returned to the razed neighbourhood of Mingalar Zayone in Meikhtila, where the madrasa had been destroyed and the pile of bodies set aflame, they discovered that they were forbidden from rebuilding their homes on the land they once inhabited. Nearly three years on from the violence, when I visited Meikhtila for the second time, a camp holding just over 100 Muslims, mostly residents of Mingalar Zayone, remained next to a football stadium on the edge of town. Inhabitants there had been told by government officials that they would be rehoused by the end of 2014, but this hadn't materialised. Several months after I met with the camp inhabitants in late 2015, a number tried again to return to their neighbourhoods, but Ma Ba Tha supporters petitioned local authorities to block them. Authorities told the displaced Muslims that they would not be able to guarantee their security should they try to set up home there once again, and so they returned to their shacks on the edge of town.

During my second visit to Meikhtila I decided to go back to Mingalar Zayone, having known it before only as a mass of rubble and charred household possessions. My translator and I parked our bike at the edge of the quarter early one afternoon in November 2015 and walked in. The debris that once covered the area had been cleared away, but the skeletal walls of several houses were still standing. We approached one man, a Buddhist, outside his home and asked what relations had been like between the inhabitants of the quarter before the violence. "We were like brothers and sisters," he said. "Like a family. There was no conflict." He pointed to nearby patches of land marked by faint rectangular outlines where Muslim houses had once stood. One of them belonged to a man, his neighbour, who had been killed. Another was the home of a 13-year-old boy, also a victim of the mobs.

We continued to move around the quarter. I snapped some photographs, and we climbed up the bank at the western edge to the point on the road where crowds had gathered two and a half years before to direct the killers below them. After several minutes we dropped back down and headed back across the quarter in the direction of our bike. A man quickly rode up behind us and muttered something to my translator, and stuffed a note in her hand. She grew agitated, and told me that we needed to leave quickly. We made for the bike, and she hurriedly relayed how the man had warned her we were being followed. He said he was a Muslim community leader, and had given her his phone number.

We climbed on the bike and rode off back into town, but as we circled the same roundabout in the centre where Sandar had seen the body set aflame years before, I noticed another man in a white polo shirt riding parallel to us, casting looks in our direction. He soon disappeared into the traffic. We eventually found a teashop and ordered some food. Several minutes later the man entered and sat down at a nearby table. The food arrived, and as we ate he began to take photos of us on his phone. I assumed he was from the Special Branch wing of police intelligence, which often tracks the movements of journalists.

We finished up, paid and rode off again, agreeing that it would be unwise to continue working that day. I had scheduled a follow-up interview with a man I'd met the previous day whose adopted son was killed in the madrasa massacre, but the risk that we might lead our pursuer to him seemed too great. So we rode out of town to a temple complex where we parked up and considered what to do next. It was mid-afternoon and the temple was empty. We walked to a pagoda inside the complex, and at the base of it sat down on some steps, shaded from the sun by a canopy overhead. Several minutes passed. Then, to our right, around the corner of the pagoda, the man appeared. He was smiling, and motioned to the step next to where the translator sat. I gestured for him to sit down. He was soft-spoken, polite, and asked my translator to explain who I was. We knew him to be police, but still asked the same question back. He was indeed Special Branch, and had seen us in Mingalar Zayone. He took down our passport and ID card details as we spoke – a common procedure for foreign journalists in Myanmar – and enquired as to why we had visited the quarter. The 2015 elections were only a week away, I said, and we had been speaking to locals about their hopes for the vote and what might come after. He seemed amiable, and I asked why he had felt the need to follow us. Because the destroyed neighbourhood in which we were spotted was a sensitive site, he said, and what had taken place there remained a delicate issue. Police didn't want journalists poking around. Evidently there was an effort to block new information from getting out there.

I never did manage to meet again with the father of the slain child. The boy had been 15 years old at the time. He was among those led out of the school by the police on the morning of 21 March 2013, but was picked off before he reached safety. His adopted father thought police had intended to protect the students, but had been unable to contain the mobs that grew with each passing minute. The son, who had moved to Meikhtila in 2005 after the death of his biological father, was left behind in the grass as the police line moved on and out of the quarter.

A number of students who survived the madrasa attack had since moved to Thailand, while inhabitants of houses in Thiri Mingalar quarter that were destroyed were relocated to Kyaukse, 90 kilometres to the north. The knock-on effects of the violence in central Myanmar were less overt than the system of apartheid that had been implemented across Rakhine State. But it remained an acutely sensitive matter, not only for locals, but evidently too for the police, who had attracted so much suspicion for their puzzling actions during the butchery of March 2013. Even long after the town had returned to a semblance of normality, save for the still-displaced Muslims, there seemed to be an effort to control the collective memory of those events.

The violence of 2013 in central Myanmar had given rise to groups like 969 and Ma Ba Tha who were able to influence the national conversation about Muslims and to apply pressure at the political level, but there were more subtle day-to-day impacts too. The young student I'd met in Yangon who had lamented how she was required to attend Buddhist ceremonies at school despite being Muslim said that the violence had left her feeling more exposed. She had been one of the only Muslims in her school, and it began to affect her relations with classmates; not explicitly, but in understated ways.

"A friend came up to me after the Meikhtila violence and said 'You're Muslim right? You heard about what happened?'"

She knew the friend meant no ill will, but she began to feel as if she stood out in a way she hadn't before.

★ ★ ★

At his house in Thet Kae Pyin camp on the Rakhine State coast, Mohammed Ismail, the young teacher who had escaped Nasi quarter in Sittwe as mobs descended in June 2012, spoke of those left behind. While the majority of his neighbours had fled to the camps, a few moved into the homes of relatives in Aung Mingalar quarter, further towards the centre of town. But the tight restrictions on their ability to leave the quarter gave rise to a malaise that hung heavy over the neighbourhood. You can feel it when you go there now – a greyness in the eyes of those looking out from their doorways, and a depression that tugs at the body.

"People who live in Aung Mingalar, their minds are not normal," Mohammed Ismail had said. "They worry about more violence."

The official combined death toll from both waves of attacks in 2012 didn't break 300. Such figures from the Myanmar government are always grounds for scepticism, eager as it is to fudge any statistics from episodes of unrest lest it reflect poorly on its ability to wield authority. But either way, in the grand scheme of group violence, it seemed small. Hundreds, possibly thousands, died at sea as they crammed onto wooden boats docked in the shallow waters off the Sittwe coastline and sailed to Thailand, Malaysia and beyond, drowning under the weight of numbers.

But the figures of the dead failed to illuminate the true cost of the events of 2012. The barricades set up around Aung Mingalar became psychological barriers too, as did the checkpoints that came to demarcate the zones of movement for Rohingya across the state. What lay beyond them, in land they could no longer access, became the stuff of nightmarish rumour. When Aarif returned to his village near Kyauktaw from the hospital in Sittwe, he would have told of how his wife had been taken from him by the people charged with saving her. What exactly occurred in the hospital wasn't clear, yet stories like that became "proof" that doctors were killing Rohingya, and therefore that a trip to hospital would put the final seal on one's fate. This fear of what went on inside Sittwe hospital was echoed time and again, and meant that Rohingya increasingly began to refuse treatment for life-threatening illnesses. The health crises that came about as a direct result of the restrictions on access to healthcare were predictable, but I hadn't foreseen the extent to which the system of segregation that was implemented after 2012 would work its way so deeply into the mental state of Rohingya there.

In a hut in a village not far from Aarif's lay Khine Begum.[4] She was in her mid-forties, and had developed a lump on her stomach that the village medic had said was cancerous. It sat just below her belly button, around the size of the palm of a hand and protruded a centimetre out. The medic had little training though, and there wasn't any way to substantiate the diagnosis. Being Rohingya, she was barred from travelling to Kyauktaw hospital for a scan, and visiting medics couldn't transport equipment in. Had she requested travel to Sittwe hospital?

"I'm afraid of going to Sittwe," she said. "If somebody goes they die in Sittwe hospital, and the bodies are never returned to the village."

This came to be a common refrain among Rohingya after the segregation measures were implemented. Khine Begum knew four people that she said had died inside the hospital.

> One of them was my friend and I spoke with her before she went. She couldn't give birth in the village so she went to hospital – this was a year and a half ago. The four people who died, I think the doctor poisoned them.

These stories had a snowball effect. Compounding the fact that a visit to hospital might now take up to two days, people also feared the hospital so much that they avoided visiting until right at the last minute, when the illness had advanced to the point at which death was likely. Each time that a Rohingya entered and didn't leave alive, it fed the rumours of doctors killing Muslim patients, thereby deterring more from going until it was too late, and the cycle would turn another revolution – more talk in the camps and villages of suspicious deaths, more reason to avoid seeking treatment.

The bodies that left the hospital would not be counted in the tally of deaths caused by the violence, but they were most certainly victims of it. The changes that followed 2012 led to violence of a kind different to the butchery, but no less devastating. Access to the most basic of rights was determined solely on the basis of religion. These limitations had been in effect before 2012, but to a lesser degree, and were largely restricted to the far north. Afterwards, however, they became principal elements in a system of segregation that was active across the state, and which included Kaman too.

This was violence, but not the kind that made headlines. It was structural – less spectacular, and harder to detect, but nonetheless equally catastrophic. Muslims wouldn't die on the streets, bludgeoned by machete. They would die in their homes or in their huts in the camps, slowly and quietly. The government could hide behind the excuse that the restrictions were needed to protect Muslims from attack by Rakhine, and there was some truth to this. But in drawing up this system of measures – of allowing only one adequately equipped hospital to take a population of more than a million, of forcing Rohingya to pay fees they could not afford, of determining wholly arbitrarily whose condition did and did not warrant treatment; of endless delays and countless refusals – the government was most certainly complicit.

The tightening of restrictions and the spread of checkpoints and no-go areas for Muslims amplified a process of dehumanisation that had been engineered over decades by the state, and which made more foot soldiers of Rakhine. To see Muslims being vetted at checkpoints on a daily basis and to know they were being confined to camps and villages for security reasons further animated the idea of them as a threatening presence. It wasn't just that Rohingya had also attacked Rakhine in 2012 – it was that everything that came before and after served as supposed proof of their inborn malevolence, and therefore the need to contain them en masse. In response, Rakhine took it upon themselves to police their own state, therefore acting as functionaries of the government and allowing it to step back and deflect much of the blame.

From my conversations with Rakhine, it seemed that the psychological effects that the segregation had on a population already primed to see Muslims as a threat were profound. Friends quickly became enemies because the actions of a few were portrayed as indicative of the intentions of many, and so the measures needed to address them were rolled out to all. As the communities grew further apart, there was nothing to correct these thought patterns, and they had a circular effect: the security measures could be read as evidence that Muslims had been allowed to roam free for too long; that they were always threatening, and that action was finally being taken to remedy that threat. This extended the narrative of the violent Muslim back to before the violence took place, and further justified the support Rakhine gave for the increasingly severe controls placed on the group. The son of the Par Da Lek village administrator had come to see "bad blood" in his Rohingya friend. He may not have been violent, but his group, his bloodline, was. The friend was susceptible, and therefore required confinement to a camp, as did all Rohingya.

★ ★ ★

Long after the violence there still emerged stories from time to time of Rakhine amassing near Rohingya communities, or mysterious disappearances of Rohingya from camps. But for several years after 2013, there were no repeats of the massacres, and the western coastal region of Myanmar seemed, in the eyes of the government, to have returned to normalcy.

Yet the conditions to which the violence had given birth – the camps and the ghettos; the intricate architecture of control that denied healthcare to the dying – were in some ways more distressing and more embittering than even the most gruesome accounts of the bloodletting I'd heard from 2012 and after. It took a while to figure out why, but something gradually took form. When the hand of higher powers in episodes of violence is hidden by the hordes of people on the ground that deliver it, one can explain it away as the work of a collective of extremist individuals. The patterns the violence forms a part of aren't so clear, and the measure of hostility faced by the victims doesn't get a true reading. They might be recurrent, but they seem isolated from broader structures of power, and the animosity that feeds it appears localised.

But as the extent of the reorganisation of the landscape in Rakhine State became clearer, that illusion was broken. The mobs that wrecked the aid infrastructure in Sittwe in March 2014 provided a more visible manifestation of processes that were quietly underway all across the state, whereby access to life-saving treatment is controlled and greatly limited on the basis of identity, whether it be ethnicity or religion. It amounts to a system of racialised healthcare, purposeful and carefully designed, in its most extreme form. And because it is a system, with an enforced command structure – from the village administrator required to telephone health officials who then bring in police to determine the fate of the individual – the hand of the state is plain to see. It, and not Rakhine civilians, decides how healthcare is distributed among the population. This system, and the methods of control that are integral to it, appears calculated to ensure that the existence of the Rohingya community there is as fragile as possible.

It seems like the cruellest punishment, to delay or deny treatment for someone not because as an individual they have done wrong, but because they belong to a group considered collectively wrong. This was perhaps why those accounts were so affecting – through that lens, the young too are as guilty as the old, and the government, the supposed guardian of a populace, shared that view as much as the extremists on the ground that helped to enforce it. The stories from the Rohingya villages around Kyauktaw and Mrauk U were not as sensational as those told from the sites of massacres in 2012 and thereafter, and they won't make headlines. They are, I suppose, the silent continuation of a campaign of violence that began long before 2012 and proceeds today, out of the public eye. But in its impact it is no less appalling.

10

U Maung Soe: an outcast in disguise

In Yangon I met a man whose own curious story seemed as reflective of the mysterious ways in which power functions in Myanmar as anything I'd come across. He had neither witnessed any of the violence of the transition, nor was he directly affected by it. Yet he seemed to illustrate that, for all the blood spilled in the contestations over identity in Myanmar, there was an element of the absurd in the way the regime determined who did and did not belong in the country. Even individuals from the most detested group – spurned by the majority, and cast to the farthest edges of society – could, with a bit of work, not only become members of the national community, but rise to a position of authority within its most prestigious institution.

U Maung Soe was born in Buthidaung in 1966. At the time of his birth, his father was away on the other side of the country, fighting the Chinese nationalist Kuomintang army, who a decade earlier had been routed by Mao's forces and fled across the border into Myanmar. In late 1966, the father received word that he would be transferred again, and so he travelled back to Buthidaung to collect his family. He met U Maung Soe for the first time, and together with his wife, the three of them moved to Yangon.

Both sides of the family could trace a lineage in northern Rakhine State back several generations. U Maung Soe's

great grandparents had been born there, and worked as
farmers. His mother's family hailed from the countryside to
the north of Buthidaung, and his father's from the south. U
Maung Soe had always known both sides of the family to
be Rohingya, but either way, in his parents' day the regime
hadn't required ethnicity to be recorded on ID cards. To
officials, they were known only by their place of birth:
"BTH," or Buthidaung.

I'd gone to meet U Maung Soe because he, like his father,
had fought in the army. It was a rarity to find someone from
such a derided group brought into that institution, and I was
intrigued as to how he managed it, and why. It seemed odd
that the army, whose principal task since independence had
been the ethnic and religious homogenisation of Myanmar,
would allow a Rohingya to join its ranks; even odder that
he wanted a part in that project in the first place.

The severity of Ne Win's crusade against ethnic diversity
had taken a while to become apparent. Born four years after
the general took power, U Maung Soe was, for much of
his early life, unburdened by his ethnicity. But when he
turned 12 and was required to obtain his first ID card, the
problems began. That was 1978, the year Rohingya were
forced to carry Foreign Registration Cards, and when more
than 200,000 were driven into Bangladesh following heavy-
handed verification checks by the military. But rather than
maintain his Rohingya identity and risk being swept up in
the pogrom of that year, he and his parents fudged their
ethnicity. He "became" a Rakhine Muslim, a recognised
category prior to the 1983 census, in the same way Hla Hla
had transitioned from a Mon to a Bamar when she moved
to Yangon, by convincing immigration officials otherwise.
In doing so he secured citizenship, while his fellow ethnics

came to know the particular pains of statelessness. It was a simple calculation for U Maung Soe and his family: to remain a Rohingya in the eyes of officials was to lose all the rights enjoyed by those groups that, in their various degrees of belonging, were accepted as part of the nation.

By his early twenties, U Maung Soe had passed through university in Yangon and joined Ne Win's Burma Socialist Programme Party, where he worked as an office clerk in the northern suburbs. Myanmar was a one-party state at the time, and his decision to join came down to a simple matter of knowing that a secure career path lay with the government. The pragmatic streak shown by his parents in their decision to switch ethnicities seemed to have passed down to their son, who understood that his immediate chances in life would be bettered if he worked in the offices of the government. He wasn't there for long, however. The uprising of 1988 toppled Ne Win and his party, and U Maung Soe became jobless. Several months later, aged 22, he found himself running errands for the National Unity Party, the civilian face of the military leadership that took Ne Win's place. And then, in February 1989, he decided to join the army.

"I didn't think the military was positive," he said. "I just wanted to learn the arts. There should be someone who knows military skills among my people. That was my father's ambition. He said that joining the military is a good thing to do."

In his day, U Maung Soe's father had fought alongside other Rohingya in the army. At that time, in the decade after independence, the institution hadn't discriminated so heavily on the basis of religion and ethnicity. Only later were the ranks purified.

"He joined the military to protect the land of his ethnic people and earn the pride for his people, just as there were Rohingya people who served the government as teachers, doctors, government servants and police with that same spirit," U Maung Soe said.

But much had changed in the four decades between his father signing up and U Maung Soe following suit. He may have undergone one identity shift to spare him the fate of other Rohingya, but Muslims were still barred from joining the military. He went to the draft office in Yangon in early 1989 where his friend, a Buddhist, was staff. The friend agreed to write on the draft form that U Maung Soe was Rakhine Buddhist, initiating a second transformation of identity – on paper at least. That kind of deceit between official and civilian was by no means unheard of in Myanmar. Nepotism, corruption and their many varied forms were par for the course, and shortly before turning 23, U Maung Soe enrolled and was sent to Kayin State. By the time immigration officials came to his barracks in 1990, after a new round of National Registration Cards had been ordered, he was able to provide "proof," in the shape of his army form, that he was now a Buddhist. The ID card handed to him soon after brought this new reality into being.

Once in the military, troops aren't given the luxury of choice – they go where they are told. U Maung Soe spent two years in Kayin State, fighting soldiers from the Karen National Liberation Army, before being sent back across the country to Kyauktaw in Rakhine State, close to his birthplace. Soon after arriving there in 1991, his battalion was tasked with assisting the newly formed Na Sa Ka, the security unit composed of army, police and immigration

officials that was formed to man the Bangladeshi border and
to implement control measures on Rohingya. That unit
came to be widely feared among the community for the
abuse they freely inflicted on them, and at this point in
his recollection of events, U Maung Soe became sparing
with the detail. He was a Rohingya, aiding a security force
preoccupied chiefly with suppressing the Rohingya. Na Sa
Ka had helped to orchestrate the second pogrom against
Rohingya that, by March 1992, had sent some 250,000
people fleeing into Bangladesh. U Maung Soe said that he
largely remained stationed in the barracks in Kyauktaw,
but would sometimes provide additional security for Na
Sa Ka. His unit entered Rohingya-inhabited areas prior to
the arrival of immigration officials, who conducted regular
checks on Rohingya, and locked down the area entirely,
preventing any movement. On one occasion in 1992, a
group of nine young Rohingya had managed to leave their
homes in Buthidaung, without permission and undetected
by authorities, with the intention of reaching Yangon. They
passed through Kyauktaw and made it as far as Mrauk U,
where they were caught. Over the radio, U Maung Soe
could hear the commander in Mrauk U ordering his soldiers
to dig graves for the nine men and beat them to death.
"The Western Command division commander ordered to
kill them all. We could hear it from the communication
device we had."

I asked him what guilt he felt about incidents like these,
but he would never be drawn. "I did feel sad. More than
sad – tragic." But that was all. The thought of quitting the
army hadn't crossed his mind, he said. He wanted to learn
all the skills the army might equip him with. He felt a sense
of solidarity with the Rohingya, but at the same time, he

was happy that he had been deployed to Rakhine State. He was close to home there, and from time to time he would go to see his father in Buthidaung. He knew the abuse that soldiers were inflicting on Rohingya, something he said he never took part in, but he would give medicine and other goods to Rohingya families and that would alleviate some of the bad feeling he had.

Over the years, U Maung Soe – a Buddhist, in the eyes of his colleagues in the army – rose up the ranks. By the time he left the military in 2006, he was a captain. He was proud of his ascent, and handed me the military ID card he still carried. The photo showed him smiling, dressed in uniform, his epaulettes studded with three stars. But after leaving the army, his life took an even more unlikely turn. "It was just my fate," he said. "When I turned 40, I was transferred."

It was common practice to reassign officers in the army to ministries, for the line between military and political life in Myanmar had long ago dissolved. Having retired from active duty in 2006, he was sent to the Ministry of Religious Affairs. At the time, the ministry was divided into two main departments. The Department for Religious Affairs ostensibly handled the affairs of the four major faith groups in Myanmar, but in reality served as an administration department for Buddhism, printing texts, holding exams for monks and administering schools and monasteries. The latter was more focused. Named the Department for the Promotion and Propagation of Sāsana, its principal function was to vigorously promote Buddhism, particularly in the mountainous border regions where Christianity was strong.

It was to this department that U Maung Soe was assigned, and in 2006, he took up residence in an office in Kengtung, in the hills of southern Shan State where Baptist missionaries more than a century before had made converts of the Lahu, the Akha and other communities. The Department dispatched monks, the counter-missionaries of the regime, to their villages and it endowed Buddhist monastery schools in the hills with texts translated from Pali, the language used in many of the earliest Buddhist texts. U Maung Soe greeted these travelling holy men and set them up in newly built monasteries in the villages around Kengtung.

But he soon came to learn of another function of the Department. In those tiny villages it held mass conversion ceremonies for Christians and animists. They would line up in fields in front of stages made of bamboo and, to the monks that sat above them, pledge their commitment to Buddhism. And in return they would receive a National Registration Card. It was in spectacles like this that U Maung Soe, who still considered himself a Rohingya and a devout Muslim, would play an organising role.

"In the conversion ceremonies, I had to perform as a ceremony master," he explained. "The people who converted received bags of rice, salt and cooking oil, and the last thing they received was the NRC, which had 'Buddhist' written on it." In the lead-up to the ceremonies, the monks sent by the Department to the villages would hold sermons on Buddhism and, along with the township authorities and religious affairs officers like U Maung Soe, explain to the villagers what rewards would be given for conversion. "They could persuade the poor who had no food to eat and the people who had no NRC to convert."

But there was a more mundane element to it all. The monks would read from the scriptures and then detail the incentives for conversion. Having garnered interest from the Christian communities, the township authorities then organised the conversion ceremonies, over which the governor presided.

> At that time, it was the period of the military regime. In those days, the township governor hosted the big conversion ceremonies to gain credit. If he could report to Senior General Than Shwe how many people he converted to Buddhism, he received credit. He wanted acknowledgement for how much work he did.

U Maung Soe understood the irony of it all. There he was, someone who had undergone a similar process of transformation in order that he could serve as an equal in society, standing at the side of a stage overseeing the coercion of thousands of others to do the same. The conversions were not ordered at gunpoint, but in the sense that options for the religious pariah would be severely limited unless they submitted, they were not voluntary. Without showing fealty to Buddhism, these people would not receive their National Registration Card, and would forever be branded by the regime as outsiders.

"When I saw these events, it made me unhappy," U Maung Soe said. "A person should be able to live freely. A citizen should be able to live freely due to his citizenship. A citizen should have freedom of religion as well."

The Lahu and the Akha weren't in quite the same league of disenfranchisement as the Rohingya. Like many of the smaller minorities, they were recognised among the 135 national races. Yet, U Maung Soe explained, many were uneducated as to their legal rights to a National Registration Card. Their community leaders often didn't understand the processes involved, nor that they actually qualified for one, and so could be readily exploited by officials seeking prestige. U Maung Soe saw it as a mutually beneficial arrangement: they would gain legal status, and in return the regime would get a new tribe of loyal Buddhist followers.

Like all the accounts of people in Myanmar who swapped their ethnic or religious identity, there was a strong element of the superficial to it all. For these villagers, it seemed to be a pure formality. They would often attend the monastery for a month or two, U Maung Soe said, before their commitment seemed to peter out. The monks would move on to other villages, and township authorities didn't have the resources, or perhaps even the will, to check the attendance of the converts at monasteries. It seemed instead to be largely a matter of numbers – a way for local officials to convince higher powers that their project to create a uniform state was bearing fruit via the exhaustive efforts of their men on the ground. The transaction being offered – a National Registration Card for non-Buddhists in return for joining the fold – was blackmail, but in a sense, the villagers knew how to play the game. They would gather in front of the stage and pledge their newfound fidelity to Buddhism, and be handed that most precious of cards, an emblem of belonging. Those cards kept their value, even when their holders quietly returned to their Christian practice. It illuminated just how farcical nation building in Myanmar could be, when that primary goal of developing a cohesive and permanent political unit required the use of communities whose devotion to that project had been no more than a temporary show of submission.

Yet there was an irony to the whole charade. Untold numbers of people have been killed in Myanmar for being on the wrong side of the ethnic and religious divide. But if the villagers, and indeed U Maung Soe himself, could, under the watch of the regime, become members of the nation by adopting a new label without then *being* it and *living* it, then perhaps it showed that the regime saw little substance to those labels. They were just quotas to be filled to strengthen the illusion of Myanmar moving in the direction of a unified, harmonious state under the military. That would bring into sharper focus the minority of those who refused to join, for it was they who justified the relevance of military rule.

After a year in Kengtung, U Maung Soe was transferred again, to Naypyidaw. There, he served as an assistant to the Deputy Religious Affairs Minister, Thura Aung Ko, whom the National League for Democracy chose to head the ministry when it came to power in 2016. Shortly afterwards he became an administrator at the State Pariyatti Sāsana University in Yangon, helping to organise the trips made by monks out to the border regions to set up monasteries among Christians and begin the process of conversion. And by 2013, he was out of the Ministry of Religious Affairs for good. He took an altogether different path, setting up a construction firm, and it was in the company's head office in downtown Yangon that I had listened to his story.

★ ★ ★

His passage into the military had been my first point of interest. It seemed strange that someone from an ethnicity that well understood the wrath of that institution had wanted to join its ranks. It was clear he possessed a keen interest in the art of warfare. That passion was inherited from his father, who had signed up as a Muslim at a time when religion and ethnicity were less divisive than they are now. U Maung Soe had spent a large chunk of his early childhood in military barracks surrounded by people of all religions, and then in neighbourhoods in Yangon where different groups mixed. He knew the texts of Buddhism and its history well, and this provided a useful platform when it came to convincing colleagues that he was Buddhist. But either way it seemed they hadn't probed too deeply. Only Buddhists could join the military – they just assumed he was one of them.

Yet how had he reconciled himself with the knowledge that, once in the military, he would be aiding its almost obsessive pursuit of a racially uniform country, one that Rohingya, perhaps more than any other in Myanmar, were not to be a part of? That seemed to be the big question.

> The important thing for me was that I love my country and I love my birth place. That is why I joined the military. I defended the country by serving in the military. I didn't care how I was defined or regarded in terms of race and religion. I needed to represent proudly that I am a Myanmar citizen.

There was an underlying message there that seemed to apply to all contexts in which religion or race determined one's chances in life. For the dictatorship in Myanmar, total commitment to the nation was best proven by membership of the one institution that would ensure protection of the nation. Yet U Maung Soe, who as a Rohingya and a Muslim was both a religious and ethnic pariah, was able not only to enter the military and make a contribution on a par with his fellow Buddhist soldiers, but was made a captain for it. He may have done it to prove he could be as much a part of the national community as anyone, or he may have merely wanted to follow in his father's footsteps. Perhaps, even, his decision was the product of an opportunism so fierce that he was willing to aid the brutalisation of his own ethnicity in order to boost his prospects in life. It was difficult to detect any single motive, and he had always been evasive when I tried to discern any moral angst in the decisions he made. "Duty is duty," he would often say.

But in the context of nation building in Myanmar, what seemed to matter more than his own reasons for joining was the fact that, even in the climate of deep hostility towards Muslims, Rohingya in particular, cultivated by Ne Win, U Maung Soe was accepted into that institution, and rose up within it. He hadn't needed to change anything deep within himself in order to do so. Rather, it needed only a false statement on a form, and suddenly he was in.

There was something in the experience of this individual that seemed universal. "In a democracy," he had said, "all the diverse people can cooperate with each other. I proved it myself." His passage from the far fringes of Myanmar society into its centre countered the assumption that ethnicity and religion were markers of deep and irresolvable differences in the core characters of the individuals that inhabited those groups. It was this lie that, in Myanmar, had determined so radically whether one was accepted into the nation, or violently cast beyond its boundaries. U Maung Soe seemed to be proof of that lie.

11

In the old cinema hut: fear, hope and the heroes we forget

Not all of Myanmar experienced violence between Buddhists and Muslims, and for tens of thousands of villages and towns across the country, life continued on in its own particular fashion. Conflicts between the military and armed ethnic groups that had dogged the country for decades raged across the transition, but these were different in nature to the bloodletting that occurred in Rakhine State, Meikhtila and elsewhere. What distinguished this violence was its communal quality. In a snap, neighbours turned to strangers, and years of shared friendships receded so sharply they were forgotten.

But it hadn't been that way everywhere. Even in Rakhine State, where enmity between Buddhists and Muslims had been most bitter, there were towns that hadn't fissured violently. They seemed to hang together, if at times only by a thread, and they came to provide interesting zones of inquiry for how the two communities might, if conditions could be altered, be brought back together.

The small town of Buthidaung in northern Rakhine State, where Muslims outnumber Buddhists, experienced neither the violence nor the segregation that Sittwe and other towns did. Journalists who fly into the state capital and visit the camps and the ghettos often report it as a microcosm of the wider racial geography of the region, but that isn't entirely the case. Segregation persists where it is viable; where a calculation determines that the group pushing for a divide would be better off without the other in their midst. The logic that drove Buddhist Rakhine to demand separate enclaves for Muslims elsewhere in the state was underpinned by a conviction that their wellbeing was negatively affected by the proximity of this Muslim community, whose ideologies were corrosive and whose hunger for resources competed with their own. Restricting them to camps, villages and ghettos, and thereby removing this scourge, would improve the condition of the Buddhist population.

But if that condition instead worsens in the wake of isolation, then popular support for segregation won't last long. Buthidaung seemed to have realised this quickly. As communities elsewhere in Rakhine State moved apart, the town remained more or less as it was prior to 2012. The two communities still interacted, in the teashops and in the schools and marketplace, and Rakhine still employed Rohingya, as they had done before. Tensions had emerged that were particular to this town, but the rupturing of the two communities that occurred elsewhere had not been so powerful here.

★ ★ ★

One evening in Buthidaung I left my guesthouse and headed with a Rakhine friend to the local cinema hut. It was one of the few places that stayed open beyond 11.30pm, the hour each night when the power was cut and darkness fell over the town. It was early in the English Premier League season, and on that night Arsenal was playing Manchester United. We knew the place would be busy, for football is astonishingly popular in Myanmar, and the appetite for European leagues is particularly intense. As we turned onto the street where the hut was, we saw groups of people heading through a narrow doorway up ahead. Outside the entrance, illuminated by a bulb, a man was selling cans of beer from a stall. We bought enough for the game and headed through the doorway. Rows of benches and chairs were set up inside, most of them already taken up, and a hulking old projector beamed the preparations for the game onto the wall at the front. The building was musty and dilapidated in the way I'd imagine an old Victorian theatre to be, with its high ceiling, peeling walls and its hotchpotch of loosely arranged seats. As people crammed in, the volume of noise grew and the game got underway.

It was one of the few places I came across in the state where Rohingya and Rakhine still came together, not to trade goods or to labour alongside one another, but as social peers. They sat side by side on the benches, hollering as the game fizzed on in all its intensity. The hut didn't have the functional basis of a marketplace – it was a zone of purely voluntary interaction where religious or ethnic identity seemingly had no bearing. I noticed a camaraderie inside the hut that surprised me, and the lines of division that had been so visible elsewhere in the state were less evident here. At the end of the game, they got up and poured out into the pitch-dark street. They mingled for a brief moment, and before long, using the light from their phones, they walked back home.

Late the next morning I went to the house of Abdul, a young Rohingya acquaintance of my friend. You can spot which houses in Buthidaung belong to Rohingya by the small arched cover, like a miniature roof, that sits above the front gates of their houses and protects the wood from sun and rain. A number of the homes along his street had those, but others didn't, and that marked them out as Rakhine. Abdul had gathered a group of people from both communities together for lunch, and we sat in the cool dark upstairs room of the house as his sisters prepared food in the kitchen. A corresponding lunch would have been unimaginable in Sittwe, with Rohingya inviting Rakhine into their home and Rakhine eating food cooked by Rohingya.

Among the two Buddhist Rakhine who sat with us was Aung Tun. He ran a business selling bamboo, and worked for the General Administration Department, the expansive local-level state body that administers villages and towns across Myanmar. He grew up in a village outside Buthidaung where Rohingya were a majority. He could practise his religion there freely, he said, and exhibited no prejudice. The majority of his staff were Rohingya; their labour was cheaper.

Buthidaung lies north of the Mayu River, in that area the government and many Rakhine believed had become a Muslim stronghold, one step away from secession. But the demographic difference that saw Muslims outnumber Buddhists here seemed to have a converse effect, in the towns at least: after the violence of 2012, Buthidaung in particular remained more integrated than many other places in the state. Aung Tun's business would not have survived if Rohingya here had been herded into camps, or if the stigma of maintaining contact between Buddhists and Muslims had been as strong here as it was further south. He was reliant on that contact and all that came with it – a dependable workforce and buyers within both communities. It would have taken a pogrom of unimaginable intensity to drive Rohingya out of Buthidaung. But there was perhaps another, more mundane reason why Buthidaung didn't follow the fate of Sittwe and other towns. Because Rohingya were a majority, and provided much of the workforce, the damage to the economy would have been too great. This meant the project of segregation wasn't viable here – too much would have been lost on both sides.

No one theory for explaining ethno-religious violence, or cooperation, can be applied to all who have a stake in it and are affected by it. There were Rakhine and Rohingya in Buthidaung who disdained one another as much as they did anywhere in the state. But that disdain wasn't able to mutate into a total reconfiguration of the social landscape of the town, as it had done in Sittwe. Instead the two communities remained in contact, and as levels of trust slowly built as a result of that continued interaction, it meant they didn't fear one another to the same extent. Aung Tun said he worried about going to remote Muslim villages beyond the town limits; there were greater unknowns, and thus greater fears, the further one ventured from the familiar. But in and around Buthidaung he, like other inhabitants of the town, felt relatively comfortable among Rohingya. They knew each other here, and that made it harder for the kind of unsettling rumours that gained traction elsewhere in the state to impact so heavily on relations. So they continued to mingle together, not just in the marketplace, but in the teashops and in the old cinema hut.

That hadn't been the case in Sittwe. After it became segregated, whatever trust had existed was shattered, making the eventual job of bringing the two communities back together that much harder. But there were slivers of hope. One day during a visit in early 2016 I headed out of Sittwe to the village of East Tonbyin. I was still looking for people who had witnessed or participated in the violence, and East Tonbyin sat back from the same road that had served as a thoroughfare for the buses that ferried Rakhine mobs into Sittwe three years earlier.

Our strategy for finding participants was somewhat crude: we would locate the house of the village administrator, knock on the door, and if he was receptive, sit down and begin talking more generally about the political situation in Rakhine State and development in the area. This provided context for the grievances Rakhine held towards both Rohingya and the central government, and from there we could steer the conversation towards the events of 2012 – how had the village been affected, and who had been caught up in the violence?

In East Tonbyin that day the administrator was away, so we wandered around the village and came across a man in the process of erecting sections of a large wooden frame for a two-storey house. Behind his yard was a field, and on the other side, some 200 metres away, lay the village of South Tonbyin, populated largely by Rohingya. Win Zaw was a jeweller in Sittwe and earned around $6 a day. His wife, who had been sitting at the back of the yard as we came in, didn't work, and instead tended to the house and garden. The 2015 elections had taken place three months before, and they had both voted for the Arakan National Party, which had formed from a merger of the Rakhine Nationalities

Development Party and the Arakan League for Democracy. The previous government of the Union Solidarity and Development Party had brought some improvements to the region, he said – school textbooks for his two children were now free of charge. But the USDP was still backed by the military, and was too distant a presence. It did nothing on the ground in Rakhine State, and nothing for working people there.

On the third day of the violence in June 2012, a large group of Rohingya had converged on East Tonbyin, armed with sticks and machetes. Win Zaw had seen them but didn't recognise among them any inhabitants of the village across the field. He thought the majority had come from Thet Kae Pyin village, around which the camp for displaced Rohingya later sprang up. There was a temporary standoff, before a unit of soldiers nearby intervened, stationing themselves between the two groups. The Rohingya mob eventually dispersed.

That had been the only time the village came under threat. Before that day, relations between East and South Tonbyin had been good. Rakhine from this village would cross the field and sit in the teashops of South Tonbyin, and Rohingya would come here to sell fish and vegetables. But even though none of the mob had come from South Tonbyin, that exchange stopped altogether after the violence and the field separating the villages became a no man's land between the two communities. Win Zaw said that they stopped trusting their neighbours and no longer sat in their teashops. Three motorbikes and two cows had gone missing from East Tonbyin the previous year, and he suspected it was the work of Rohingya.

Win Zaw had said earlier in our conversation that he didn't trust Muslims. With that curious mathematical specificity I'd heard elsewhere, he explained that 70 per cent of them were dishonest. As we spoke, his wife wandered over. Mya was more sympathetic. By late 2013, Rohingya had begun returning to the village to sell fish and vegetables, and she would say hello to them when they passed by. She still avoided going over to South Tonbyin, even when old friends invited her. It wasn't that she feared the residents, but instead that Muslims from the camps might be in the village, and that meant trouble for Rakhine. The peril of the unknown was there again – something to fear in unfamiliar faces.

As she spoke, a young man in his early twenties arrived at the gate of the yard. He carried two buckets of fish, each hanging by a rope from either end of a wooden plank that rested across his shoulders. He was Rohingya, and had come that morning from his home in South Tonbyin to do the rounds of houses where he knew he could offload his catch. He had been selling fish to Win Zaw and Mya for several years. We ushered him into the yard, and he came in slowly and sat down next to Mya. He was sweating heavily. The day was a hot one, but this seemed like a fever, and his eyes were glazed and heavy. It was malaria, he thought. "You're always sick when I see you," Mya told him. They talked together with an air of familiarity. The young man had been unwell for several days and the medicine he was taking hadn't worked. That medicine was for the stomach, not a fever, Win Zaw said. Fever and stomach pain are different. They knew he couldn't go to Sittwe hospital – malaria wasn't considered threatening enough to override the restrictions on Muslims receiving treatment there – and I asked if there was a clinic around here he could access. "*Ya-deh, ya-deh,*" they both said. No problem, no problem.

Mya would contact a doctor in a nearby Rakhine village to see if he could visit there.

Later as I walked with my translator back to our bike, he told how he had met the family a year before. Back then Win Zaw had spoken with far greater contempt of Muslims than he had the day I met him. It seemed that time had dampened his disdain – he was milder now, and although he was evidently still suspicious of Muslims, he had shown an attentiveness towards the ailing Rohingya man that surprised my translator. I wondered how my conversation with them might have gone if we had met in the year after the violence, when interaction between the two villages had broken off entirely. The mental wounds from the attempted attack by Rohingya would have been fresher, as would the stories that had come in from nearby villages where violence had taken place. But so too would their anxieties have been compounded by the absence of any contact with the objects of that anxiety.

When Rohingya began returning to East Tonbyin a year after the violence, the intensity of those emotions began to ease. There seemed to be a lesson here. Might not the behavioural traits in people that are often read as signs of a deeply ingrained prejudice instead be more visceral, temporary responses to the tensions around them? And might that hatred not change if those tensions were to subside? The emotions that underpin prejudice – the fear and the resentment of those considered rivals – are exploited by nationalist leaders to create foot soldiers of a community. But were those emotions to be dampened, either by proactively cultivating greater interaction, or by merely allowing communities to naturally coalesce again, instead of segregating them, then whatever fears had arisen in the meantime could be countered. As a result, the job of recruitment might become harder, for the resources needed to whip up rage wouldn't be so readily available.

Win Zaw worried that the violence would come again, and that meant he couldn't relax. He was angry too about the theft of the bikes and cows. Yet still, East Tonbyin was a pocket of relative communal calm in a landscape where, even when I had visited again three and a half years after the violence, hostility seemed to be the abiding sentiment. But the fact that the communities in this small village tract had come to know that coexistence, albeit limited, didn't spell the end of their community meant that the divisions opened by the events of 2012 might not necessarily endure. It could, in time, be bridged if they could only come to understand in the other that their ethnicity or religion wasn't innately fearsome. And, even, that both communities might prosper as a result of renewed interaction.

Towards the end of my conversation with Win Zaw and Mya, another Rohingya man walked past the gate with baskets of vegetables. He paused outside, looking inquisitively in, and Mya called him to come and sit down. Mohammed Rafique also came from South Tonbyin, and could remember the time nearly three decades before when this sister village was built over a crop field. He had known this family almost as long as that. But for a year after the violence he too stopped coming here, as had everyone else in South Tonbyin. They were afraid of this village and this village was afraid of them. But he sat there now, next to the Rakhine husband and wife, and he seemed at ease, save for the endless questions being asked of him by a foreign journalist.

★ ★ ★

While space did gradually open in small pockets of Rakhine State for the kind of day-to-day interactions that occurred in East Tonbyin, there could be no overt peace-building efforts. The circulation of the names of Rakhine who worked for organisations assisting Rohingya in the aftermath of the anti-NGO attacks in Sittwe in March 2014 had been deeply unnerving, for it indicated the dangers that came with displaying any sympathy for Muslims. A number of organisations held occasional games of football or film screenings where the two communities could come together, but it was undertaken cautiously, and quietly. Rakhine nationalists were primed to consider any such efforts as traitorous.

The stigma of contact between Buddhists and Muslims wasn't so powerful in the towns of central Myanmar struck by the violence. A year after the killings in Mandalay in July 2014, the young Muslim interfaith activist, Myo, went to work in the villages that lay on the edge of the city, almost indistinguishable from the suburbs that sprawled south from the centre in their endless grid patterns. The death threats sent to his phone after the workshop he gave to monks and nuns in the middle of 2015 had served as a warning that he needed to change his strategy. Rather than addressing directly the religious tensions in central Myanmar, he opted for a more mundane approach. Joined by a small team of activists and educators, he began surveying residents of Kan Ywar village. It had been founded more than two centuries before as a place for the Kaman Muslims who had brought the statue of the Mahamuni Buddha to Mandalay from Rakhine State to live under the favour of the king. The Muslims here knew they descended from Kaman, but now largely considered themselves Bamar. Buddhists, also

Bamar, moved there soon after it was settled, and they had lived side by side ever since.

One day during the violence in downtown Mandalay, a group of men had entered the village carrying stones. They loitered briefly in the street, sizing up their surrounds, and were spotted by residents of nearby houses who ran out to confront them. They quickly dispersed and never returned. That was the only instance of near-violence that Kan Ywar had experienced, but the village was already living in uncertain times. Mysterious rumours had been circulating among both Buddhist and Muslim communities since the 2012 carnage in Rakhine State, warning that each would be attacked by the other. No one knew their origin – they seemed to have carried in on the wind and worked their way through the streets and alleyways, unnerving the communities so much that they shrank within themselves. It sent a chill through the village: Muslims became doubly careful not to cause any accidents that might harm Buddhists, like the girl in Okkan who the year before had bumped into a novice monk while riding her bicycle, sparking a day of attacks. Buddhists grew wary of walking through streets where Muslim households were concentrated, and kept to themselves. These were nagging doubts, in no way explicit, but they accumulated as the rumours kept coming, and slowly a wall of distrust began to snake its way through the village.

One afternoon in early 2016 I travelled with Myo to Kan Ywar. He had come here for the first time eight months before and gathered community leaders from both sides together. They had discussed what problems there were in the village – not religious, but day-to-day concerns: too much litter, not enough greenery. Those were the issues that united the communities in their frustration, thereby bridging the religious divide that had opened as the violence in the city sent ripples out to its periphery.

The day I visited, Myo was holding a workshop in a madrasa there. The following week it would take place in the monastery, and thereafter alternate between the two. Twenty people, both Muslim and Buddhist, had enrolled, the majority of whom worked in the community, in library or funeral services or blood donation groups. These were the kinds of civil society organisations that had been tolerated by the junta – apolitical, but nonetheless ones that provided people in Myanmar with a sense of cooperation across lines of difference. Amid violence of the sort that erupted in the wake of the junta's retreat from power, these preexisting links would prove vital in the effort to reintegrate communities.

The discussion in the madrasa that day focused on the shape and function of a democratic government: the separation of powers between the executive and judiciary, and fundamental rights for citizens. Slides were beamed onto a screen, and a Buddhist educator brought up from Yangon asked questions of the attendees. This pool of participants was in the latter stages of the programme. They had already looked at strategies to address waste management in the village, and as time went on, the topics moved more towards the rights of the communities. Myo said there were two principal aims to the programme: to bring the two groups together along lines of common interest, and to help them finally engage with the political system in Myanmar. Talk of religion was generally avoided. But occasionally arguments would break out. Two months before they had discussed LGBT rights. Myanmar retains a deeply conservative streak when it comes to sexuality, and the class descended into a row. Another time, Myo had organised tours for the whole group to visit their respective religious buildings, and the group became tense.

A pause came midway through the workshop. With Myo, I approached a Muslim man in his early thirties and began to talk. He knew the history of the village well. Before it became Kan Ywar, it was known as "Kaman Village," and in the early days the two communities had lived among one another to a far greater extent than they did now. Buddhists occupied houses directly in front of the mosque where the workshop had taken place. Over time they had retreated into somewhat separate enclaves, yet still, until 2014, he would stay at the homes of Buddhist friends, and they would stay at his. It was only after the Mandalay violence that this was stopped, when a deeper distrust, fed by the swirl of rumours, began to pervade relations.

The workshops had achieved several things, the man explained. The mere act of mixing allowed attendees to get to know one another again – not only on an individual basis, but in a way that helped to de-stigmatise the broader identity of the other community. It gave birth to a kind of neighbourhood watch initiative, whereby leaders from each side held meetings whenever signs of tension arose and pledged to the other that they would not attack.

"We know these rumours come from the outside," the man had said. "This community is very closed. We don't have much information coming in and these rumours create fear."

All that police did when stories began to circulate was to order people to stay inside their homes; they offered nothing in the way of organic trust building. The workshops had filled that void – they served as a space in which that vital mechanism for communal healing could begin to be generated.

One of the great paradoxes of group violence is that, so often, a key driver is the misplaced anger that results from disenfranchisement of one or both groups by the political leadership. During the rule of the military, all communities in Myanmar were denied the ability to negotiate their grievances through institutional channels. Those had been closed off entirely. For some, like the ethnic minority groups who rose up one by one in the decades after independence, violence towards the junta appeared the only viable alternative expression. But if that leadership could redirect the target of that anger away from itself and towards a rival group, framing it as a competitor for the scarce political and economic capital being sought by the in-group, then the violence would play out on a more horizontal axis. That would deflect animosity away from the leadership and towards the more immediate threat – one's neighbours.

The Muslim man at the workshop had said that local authorities continually harassed residents of Kan Ywar: not only Muslim, but Buddhists too. When it came to managing the local population here, they discriminated little. But through the workshops he and the other attendees had come to know of their legal rights and could communicate this to their communities. In the process, those channels were opened up. Residents of Kan Ywar became both able, and more emboldened, to address issues of neglect or abuse by the state directly, rather than leaving frustrations to fester in a way that could turn up the heat inside the village. "We have become united and we can now elect our own village heads," he had said, and the outcome of this empowerment was quick to bear fruit: a youth from the village had been arrested several weeks before on what the man believed was a spurious charge – he didn't say what exactly – and he had gone to the station and spoken with the police, who then ordered the youth's release.

Among the workshop participants who had been left embittered by the class Myo gave on LGBT rights were several poets. Months on from the row that erupted during their discussion, these poets began contributing their work to an LGBT magazine. Here and there, small victories were being won, but these were early days. After Kan Ywar, Myo planned to take the initiative out to other villages similarly affected by the ripple of violence. In some of these, the ultra-nationalist monks of the Ma Ba Tha movement had grown influential in the two years prior and that had meant a widening of the divide.

"We first need to get them into an environment where they can collaborate," he said of the villagers, "and then we can work on cohesion." It would be a step–by–step process, slow, painful and beset by suspicions that were amplified by the propagandising of Ma Ba Tha and other nationalist groups. The hope was that the contact rekindled in the workshops between the Buddhists and Muslims of Kan Ywar would filter into communal interactions outside of that space, gradually defusing the tensions that had built in the preceding years. Greater knowledge of their legal rights would give the communities a degree of ownership of their fate that had long been denied to them, and that would slowly ease the feeling of vulnerability that was so intimately connected with the fears Buddhists and Muslims here felt of one another.

★ ★ ★

These were small causes for optimism in a political context marred by turbulence and deep uncertainty. The transition had ushered in unprecedented freedoms for many in Myanmar, and the significance of this struck home as I watched people gathering in the mosque in Kan Ywar to understand better how a democratic system should work. The ability to organise and be educated in the arts of making demands on authority is a wholly new development in Myanmar, and there was a time not so long ago when Myo and the 20 participants would have been herded into prison vans long before the workshop had even begun.

But the violence of recent years, and the movements that sprang up around it, made clear that demons had also been unleashed. Myo was an activist as a student, and his uncle had been close to Aung San Suu Kyi in the decades when the junta saw the opposition as a criminal operation. He knew the risks back then, but also understood one of the great ironies thrown up as the landscape began to shift in Myanmar after 2010: that a principal source of danger for activists like himself no longer came chiefly from the men in green uniform, but from the men in their saffron robes who appeared bent on engineering a shift to a religiously uniform state. The militant monks, as well as the supposed democrats whose fierce nationalism seemed to overwhelm any commitment to equality, saw his attempts to generate space in which multiple belief systems could coexist as an act of sabotage of the nation.

The project of nationalist leaders who preach purification of the social order nears completion when it infects the minds of the majority of the population. Yet whether the likes of Ma Ba Tha or the Rakhine political leaders had tapped into a majoritarian sentiment is impossible to say.

There have always been different nationalisms at play in Myanmar whose targets change according to the particular context of the age. Many are the result of a residual anger towards the corrosive legacy of British colonial rule or the colonising projects of the Bamar leadership that followed. Yet the democratisation process, and the fears of societal change it prompted, have allowed these to be updated with a new target. As the transition progressed, the purveyors of an exclusionary ideology seemed to excel in transforming differences into divisions, yet they also managed something else. In recruiting millions to their cause, they were able to take the focus of those who subscribed to this ideology away from the individual struggles that all in Myanmar are burdened with, and onto something far larger and far harder to rein in. That was something the military tried for so long to do, with little success, making the achievements of this movement over recent years all the more saddening.

But they, Ma Ba Tha in particular, had also been able to cow the political leadership into a state of near submission. When I'd gone to meet with U Win Htein from the National League for Democracy in early 2016, shortly before the party took power, I asked about its refusal to field Muslim candidates in elections the year before. It seemed the surest sign of an abject failure, a dereliction of duty, on the part of this mighty democratic force. The NLD had never stated clearly its reason for the decision, knowing the damage it would do to its image as a progressive, inclusive party. But U Win Htein didn't tiptoe around the issue. "We don't want to sell the bullet to Ma Ba Tha," he had said. The one they would shoot at you, I asked? "Yes," he laughed.

Ma Ba Tha's power had grown unchecked for too long, aided by the symbiotic relationship it enjoyed with the chief power holders in Myanmar, the military. But there was also the fact that, in the void created by the silence from pro-democracy quarters, it was able to grow in confidence and clout to a point where it felt it might be able to steer the transition – by undermining the NLD, emboldening military-aligned forces, and legislating for discriminatory laws to be implemented. Its manoeuvring made a delicate transition all the more fragile. Yet somewhere in the long-term strategy of the NLD must be an acknowledgement that continued violence will only serve to reinvigorate the military. In that sense, whatever prejudices towards non-Buddhists are held by figures within the NLD and the democratic movement more broadly, there still remains the fact that harmony between the country's many different communities is politically beneficial for a civilian government, while violence will eat away at its legitimacy. This should provide a point of optimism, however muted it may be, amid all the justifiable frustration directed at Aung San Suu Kyi and her colleagues, who initially provided such little resistance towards a movement that tried so vigorously to undo the democratic opening. If the primary goal of the party is civilian governance, then its interests will not be served by the kind of divisions that its silence has encouraged.

Yet for all the hope that the NLD would mark a break with the military's treatment of minority groups, it would appear there is some alignment between the two on one issue. In April 2016, Suu Kyi took on the newly created State Counsellor position, one that granted her far-reaching powers in government while bypassing the constitutional block on anyone with a foreign spouse becoming president. A short while later she asked the US ambassador to Myanmar not to use the word "Rohingya" in public addresses. Neither would the NLD-led government. Government officials were also asked to cease labelling them "Bengali." Instead, they would henceforth be referred to as the "Muslims of Rakhine."

Suu Kyi's request to the US ambassador, while likely aimed at countering the emphasis on ethnic identity, explosive as it has been – and protecting the party from accusations of support for the group – in many ways mirrored the denialism practised by the previous government, which had blocked any registration of Rohingya in the national census of 2014. That rejection of an identity, pursued first by Ne Win and now by the civilian government, is not only a form of persecution in itself, but provides a basis for a wider array of abuses. By denying them the name they claim, they are denied a place in the national community they avow membership of. The effect is to place them outside the purview of the state and the security it is obliged to offer. In doing so it helps to legitimate violence by local actors – namely, those Rakhine who interpret the continued subordination of the group as indicative of the subhuman nature of its members.

The NLD, and the broader intellectual community in Myanmar, could approach all this differently. A departure from military rule brings with it the opportunity to break with a principal narrative it used to bolster its power – that the country's ethnic and religious diversity posed a threat to unity and stability, and could be managed only by a strong and violent leadership. The "national races" index and the tiers of belonging created by Ne Win were fundamental to this narrative, yet their legacy has weakened the potential for a civilian government to consolidate its rule. Perhaps it seems futile to reintroduce the debate so long after Myanmar's ethnic landscape was "established," yet it was precisely this process of codifying a bogus order of groups that has determined way down the line who is included in the national community, and who is not. The resulting effect, strengthened over so many decades by the military – and now, it seems, helped on by the NLD – has been to equate foreignness with threat; that anyone of an alien appearance, belief, practice – whatever measure is used to demarcate the "us" and the "them" in Myanmar – is a contaminant in society. Addressing the fallacies that underlie the ethnic landscape could help to cultivate a nationalism based on civic values rather than exclusionary ideologies, and would in turn strengthen the NLD's ability to govern effectively.

But a challenge to the military's blueprint for society is evidently not on the NLD's table. Given that the party's ranks are populated largely by Bamar, privileged as they are in the hierarchy of belonging in Myanmar, perhaps there is an ulterior reason as to why it has never challenged the ethnic order of the country. The NLD has instead looked elsewhere for remedies for Rakhine State. Rule of law must be respected, it has said, and funds must be channelled into developing infrastructure and bettering livelihoods for both Rakhine and Rohingya. These, the party has argued, will help defuse tensions and give each community greater ownership of their fate. Yet these can only go so far. Without any effort to de-stigmatise and de-politicise the Rohingya identity, and to make clear that identity should not provide a basis for discrimination by the state, these cycles of violence risk repeating themselves.

Instead of this happening, another process continues to play out. So deft have the machinations of power in Myanmar been that both the Rakhine and Rohingya consider the other as privileged – Rakhine as superior in the hierarchy of status in Myanmar; Rohingya as the beneficiaries of international sympathy and support. Neither sees the other as a victim of the military, and so the history of shared suffering is obscured. Like the Chin Buddhists in the village near Mindat who turned on Naing Ki after his conversion to Christianity, the triangulation of communal animosities has been a crowning achievement of the military's nation-building efforts. It deflects attention away from its own manoeuvrings and sows the potential for unrest that it can profit from well into the future.

★ ★ ★

With each year that has passed since 2012, the overall condition of the million or so Rohingya living on Myanmar's western coast has worsened. While a number of pilot schemes were launched by the National League for Democracy to test how Rakhine reacted to the return of displaced Rohingya to their villages, the group continued to be denied the freedoms that other communities cautiously began to exercise under civilian rule: a political voice, the ability to move, to worship, to claim greater bargaining rights from the government. If the intention was to empty Rakhine State of Rohingya, then it achieved a degree of success: in the three years after the violence, as the control measures were tightened and their isolation grew more acute, tens of thousands of Rohingya left the country on boats, crossing the Bay of Bengal to seek sanctuary elsewhere.[1] As they went, an industry developed to meet their demands: trafficking rackets deployed vessels equipped with desalination plants to the waters off Myanmar and Thailand, thereby allowing trafficked Rohingya to stay at sea for months until they could be shipped or sold elsewhere. But the effects of this mass flight were felt only locally, in villages in Rakhine State whose populations thinned, or by families who lost members beneath the waves. For the nation more broadly, they were not missed. The sum total of the loss of tens of thousands of people has come to nothing.

For those who remained, perhaps hopeful that a civilian government would finally end their decades of disenfranchisement, an altogether different problem developed. In early October 2016, hundreds of armed Rohingya attacked three police outposts in Maungdaw township, seizing weaponry and ammunition and leaving nine policemen dead. Several videos were circulated in the aftermath. In one, a group of armed men speaking the Rohingya dialect, who went by the name Harakah al-Yaqin, or Faith Movement – and later changed to the Arakan Rohingya Salvation Army – called upon Rohingya around the world to "get ready for Jihad" – perhaps the first time the word has been used as a rallying cry by a local group in Myanmar – and deployed the same religious justification for martyrdom that Islamist militants elsewhere have done. Another video featured a man, flanked by armed men, also claiming to represent Harakah al-Yaqin. His message was different: the group is "free from all elements of terror in any nature," he explained, "but seeks fundamental and legitimate rights for all Arakanese, including our innocent Rohingyas and other civilians dying from the continuous military assault." It demands that Rohingya be released from the camps, and that all military offensives against ethnic minorities be ceased.

So fragile is the condition of the Rohingya that any stirrings of armed rebellion within the community could prove suicidal. Their position is utterly unique in Myanmar: where other ethnicities that rose up against the state had the broad ideological, if not material, support of the populace, the Rohingya have none. Many Buddhists in the country now appear to consider them more threatening than the military, and in the aftermath of the October 2016 attacks, the implications of this perception were quick to materialise. As soldiers swept through the north of Rakhine State and deployed helicopter gunships to fire on villages where participants were rumoured to be hiding, civilian support for the army grew in volume. The government of Aung San Suu Kyi then gave the go-ahead for the formation of armed civilian militias made up of Rakhine locals. Journalists who reported on allegations that troops had raped and killed Rohingya were rounded on by the government and civilians, for their reports were seen to slander a military that had been sent to northern Rakhine State to protect the area – and, perhaps, Myanmar as a whole – from the Muslim menace.

In decades past, similar acts of debasement carried out by the military against other ethnic minorities were read as evidence of a sickness at the core of the institution. But in Rakhine State, the claims made by Rohingya – of the gang-rape of women by soldiers, the execution of children – and later corroborated by the UN, were seen as mere fabrications designed to sully the image of the army and garner support for the victims. Where insurgencies by the likes of the Kachin and Shan ethnicities were popularly considered to be assaults on a military that had brought so much ruin to the country, any mobilisation by Rohingya "invaders" is read as an attack on the nation, and all within it. As tens of thousands of Rohingya fled to Bangladesh amid claims from the UN that crimes against humanity were likely being committed, state media in Myanmar made this deduction explicit: Rohingya were not victims, but perpetrators. An article in the state-run *New Light of Myanmar* newspaper warned that the country was "facing the danger of the human fleas" that "we greatly loathe for their stench and for sucking our blood,"[2] an analogy used by the Nazis to refer to Jews. Another article alluding to the Rohingya was entitled, "The Thorn Needs Removing If It Pierces!"[3]

In creating an image of the bloodthirsty Rohingya bent on taking control of the country, the military was gifted a moral foundation for its campaign of violence in Rakhine State. The effect of this was to encourage many in Myanmar, for so long deeply cynical about the military's intentions, to unite behind it.

Therein lay another irony to the turmoil that has engulfed the country after its passage to democracy began. For decades the military had spun its campaigns in the borderlands as motivated by a need to defend the people against what it called "internal destructive elements," but the propaganda had always fallen on the deaf ears of a public that seemed to know its trickery well. Now, however, it is finally gaining traction, at a time when the military is supposed to be in retreat. This change in public perceptions of the military has been a mere side story in the narratives of the violence that has rocked Myanmar since 2012, but it may turn out to be among its most significant, and yet saddening, by-products.

★ ★ ★

For some in Myanmar, it will be beneficial – politically, strategically and ideologically – to ensure these communal fissures remain in place. While the violence that began in northern Rakhine State in October 2016 has set back the clock considerably, there are indications, however cautiously they should be treated, that efforts to resolve bitter differences are bearing fruit. East Tonbyin village, Kan Ywar village, the cinema hut in Buthidaung – these are small pockets of space in which the two communities are beginning slowly to rediscover that their wellbeing is closely intertwined.

Even in areas where the project of divide and rule and the deliberate weakening of Muslim communities had been most acute, there were Buddhists and Muslims who still crossed the divide. One afternoon in late 2015 I drove out of one of the Na Ta La villages south of Maungdaw and came to a road that cut through a wide plain of paddy fields. Up ahead a line of hills climbed and fell across the horizon. Soon after joining the road we passed a group of six men in a cleared corner of one field playing *chinlone*, leaping high off the ground as they scissor-kicked the small woven wooden ball through the air and over the net. We slowed to watch them play and saw that it was a mixed group, Rohingya and Rakhine. Behind them a rainbow arced over the hills. It had been raining all morning, easing only an hour before, and the droplets that lingered high in the sky conspired with the brilliant late afternoon light to form a backdrop of the most enchanting and symbolically resonant kind.

All around this group of people, for 20 years and more, a social engineering project of the most cynical design had been undertaken, and still continued. The myriad points of blight on the landscape there – the stolen land on which the

Na Ta La villages were built, the checkpoints and the ritual humiliation of Rohingya, the freely abusive police and army – signified that one group, more than the many others in Myanmar who have felt the pain of not truly belonging, were considered unworthy of membership of the national community. Yet to do as these young men in the corner of the paddy field had done and keep a connection going across an ethnic and religious divide that powerful forces had tried so hard and for so long to deepen, showed that, to some, these cleavages mattered less than others might hope.

As dictatorial rule recedes, the agency of individuals is strengthened. This can be as much a force for positive empowerment as it can be a force to bring ruin to a fragile and changing society. But the leaders of today and tomorrow in Myanmar would do well to take note of scenes such as that one in northern Rakhine State, for the arc of colour that spanned the hills that afternoon seemed apt for the exchange happening beneath it. Myanmar is a rainbow nation, and its vast array of different cultures and belief systems could all make a unique and important contribution to its future, if they were allowed.

Those on the ground in Myanmar who recoil from that vision have sought to steer the country away from being an inclusive society, and in doing so have allowed the vestiges of the old order, and the mentality it cultivated, to remain. They have garnered such attention because their actions seemed so contrary to what we thought we knew of Myanmar – of the steadfast Buddhist values held by the majority, and of the long and laudable history of resistance to the trickery and bullying of the powerful. But by no means did they represent everyone, and amid the carnage that swept towns and cities, there were heroes. Perhaps they knew that to be seen acting against the forces driving the violence would imperil them too, and cast them as enemies of the nation. So they went about their work quietly. But their acts, and the sentiment expressed within them, should be amplified the loudest, and so I'll end with the story of one of these.

It wasn't until long after I first visited Meikhtila that I heard of the abbot, U Witthuda. As the casualties from the violence in late March 2013 rose and more families fled their homes, he opened the gates of his monastery. Along the dusty road they came, first in groups of ten or so that had made the three-mile walk there from downtown, and then in their hundreds. None were denied, neither Buddhist nor Muslim, and under the abbot's watch they entered and found refuge there as the town around them split apart.

I went to meet U Witthuda one day in late 2015. The grounds of the Yadanar Oo Monastery were bathed in a crisp sunlight, and inside those walls, young novice monks, barely out of childhood, quietly went about their day. There was an affecting stillness to the place – the sounds of traffic had died out long before I reached the gates, replaced by the song of birds nesting in the trees that dotted the compound. As we entered he approached us slowly, with a curious smile on his face. We followed him inside the main hall and sat on the floor, my translator and I opposite the abbot. I asked him to recount the events of those few days. As we waited, he lit a cheroot, and in the measured, almost soporific tone that is the manner of monks, he explained what had happened.

There was a police station close to the monastery. But at the time of the violence the police had received no orders to protect the Muslims that had fled there, and turned them away. So U Witthuda told the officers to send them to his monastery, and there they went: 40 on the first day, and nearly 400 on the second. By the third day there were 800 people inside, and still more came. He asked men from his ward to search for others who had remained in hiding nearby, and they went out from the monastery each morning, afternoon and evening and looked high and low.

"Some were in the paddy fields and in the trees. They were afraid," the monk recounted.

> And I told those people inside the monastery to call their relatives to come and stay at this monastery. Some told me that there were this and that who were too scared to even get out of their houses, and I asked certain people to rescue them.

Among the group that had arrived on the first day was the family of the owner of the gold shop. It was the brawl there between the Buddhist customer and Muslim owner that had triggered attacks across the town in early 2013. U Witthuda had once lived near to the shop and knew the owner's son, and when they came he ushered them into the monastery. Yet news of the family's arrival there soon reached the wrong people. In the early hours of the morning of 21 March, a group gathered outside the gates.

"They asked me, 'Bring out those Muslims in the monastery.'" He refused. "I am helping those people who are in trouble. I can't. If you want to get them, you have to kill me first. I can't bring them out."

There were two people at the front of the group who began to shout. "Who are you? Are you a Muslim monk?" But, said the abbot, there were around 35 monks in his monastery. "Those monks were standing beside me. So the group didn't dare come inside the monastery, and turned their backs. And they didn't come again."

By the fourth day, 940 people were sheltering inside the compound. The two communities were initially separated, but in time they came to be among one another. For the first two days, many of the Muslims hadn't eaten. "They were that scared. They told me later that when they first came to this place they thought this monk had kept them here to kill them all."

Their fear soon faded and they accepted food, but it was a tumultuous few days. There were alcoholics who, bereft of liquor, shouted in the night, shattering the silence that descended as people huddled on the floor sleeping. Several women gave birth inside the monastery. And there was an elderly man who died from an illness he had brought with him. It was heart disease, U Witthuda thought. He had arrived with his family, and knew his time was near.

> What can I say? I think it is his fate that brought him to this monastery and defined this as his final resting place. And those whose fate defined this monastery as their birthplace were born here as well. You can view it that way, you know? We don't know where we will be born and where we will die, do we?

U Witthuda spoke of the people whose lives he had saved with an arresting tenderness. And as he did so I thought that he might be that rare kind who had staved off the malignity that seemed to have infected segments of the Buddhist order so virulently in the turbulent early years of the transition. At times it felt as if those who had stayed true to the core humanist qualities inherent in the Buddha's teachings were a minority. Perhaps that was the case. Or perhaps, rather than a matter of numbers, it was the volume of those preaching division. They seemed to have drowned out the voices of the monks and their followers, like U Witthuda and the many others who resisted the call of the mobs, that wholly rejected it.

Wouldn't it be heartening if the next stage of Myanmar's future could begin with that picture in mind, of a monastery bathed in sunlight, the gates open, offering a space in which people of different faiths could do as they had done before the madness came to their town: finding sanctuary and solidarity among one another, sharing their food and their quarters?

Notes

2 SONS OF WHOSE SOIL?

1. Yegar, Moshe. (1972). *The Muslims of Burma: A Study of a Minority Group.* Otto Harrassowitz. Page 6.
2. Yegar, Moshe. (1972). *The Muslims of Burma: A Study of a Minority Group.* Otto Harrassowitz. Page 2.
3. Tin Maung Maung Than. (1993). "Some Aspects of Indians in Rangoon." In *Indian Communities in Southeast Asia.* Sandhu, K.S. and Mani, A. (Eds). ISEAS Times Academic Press. Page 586.
4. Smith, D.E. (1965). *Religion and Politics in Burma.* Princeton University Press. Page 27.
5. Spiro, M.E. (1970). *Buddhism and Society: A Great Tradition and Its Burmese Vicissitudes.* Harper & Row. Page 379.
6. Smeaton, D.M. (1887). *The Loyal Karens of Burma.* Kegan Paul, Trench. Page 4. Quoted in Smith, D.E. (1965). *Religion and Politics in Burma.* Princeton University Press. Page 45.
7. Smith, D.E. (1965). *Religion and Politics in Burma.* Princeton University Press. Pages 92–93.
8. Yegar, Moshe. (1972). *The Muslims of Burma: A Study of a Minority Group.* Otto Harrassowitz. Page 31.
9. Riot Inquiry Committee. (1939). "Final Report of the Riot Inquiry Committee." Supdt., Govt. Printing and Stationery, Burma. Page 6.
10. Riot Inquiry Committee. (1939). "Final Report of the Riot Inquiry Committee." Supdt., Govt. Printing and Stationery, Burma. Page 8.
11. Riot Inquiry Committee. (1939). "Final Report of the Riot Inquiry Committee." Supdt., Govt. Printing and Stationery, Burma. Appendix 2, page x.
12. "Burman" is the old terminology for the "Bamar," Myanmar's majority ethnic group.

3 THE ART OF BELONGING

1. *Minye Kaungbon.* (1994). Pages 168, 178. Quoted in Houtman, G. (1999). *Mental Culture in Burmese Crisis Politics: Aung San Suu Kyi and the National League for Democracy.* ICLAA Study of Languages and Cultures of Asia and Africa Monograph

Series No. 33. Page 68. Accessed at www.burmalibrary.org/docs19/Houtman-1999-Mental_Culture_in_Burmese_Crisis_Politics.pdf

2. Lieberman, V.B. (1978). "Ethnic Politics in Eighteenth-Century Burma." *Modern Asian Studies*, Vol. 12, No. 3. Page 457.

3. Smith, M. (1991). *Burma: Insurgency and the Politics of Ethnicity*. Zed Books. Pages 34–35.

4. Scott, J.C. (2009). *The Art of Not Being Governed*. Yale University Press. Page 238.

5. Buadaeng, K. (2007). "Ethnic Identities of the Karen Peoples in Burma and Thailand." In *Identity Matters: Ethnic and Sectarian Conflict*. Peacock, J.L., Thornton, P.M. and Inman, P.B. (Eds). Berghahn. Page 75.

6. Thiong'o, N.W. (1986). *Decolonising the Mind: The Politics of Language in African Literature*. James Currey. Page 16.

7. Cheesman, N. (2015). "Problems with Facts about Rohingya Statelessness." E-International Relations. Accessed at www.e-ir.info/2015/12/08/problems-with-facts-about-rohingya-statelessness/

8. Callahan, M. (2004). "Language, Territoriality and Belonging in Burma." In *Boundaries and Belonging: States and Societies in the Struggle to Shape Identities and Local Practices*. Migal, J.S. (Ed.). Cambridge University Press. Page 108.

9. Taylor, R.H. (2015). *General Ne Win: A Political Biography*. ISEAS Publishing. Page 484.

10. Gravers, M. (1999). *Nationalism as Political Paranoia in Burma: An Essay on the Historical Practice of Power*. NIAS Report No. 11. Copenhagen. Nordic Institute of Asian Studies. Page 56.

11. Smith, M. (1991). *Burma: Insurgency and the Politics of Ethnicity*. Zed Books. Page 37.

4   US AND THEM

1. Gutman, P. (2001). *Burma's Lost Kingdoms: Splendours of Arakan*. Orchid Press. Page 21.

2. Harvey, G.E. (1967). *History of Burma: From the Earliest Times to 10 March 1824: The Beginning of the English Conquest*. Frank Cass. Page 267.

3. Seekins, D.M. (2006). *Historical Dictionary of Burma (Myanmar)*. The Scarecrow Press. Page 278.

4. Seekins, D.M. (2006). *Historical Dictionary of Burma (Myanmar)*. The Scarecrow Press. Page 278.

5. Charney, M.W. (1999). *"Where Jambudipa and Islamdom Converged: Religious Change and the Emergence of Buddhist Communalism in Early Modern Arakan, 15th–19th Centuries."* PhD thesis. University of Michigan. Page 260. Accessed at www.burmalibrary.org/docs21/Charney-1999_thesis-Where_Jambudipa&Islamdom_Converged-red-tu.pdf

6. Scott, J.C. (2009). *The Art of Not Being Governed*. Yale University Press. Page 7.

7. Haque, S.A. (2012). "An Assessment of the Question of Rohingyas' Nationality: Legal Nexus Between Rohingya and the State." Page 2. Accessed at www.

burmalibrary.org/docs14/ARAKAN-%20Question_of_Rohingyas_Nationality-red.pdf

8. Arendt, H. (1986). *The Origins of Totalitarianism*. Andre Deutsch. Page 300.

5 RULING THE UNRULY

1. Charney, M.W. (1998). "Crisis and Reformation in a Maritime Kingdom of Southeast Asia: Forces of Instability and Political Disintegration in Western Burma (Arakan), 1603–1701." *Journal of the Economic and Social History of the Orient*, Vol. 41, No. 2. Page 164.

2. A copy of the original document was provided to me by Phil Rees and Al Jazeera. I am grateful for this and the accompanying information.

3. Development of Border Areas and National Races. Website of the Embassy of Myanmar in Brazil. Accessed at www.myanmarbsb.org/development_of_border_areas_and.htm

4. Pearn, R.B. (1952). "The Mujahid Revolt in Arakan." Research Department, Foreign Office. 31 December 1952. Page 9. Accessed at http://web.archive.org/web/20160430034640/http:/www.networkmyanmar.org/images/stories/PDF18/Pearn-1952-rev.pdf

5. Adloff, R. and Thompson, V. (1955). *Minority Problems in Southeast Asia*. Stanford University Press. Page 154.

6. Yegar, M. (2006). "The Crescent in Arakan." Accessed at www.kaladanpress.org/index.php/scholar-column-mainmenu-36/36-rohingya/216-the-crescent-in-arakan.html

7. Yegar, M. (2002). *Between Integration and Succession: The Muslim Communities of the Southern Philippines, Southern Thailand and Western Burma/Myanmar*. Lexington Books. Page 35.

8. Pearn, R.B. (1952). "The Mujahid Revolt in Arakan." Research Department, Foreign Office. 31 December 1952. Page 9. Accessed at http://web.archive.org/web/20160430034640/http:/www.networkmyanmar.org/images/stories/PDF18/Pearn-1952-rev.pdf

9. Pearn, R.B. (1952). "The Mujahid Revolt in Arakan." Research Department, Foreign Office. 31 December 1952. Page 9. Accessed at http://web.archive.org/web/20160430034640/http:/www.networkmyanmar.org/images/stories/PDF18/Pearn-1952-rev.pdf

10. Chin Human Rights Organisation. *Threats to Our Existence: Persecution of Ethnic Chin Christians in Burma*. Page xiv. Accessed at www.chro.ca/images/stories/files/PDF/Threats_to_Our_Existence.pdf

11. *New Light of Myanmar*. (2011). "Second Regular Session of First Amyotha Hluttaw Continues for 17th Day." 14 September 2011. Page 9. Accessed at www.burmalibrary.org/docs11/NLM2011-09-14.pdf

12. UNICEF. "Chin State: A Snapshot of Child Wellbeing." Page 1. Accessed at www.unicef.org/myanmar/Chin_State_Profile_Final.pdf

13. Chin Human Rights Organisation. *Threats to Our Existence: Persecution of Ethnic Chin Christians in Burma*. Page 109. Accessed at www.chro.ca/images/stories/files/PDF/Threats_to_Our_Existence.pdf

14. *New Light of Myanmar.* (2011). "Second Regular Session of First Amyotha Hluttaw Continues for 17th Day." 14 September 2011. Page 9. Accessed at www. burmalibrary.org/docs11/NLM2011-09-14.pdf

15. Ministry for Home and Religious Affairs statement, 16 November 1977. Quoted in Human Rights Watch. (1996). "Burma: The Rohingya Muslims: Ending a Cycle of Exodus?" Accessed at www.refworld.org/docid/3ae6a84a2.html

16. Fuller, A., Leaning, J., Mahmood, S.S. and Wroe, E. (2016). "The Rohingya People of Myanmar: Health, Human Rights, and Identity." *The Lancet.* Page 6.

17. Human Rights Watch. (1996). "Burma: The Rohingya Muslims: Ending a Cycle of Exodus?" Accessed at www.refworld.org/docid/3ae6a84a2.html

18. Fortify Rights. (2014). "Policies of Persecution: Ending Abusive State Policies Against Muslims in Myanmar." Page 24.

19. Fortify Rights. (2014). "Policies of Persecution: Ending Abusive State Policies Against Muslims in Myanmar." Page 24.

20. Rakhine Inquiry Commission. (2013). "Final Report of Inquiry Commission on Sectarian Violence in Rakhine State." Cited in Fuller, A., Leaning, J., Mahmood, S.S. and Wroe, E. (2016). "The Rohingya People of Myanmar: Health, Human Rights, and Identity." *The Lancet.* Page 5.

21. Rakhine Inquiry Commission. (2013). "Final Report of Inquiry Commission on Sectarian Violence in Rakhine State." Cited in Fuller, A., Leaning, J., Mahmood, S.S. and Wroe, E. (2016). "The Rohingya People of Myanmar: Health, Human Rights, and Identity." *The Lancet.* Page 6.

22. See de la Cour-Venning, A., Green, P. and MacManus, T. (2015). *Countdown to Annihilation: Genocide in Myanmar.* Report by the International State Crime Initiative.

23. Brown, W. (2016). "Where There Is Police, There Is Persecution: Government Security Forces and Human Rights Abuses in Myanmar's Northern Rakhine State." Physicians for Human Rights Report, October 2016. Page 9. Accessed at https://s3.amazonaws.com/PHR_Reports/Burma-Rakhine-State-Oct-2016.pdf

6   2012: SEASON OF VIOLENCE

1. San Lin. (2011). "Seminar Held to Protest Misuse of the Term 'Arakan'." Mizzima News. Published on BNI International on 6 September 2011. Accessed at http://e-archive.bnionline.net/index.php/news/mizzima/11582-seminar-held-to-protest-misuse-of-the-term-arakan.html

2. Takaloo. (2011). "Mass Protest around Misuse of the Term 'Arakan' Arises in Arakan State." Narinjara News. Published on BNI International on 1 November 2011. Accessed at http://e-archive.bnionline.net/index.php/news/narinjara/11994-mass-protest-around-misuse-of-the-term-arakan-arises-in-arakan-state.html

3. Rakhine National Defence and Protection Organisation. (1988). Statement released by RNDPO. Accessed at www.maungzarni.net/2013/10/report-of-sentiments-of-rakhine-tai-yin.html

4. Appadurai, A. (2006). *Fear of Small Numbers: An Essay on the Geography of Anger.* Duke University Press. Page 91.

5. Appadurai, A. (2006). *Fear of Small Numbers: An Essay on the Geography of Anger.* Duke University Press. Page 91.

6. Paccima Yatwun. (2012). "What the Rohingya Is." Author unknown. Not available online. February 2012.

7. Latt, Sai. (2012). "Intolerance, Islam and the Internet in Burma." *New Mandala.* Accessed 1 April 2016.

8. Eleven Media. (2012). "Curfew Imposed in Rakhine Township amidst Rohingya Terrorist Attacks." Eleven Media. 8 June 2012. Accessed at http://aboutarakaneng. blogspot.co.uk/2012/06/curfew-imposed-in-rakhine-township.html

9. Than Htut Aung. (2012). "I Will Tell the Real Truth (3)." Eleven Media. 26 June 2012. Quoted in Human Rights Watch, *All You Can Do Is Pray.* Page 25. Accessed at www.hrw.org/sites/default/files/reports/burma0413webwcover_ 0.pdf. My requests to interview editors at the *Weekly Eleven* journal for this book were not granted.

10. Allchin, J. (2012). "The Rohingya, Myths and Misinformation." Democratic Voice of Burma. 22 June 2012. Accessed at www.dvb.no/analysis/the-rohingya-myths-and-misinformation/22597

11. Vanderbrink, R. (2012). "Call to Put Rohingya in Refugee Camps." Radio Free Asia. Accessed at www.rfa.org/english/news/rohingya-07122012185242.html

12. Human Rights Watch. (2013). *All You Can Do Is Pray.* Page 26. Accessed at www.hrw.org/sites/default/files/reports/burma0413webwcover_0.pdf

13. Human Rights Watch. (2013). *All You Can Do Is Pray.* Page 49. Accessed at www.hrw.org/sites/default/files/reports/burma0413webwcover_0.pdf

14. Human Rights Watch. (2013). *All You Can Do Is Pray.* Page 50. Accessed at www.hrw.org/sites/default/files/reports/burma0413webwcover_0.pdf

15. Rakhine Nationalities Development Party. Statement released on 26 June 2012. In author's possession. Not available online.

16. *Venus News Weekly*, Vol. 3, No. 47. 14 June 2012. Page 2. Translated from Burmese. Not available online.

17. Copy of statement in the author's possession. Not available online.

18. Copy of statement in the author's possession. Not available online.

19. Copy of statement in the author's possession. Not available online.

20. Burma Campaign UK. (2013). "Burma Briefing: Examples of Anti-Muslim Propaganda." Briefing No. 21. Page 1. Accessed at www.burmacampaign.org. uk/images/uploads/Examples_of_Anti-Muslim_Propaganda.pdf,pg.1

21. *The Nation.* (2012). "Normalcy Returns to Rakhine State." 31 October 2012. Accessed at www.nationmultimedia.com/aec/Normalcy-returns-to-Rakhine-official-30193314.html

7 AT FIRST LIGHT THE DARKNESS FELL

1. Hla Myaing. (2012). "An Open Letter to 88 Generation Students Leader Ko Ko Gyi." 30 July 2012. Translated from Burmese. Accessed at http:// myanmarmuslimsvoice.com/archives/474

2. With thanks to Elliott Prasse-Freeman for bringing this point to my attention.

3. Pasricha, A. (2012). "Aung San Suu Kyi Explains Silence on Rohingyas." Voice

of America. 15 November 2012. Accessed at www.voanews.com/a/aung-san-suu-kyi-explains-silence-on-rohingyas/1546809.html

4. UNICEF. "Rakhine State: A Snapshot of Child Wellbeing." Page 3. Accessed at www.unicef.org/myanmar/Rakhine_State_Profile_Final.pdf

5. Copy of the magazine in author's possession.

6. Economist U Myint noted in 2011 that household spending on "charity and ceremonials" had by 2001 become the third biggest outgoing.

> There are several possible reasons why C&C has become more important in the everyday life of an average Burmese city dweller. It could be that the family is performing more meritorious deeds because its members have become more interested in the next life than in the present one. Or it could be that the family is taking advantage of (or is being persuaded to take advantage of) the many new opportunities for making contributions to charities, welfare activities, community self-help schemes and other worthy causes (such as building roads and public works) that have mushroomed in the country in the process of transformation into a market-oriented economy. Or it could simply be that the household is playing an active part in numerous ceremonies, celebrations, festivals, mass rallies and rituals that have become a major national preoccupation in recent years.

Myint, U. (2011). "National Workshop on Reforms for Economic Development of Myanmar. Myanmar International Convention Center (MICC). Naypyitaw, 19–21 August, 2011. Myanmar: Pattern of Household Consumption Expenditure." Accessed at www.burmalibrary.org/docs12/NWR2011-08-Pattern_of_Household_consumption_expenditure-Myint%28en%29.pdf

7. BBC. (2013). "Burma Riots: Video Shows Police Failing to Stop Attack." British Broadcasting Corporation. 22 April 2013. Accessed at www.bbc.co.uk/news/world-asia-22243676

8. YouTube. (2013). "Anti Muslim Monk Wira Thu Talk about Meiktila before Riot." 24 March 2013. Accessed at www.youtube.com/watch?v=N7irUgGsFYw

9. Burma Campaign UK. (2013). "Burma Briefing: Examples of Anti-Muslim Propaganda." Briefing No. 21. Page 2. Accessed at www.burmacampaign.org.uk/images/uploads/Examples_of_Anti-Muslim_Propaganda.pdf,pg.1

10. I am grateful to Phil Rees and Al Jazeera for providing a copy of the leaked document.

11. Human Rights Watch. (2002). "Crackdown on Burmese Muslims: Human Rights Watch Briefing Paper: July 2002." Accessed at www.hrw.org/legacy/backgrounder/asia/burma-bck4.htm

12. Karen Human Rights Group. (2002). "Easy Target: The Persecution of Muslims in Burma." 31 May 2002. Accessed at http://khrg.org/2014/09/khrg0202/easy-targets

13. US State Department. (2001). "Annual Report on International Religious Freedom, 2001." Page 113. Accessed at www.state.gov/documents/organization/9001.pdf

14. Bookbinder, A. (2013). "969: The Strange Numerological Basis for Burma's Religious Violence." *The Atlantic*. 9 April 2013. Accessed at www.theatlantic.

com/international/archive/2013/04/969-the-strange-numerological-basis-for-burmas-religious-violence/274816/

15. Brodney, M. and Gittleman, A. (2013). "Patterns of Anti-Muslim Violence in Burma: A Call for Accountability and Prevention." Physicians for Human Rights Report, August 2013. Page 13. Accessed at https://s3.amazonaws.com/PHR_Reports/Burma-Violence-Report-August-2013.pdf

16. Burma Campaign UK. (2013). "Burma Briefing: Examples of Anti-Muslim Propaganda." Briefing No. 21. Page 6. Accessed at www.burmacampaign.org.uk/images/uploads/Examples_of_Anti-Muslim_Propaganda.pdf,pg.1

17. Atkinson, H.G. and Sollom, R. (2013). "Massacre in Central Burma: Muslim Students Terrorized and Killed in Meiktila." Physicians for Human Rights. Page 10. Accessed at https://s3.amazonaws.com/PHR_Reports/Burma-Meiktila-Massacre-Report-May-2013.pdf

18. YouTube. (2013). "Recent Violence in Meikhtila, Buddhist '969' Mob Strikes in front of Police (Part 2)." 16 April 2013. Accessed at www.youtube.com/watch?v=KEowvdIX7Bk

19. Atkinson, H.G. and Sollom, R. (2013). "Massacre in Central Burma: Muslim Students Terrorized and Killed in Meiktila." Physicians for Human Rights. Page 15. Accessed at https://s3.amazonaws.com/PHR_Reports/Burma-Meiktila-Massacre-Report-May-2013.pdf

8 "WE CAME DOWN FROM THE SKY"

1. Lawi Weng. (2015). "The Rise and Rise of the Ma Ba Tha Lobby." The Irrawaddy. 10 July 2015. Accessed at www.irrawaddy.com/commentary/the-rise-and-rise-of-the-ma-ba-tha-lobby.html

2. Lawi Weng. (2015). "Support Incumbents, Ma Ba Tha Leader Tells Monks." The Irrawaddy. 23 June 2015. Accessed at www.irrawaddy.com/election/news/support-incumbents-ma-ba-tha-leader-tells-monks

3. Ikeya, C. (2005). "The 'Traditional' High Status of Women in Burma: A Historical Reconsideration." Journal of Burma Studies, Vol. 10, 2005–2006. Page 73. Accessed at www.academia.edu/23408501/The_Traditional_High_Status_of_Women_in_Burma_A_Historical_Reconsideration

4. Democratic Voice of Burma. (2013). "Monks and Religious Leaders Back Interfaith Marriage Ban." Democratic Voice of Burma. 26 June 2013. Accessed at www.dvb.no/news/politics-news/monks-and-religious-leaders-back-interfaith-marriage-ban/28988

5. Ei Ei Toe Lwin. (2015). "Guardians of 'Race and Religion' Target NLD." The Myanmar Times. 2 October 2015. Accessed at www.mmtimes.com/index.php/national-news/16801-guardians-of-race-and-religion-target-nld.html

6. BBC. 'Aung San Suu Kyi: Burma Not Genuinely Democratic." Accessed at www.bbc.co.uk/news/world-asia-24649697

7. C4ADS. (2016). "Sticks and Stones: Hate Speech Drivers in Myanmar." C4ADS report. Page 33. Accessed at https://static1.squarespace.com/static/566ef8b4d8af107232d5358a/t/56b41f1ff8baf3b237782313/1454645026098/Sticks+and+Stones.pdf

8. Wa Lone. (2015). "USDP Candidate Donates Big to Ma Ba Tha." *The Myanmar Times*. 3 September 2015. Accessed at www.mmtimes.com/index.php/national-news/16287-usdp-candidate-donates-big-to-ma-ba-tha.html

9. Houtman, G. (1999). *Mental Culture in Burmese Crisis: Aung San Suu Kyi and the National League for Democracy*. ICLAA Study of Languages and Cultures of Asia and Africa Monograph Series No. 33. Page 119. Accessed at www.burmalibrary.org/docs19/Houtman-1999-Mental_Culture_in_Burmese_Crisis_Politics.pdf

10. Metro, M. (2016). "Students and Teachers as Agents of Democracy." In *Metamorphosis: Studies in Social and Political Change in Myanmar*. Egreteau, R. and Robinne, F. (Eds). NUS Press Singapore. Page 211.

11. Video - www.facebook.com/permalink.php?story_fbid=1691946937734537&id=100007577414909&comment_id=1697713610491203&notif_t=mentions_comment&notif_id=1467816243411247

12. Metro, M. (2016). "Students and Teachers as Agents of Democracy." In *Metamorphosis: Studies in Social and Political Change in Myanmar*. Egreteau, R. and Robinne, F. (Eds). NUS Press Singapore. Page 211.

13. C4ADS. (2016). "Sticks and Stones: Hate Speech Drivers in Myanmar." C4ADS Report. Page 15. Accessed at https://static1.squarespace.com/static/566ef8b4d8af107232d5358a/t/56b41f1ff8baf3b237782313/1454645026098/Sticks+and+Stones.pdf

14. Aung San Suu Kyi. (1990). "Freedom from Fear." Accessed at www.thirdworldtraveler.com/Burma/FreedomFromFearSpeech.html

9 APARTHEID STATE

1. Testimony provided by Amnesty International based on field research interviews conducted by the organisation in February 2016. Any conclusions drawn are my own.

2. Testimony provided by Amnesty International based on field research interviews conducted by the organisation in February 2016. Any conclusions drawn are my own.

3. Fuller, A., Leaning, J., Mahmood, S.S. and Wroe, E. (2016). "The Rohingya People of Myanmar: Health, Human Rights, and Identity." *The Lancet*. Page 6.

4. Testimony provided by Amnesty International based on field research interviews conducted by the organisation in February 2016. Any conclusions drawn are my own.

11 IN THE OLD CINEMA HUT

1. The UN High Commissioner for Refugees estimates that 170,000 people migrated across the Bay of Bengal from Rakhine State and Bangladesh between 2012 and 2015, although it is unclear how many of these fled Rakhine State alone. See "Mixed Maritime Movements in Southeast Asia," UN High Commissioner for Refugees. December 2015. Accessed at https://unhcr.atavist.com/mmm2015

2. Oo, Khin Maung. (2016). "A Flea Cannot Make a Whirl of Dust, But – ." *Global New Light of Myanmar.* 26 November 2016. Accessed at www.globalnewlightofmyanmar.com/a-flea-cannot-make-a-whirl-of-dust-but/

3. Oo, Khin Maung. (2016). "The Thorn Needs Removing If It Pierces!" *Global New Light of Myanmar.* 31 October 2016. Accessed at www.globalnewlightofmyanmar.com/the-thorn-needs-removing-if-it-pierces/

ABOUT THE AUTHOR

Francis Wade is a journalist specialising in Myanmar and Southeast Asia. He began reporting on Myanmar in 2009 with the exiled Democratic Voice of Burma news organisation, based in Northern Thailand, before going on to cover in-depth the transition from military rule and the violence that accompanied it. He has reported from across South and Southeast Asia for *The Guardian, TIME, Foreign Policy Magazine* and others. He is now based in London.